100 YARDS OF GLORY

Books from Joe Garner and Bob Costas

And the Crowd Goes Wild
And the Fans Roared
100 Yards of Glory

100 YARDS OF GLORY

THE GREATEST MOMENTS IN NFL HISTORY

JOE GARNER   BOB COSTAS

FOREWORD BY JOE MONTANA

Houghton Mifflin Harcourt

Boston | New York | 2011

For information about permission to reproduce selections from this book,
write to Permissions, Houghton Mifflin Harcourt Publishing Company,
215 Park Avenue South, New York, New York 10003.

www.hmhbooks.com

Library of Congress Cataloging-in-Publication Data
Garner, Joe.
100 yards of glory : the greatest moments in NFL history / Joe Garner and Bob Costas ;
foreword by Joe Montana.
p. cm.
Summary: The Immaculate Reception. The Ice Bowl. The Music City Miracle.
The Catch. For nearly a century, the National Football League has provided fans
with pulse-pounding moments on the gridiron. In the tradition of their
revolutionary collaboration, *And the Crowd Goes Wild*, veteran chronicler of
broadcast history Joe Garner and broadcast icon Bob Costas team up to
bring fans this one-of-a-kind compendium of NFL history in a lavishly illustrated
hardcover book, with gripping text and archival photographs, as well as an
original 10-part documentary, produced by an Emmy Award–winning team, hosted
by the inimitable Costas and featuring official NFL video highlights. From the great
dynasties to the improbable catches, the legendary coaches to the heroic QBs, the
most incredible comebacks to the most notorious flubs, *100 Yards of Glory*
relives in text and video the most unforgettable moments in the game. Also available
as an enhanced ebook, *100 Yards of Glory* is a must-have for any football fan.
Provided by publisher.
Summary: A fully illustrated book and accompanying DVD of the NFL's greatest
moments. *Provided by publisher.*
ISBN 978-0-547-54798-5 (hardback)
1. National Football League History. 2. Football United States History.
I. Costas, Bob, date. II. Title.
GV955.5.N35G38 2011
796.332'64dc22   2011009149

Book design by Stoltze Design

Printed in China

SCP 10 9 8 7 6 5 4 3 2 1

Official publication of the National Football League

Page 2: Buffalo Bills wide receiver Andre Reed is upended by Dallas Cowboys strong safety
Thomas Everett after a 13-yard reception in the third quarter of Super Bowl XXVII, Sunday,
January 31, 1993, in Pasadena. Dallas won 52–17. (AP Photo/Doug Mills)

To the players, coaches, and fans.

CONTENTS

FOREWORD

By Joe Montana

As a kid, I saw a football field as a "yellow brick road," one that would take me beyond the coal mines and steel mills surrounding me in western Pennsylvania and on to an easier life than the lives of the hardworking people around me, like my parents and grandparents.

I played basketball and baseball along with football in those days and actually liked basketball the most. But I soon figured out where my future was. Perhaps it was inevitable that, coming from an area that produced so many great quarterbacks, from Johnny Lujack and Johnny U to Joe Namath and Dan Marino, I would wind up behind the center as well.

The quarterback I rooted for back then was Terry Bradshaw. Seeing all he went through—throwing a lot of interceptions and losing more than he won the first two seasons, yet still climbing to the top—inspired me. I was always a Steelers fan and still am. Oh sure, I'm also a Niners fan, but when you are growing up, the love for your first team is ingrained in your heart, and it never really leaves you.

That's why I think this book will be so enjoyable to football fans. Whatever team, player, coach, or particular game stands out in their minds, they are likely to find them all here and have the chance to relive their most treasured memories.

We all have our special football moments as fans. I remember that, for an assignment for a junior high art class, I chose to draw the menacing figure of Dick Butkus I'd seen on a cover of *Sports Illustrated*. I remember being overwhelmed by the famous photo of quarterback Y. A. Tittle sitting on the turf, blood streaming down his face. I remember the Steel Curtain, Ray Nitschke, Walter Payton, and Jim Brown. There are certain people who just pop up in your head who epitomize the NFL.

These are the people who will pop up in this book, their storied careers brought back for an older generation that lived through those times and a younger generation that can see them for the first time.

I remember, as a kid, winning the Super Bowl in my backyard a thousand times with my neighborhood friends. From there, I was happy to get a chance to go to Notre Dame, to be drafted into the NFL, and to wind up with the 49ers, a team with a good coach and a good organization. I took it step by step. I didn't really look too far ahead.

Now I don't look too far back. I don't live a whole lot in the past. I see my pass to Dwight Clark, the play that clinched the 1981 NFC championship game and became known simply as "the Catch," every now and then because it's replayed a lot on ESPN, but other than that, I try to look forward.

The 49ers' Joe Montana celebrates his first-quarter 68-yard touchdown pass to Jerry Rice. (AP Photo/Rusty Kennedy)

It's still fun to watch the highlights of my career, but that's not the focus of my life anymore. My sons' football careers are the focus of my involvement in football now.

I try to pass on to my sons what is so great about this sport. But I tell them that they can make what they do on the field easier by spending a lot more time working off the field, looking at film and studying plays. That way, when things happen, they will have already made the decision about what they will do.

I think it's the most exciting sport of them all. I think every down is challenging physically and mentally. As a quarterback, even if you see the same defense and you run the same play against it, it's never the same. There's always something different that causes you to have to make a judgment and to do so within a three-second window. Oh, and by the way, to do so while you are dropping back.

I don't know if people understand what the league has gone through or how the players and owners have struggled to get it to where it is today. I do know it is special to play in the NFL, and it is special to share those memories with people who will never have the opportunity to play themselves. That's why I think fans will love this book.

THE DYNASTIES

Teamwork is what the Green Bay Packers were all about. They didn't do it for individual glory. They did it because they loved one another. —Vince Lombardi, NFL coach

1 | THE 2000s PATRIOTS

Patriots coach Bill Belichick. (AP Photo/ Gene J. Puskar)

In over four decades of Super Bowls, only six games have been decided by three points or less. Bill Belichick's New England Patriots played in four of those games, winning three and in the process establishing themselves as the first dynasty of the 21st century.

What does it all add up to — those 20–17, 32–29, and 24–21 victories and the fact that in those seasons the team finished just sixth, twelfth, and fourth in points scored?

Those slight margins show that the Patriots did not win because they had the most talented players, like the 1990s Cowboys or 1970s Steelers. The

2001 team had just four Pro Bowlers, and only Troy Brown was a first-team All-Pro (as a punt returner); the 2003 champions had just three Pro Bowlers and three All-Pros; while the final title team had six Pro Bowlers and two All-Pros. (By contrast, the 1975 Steelers had 11 Pro Bowlers, with five men making the cut for first-team All-Pro, and the 1993 Cowboys had 11 Pro Bowlers and three All-Pros.)

These Patriots won because they got the most out of the talent they had. To do that required superior coaching from tactical and psychological mastermind Bill Belichick. Linebacker Willie McGinest praised Belichick as "a mad scientist when it comes to breaking down teams. . . . Every week something changes. There's always something new, and there's always a little twist to it."

"He definitely is the smartest coach I've been around," said safety Rodney Harrison. "There is not one detail he overlooks."

Not only did Belichick install a brilliant defensive game plan and a solid offensive system, but he imbued his team with an unquenchable desire for winning and found players with an ability to adapt—from play to play and season to season—and to play together as a team despite the chaos wrought by the salary cap and modern free agency.

The two constants were kicker Adam Vinatieri and quarterback Tom Brady, both of whom seemed like perfect symbols of the Patriots because they

Patriots wide receiver David Patten goes high for the touchdown grab in the second quarter of Super Bowl XXXVI. (AP Photo/Kathy Willens)

New England's Tedy Bruschi (54) sacks Philadelphia Eagles quarterback Donovan McNabb (5) in the first quarter of Super Bowl XXXIX. Officials initially ruled that McNabb fumbled the ball, but the call was reversed after a challenge by Philadelphia. (AP Photo/Chris O'Meara)

played their best at the biggest moments. The team reached that first Super Bowl only because of one memorable drive in the snow against the Raiders in the playoffs—Brady led an epic drive to set up Vinatieri's game-tying field goal. The duo then repeated that magical formula in overtime.

Meanwhile, the team's primary rusher shifted from Antowain Smith to Kevin Faulk to Corey Dillon across four seasons, while Brady's main receiver went from Brown and David Patten to Deion Branch to David Givens. On defense, linebacker Tedy Bruschi was always among the team's leaders, both in personality and in tackles, while others like Mike Vrabel and Richard Seymour eventually became household names in New England. There was also a steady stream of changing faces. The 2001 leaders in tackles (Lawyer Milloy), interceptions (Otis Smith), and sacks (Bobby Hamilton) were soon gone, and the mainstays of 2003 like Ty Law (who had been with the team since 2001) and Tyrone Poole were not factors in the third championship, by which time they had been replaced by Eugene Wilson.

It isn't just that the talent is interchangeable. It is that everyone buys into Belichick's "do anything for the team" ethos: When Law and Poole got hurt, receiver Troy Brown switched sides of the football to defensive back—and contributed three interceptions. In two Super Bowls, linebacker Mike Vrabel played tight end and caught a touchdown pass.

The team's first Super Bowl win, over the St. Louis Rams in 2000, was an epic upset. "The Rams were as good as advertised," linebacker coach Rob Ryan said. "Belichick put the whole plan together. He deserves all the credit in the world."

The previous year had been Belichick's first in New England, and the Patriots had finished just 5-11. Then the 2001 season began with quarterback coach Dick Rehbein dying of a heart attack and starting quarterback Drew Bledsoe getting knocked out with an injury. Brady had barely played in his rookie year, but he stepped into the breach and led the team to the Super Bowl.

The team's golden aura following that win created great expectations, and after an off year in 2002, the Patriots fulfilled them with their next two Super Bowl wins. When Brady threw an interception in the fourth quarter deep in Carolina territory in Super Bowl XXXVIII, he and his team never wavered. When Brady came off the field, Belichick

recalled, he was not slump-shouldered but instead had "one of the most determined looks of a champion that you'd ever want to see."

Brady led the team to its third Super Bowl the following year, despite his grandmother dying and his father being hospitalized in the week before the big game.

"Everybody knows Tom Brady is a proven winner," said receiver Troy Brown. "He may not put up the big five thousand passing yards in a season and all that stuff. [But] he's proven that he's the master at putting up wins."

By the end of the third title, the team had won nine straight postseason games, with just six turnovers and 25 takeaways. This was fundamental football at its most solid.

But after a first-round playoff loss in 2005 and a loss in the 2006 AFC championship to the Indianapolis Colts, it seemed that the Patriots' time might be passing. Instead, they went into hyperdrive for 2007 and added receivers Wes Welker and Randy Moss, who caught a total of 210 passes between them in their first season in New England. That year ended in a devastating defeat at the hands of the New York Giants in the Super Bowl, yet it remains

worthy of celebration. The Patriots finished 16-0 in the regular season, just the second team in modern NFL history to attain perfection. Belichick had always been thought of as a defense-first coach, but the 2007 team averaged an NFL record 36.8 points per game, Brady finished with a 117.2 passer rating—the second-highest in league history—and he set a record by throwing 50 touchdown passes. Despite the disappointment in the Super Bowl, the season was a monumental achievement.

All of the Patriots' success can be traced back to the moment when the team took the field for their first Super Bowl in January 2002. After Belichick told the NFL that he wanted to break the custom of individual player introductions in the pregame ceremony, the NFL said no. Belichick, not surprisingly, refused to back down. And so the New England Patriots were introduced as a team. And it was as a team that they won, Tedy Bruschi once said: "When you work together—when you embrace words like 'dignity,' 'integrity,' and 'unselfishness'—great things can be accomplished."

Patriots kicker Adam Vinatieri (4). (AP Photo/Robert E. Klein)

Patriot Mike Vrabel (50) runs into the end zone past the Carolina Panthers' Deon Grant (27) on a one-yard touchdown pass in the fourth quarter of Super Bowl XXXVIII. (AP Photo/Michael Conroy)

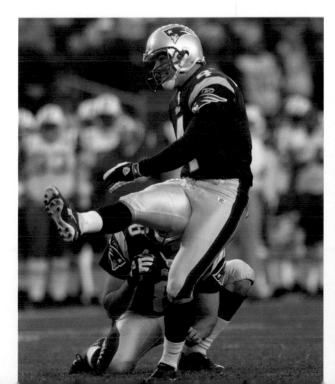

2 | THE 1990s COWBOYS

Playing Super Bowl XXVII in the Rose Bowl in Pasadena, California, Cowboys quarterback Troy Aikman (8) gets rid of the ball with Buffalo Bills defensive end Bruce Smith (78) bearing down. (AP Photo/NFL Photos)

The Dallas Cowboys were born in 1960. Their coach was Tom Landry. Within a few years, Landry had built them into an elite team, a status they held year in and year out, their success as predictable as the trademark hat on Landry's head. But after an NFL record 20 straight winning seasons, the Cowboys slipped into mediocrity, and then worse, in the late 1980s.

Landry had lost his touch. After drafting five Pro Bowlers or Hall of Famers from 1973 to 1977, Dallas came up with a string of busts, and Landry lost control of the locker room as cocaine and steroids grew prevalent and he began forgetting players' names. He also failed to adapt to a changing league, sticking with his 4-3 defense and "Flex Defense" that he had been preaching for decades while others were switching to the 3-4 or other variations.

In 1988 the Cowboys were a 3-13 disaster. A new owner, oil and gas millionaire Jerry Jones, rode into town, firing Landry unceremoniously along with two vital front-office figures, Tex Schramm and Gil Brandt. *Sports Illustrated* called Landry's dismissal "a new low in insulting a living legend."

The *Dallas Morning News* wrote that despite Landry's questionable coaching moves of late, the way the situation was handled "should stun and infuriate people who don't even follow professional sports. In a society where there still is a sometimes naive belief that great performance and loyal service will be rewarded, the callous dismissal of the Dallas Cowboys coach stings like the snap of a wet towel."

Jones took over Schramm's duties himself and hired as coach his former college football teammate Jimmy Johnson, who had won big at the University of Miami but who was seen as a crony of Jones's and someone with no NFL experience. Many fans were angered by Jones's maneuvers, and it didn't help when the team had a 1-15 season the following year, prompting some fans to wear sacks over their heads. A *Dallas Morning News* article called it "a season that set back a 30-year-old franchise 30 years."

But then the team reloaded with shocking speed. In just over two years, the Cowboys made nearly 30 trades, largely to stockpile draft picks. The most famous was born of a morning jog in the midst of that woeful '89 season when Johnson came up with the idea of trading Pro Bowl running back Herschel Walker. Johnson and Jones created a bidding war and upped the price until Minnesota handed over five players and conditional draft picks. At the time, many in Dallas and in the press thought that Johnson had made an enormous mistake, but the trade was actually a work of genius. The players never amounted to much, but Dallas used the draft picks—and Johnson's understanding of college talent—to turn the team around.

Sports Illustrated later dubbed it "the third-

Emmitt Smith (22) eludes a Buffalo Bills defender during Super Bowl XXVIII. (AP Photo/ Bob Galbraith)

Cowboys owner Jerry Jones applauds his team. (AP Photo/ Susan Weems)

The Steelers' Bam Morris (33) is stopped short of the first down by a host of Dallas Cowboys defenders in Super Bowl XXX. (AP Photo/Amy Sancetta)

worst trade in history, behind beads-for-Manhattan and Ruth-for-cash."

The 1988 draft had already yielded receiver Michael Irvin and linebacker Ken Norton Jr. With the first pick in 1989, Dallas took quarterback Troy Aikman, then grabbed fullback Daryl Johnson (thanks to a trade) and center Mark Stepnoski in later rounds. (However, Johnson foolishly drafted a second quarterback, Steve Walsh, and almost undid his dynasty before it got started by undermining Aikman.) The Walker picks were used (and traded to create more picks) for future Hall of Fame running back Emmitt Smith, future Pro Bowl safety Darren Woodson, and future Pro Bowl defensive tackle Russell Maryland, as well as cornerbacks Kevin Smith and Clayton Holmes. Using other draft picks, the Cowboys also added key components like receiver Alvin Harper, defensive linemen Chad Hennings and Tony Tolbert, and linebackers Robert Jones and Dixon Edwards.

But Jones and Johnson were also changing the persona of "America's Team." This was a bad-ass bunch from the top down. Over the long run, they would be irredeemably cocky and unbearably rambunctious, but in the short term Jones was able to take a chance on players other teams were fed up with, like safety James Washington, defensive lineman Tony Casillas, and, most importantly, Charles Haley, an emotionally unstable but immensely talented pass rusher who would transform the Cowboys defense. "What many of you have in common

is the one thing that should drive you—nobody wanted you," said Johnson to his players before the 1992 season opener.

In 1991 the Cowboys won their first playoff game of the new era. But they had finished 17th in points allowed. In 1992, with Haley leading the attack, they finished fifth, giving them the second-best point differential in the league and a 13-3 record.

"Haley put us over the top," secondary coach Dave Campo said. "He knew how to win. He was a tough guy."

These Cowboys would be far less beloved and admired than Lombardi's Packers, Noll's Steelers, or Walsh's 49ers, but they were just as feared, and for good reason. No matter how crazy the off-field antics became, the team never stopped winning for most of the next four years—an epoch in the era of free agency.

And the first jewel in the crown was, by and large, a flawless one. With 3:24 left in the first half of the 1993 Super Bowl against Buffalo, the offense scored on a 38-yard run by Smith, followed by an Aikman-to-Irvin touchdown pass. Seconds later, the defense forced a fumble—one of a record nine turnovers caused by Dallas—and Aikman hit Irvin for another touchdown. The 14–10 game was suddenly a 28–10 blowout. Dallas ended up swaggering off with a 52–17 triumph. (The sole sour note came when Leon Lett was running for a 64-yard touchdown on another fumble recovery but was so busy showboating that he didn't notice Buffalo's Don Beebe, who hustled downfield and stripped the ball away.)

The next season the Cowboys overcame Smith's holdout and Aikman's concussion to return for a Super Bowl rematch with the Bills. Dallas turned around a 13–6 halftime deficit for a 30–13 win. But a dynasty built on bad-ass attitude is hard to maintain, and the biggest rift had opened between Jones and Johnson. Each man wanted sole credit for reviving the franchise, and even Texas wasn't big enough to accommodate their two monumental egos. Shortly before shoving Johnson out the door, Jones told reporters that he believed the team could have won without Johnson. "I think there are five hundred people who could have coached this team to the Super Bowl. . . . I could have coached the hell out of this team."

So, after winning back-to-back Super Bowls, Johnson was out, replaced by another successful college coach, Barry Switzer. As he originally had done with Johnson, Jones admired Switzer's winning record and big persona. The press reaction was largely negative, however, especially because of Switzer's past, which was filled with everything from insider trading charges to DUI arrests to illegal recruiting at Oklahoma. The players soon found themselves split on the decision. Many of them welcomed the change after years of Johnson's tyrannical ways, although Switzer's more lax ethical and disciplinary approach also encouraged the worst in Dallas debauchery; the result was a team that fell short of its potential and lost to its rival, the San Francisco 49ers, for the NFC championship.

The roster was starting to turn over as age and free agency took their toll, but Jones managed to bring the Cowboys back to prime time in part by signing a player whose enormous talent and even bigger ego made him a perfect fit: Deion Sanders.

As a free agent, Sanders, who had just won the Super Bowl with San Francisco, got Jones to make him football's highest-paid defensive player. Deriding the headline-grabbing, attention-seeking move by Jones, Bob Smizik wrote in the *Pittsburgh*

Post-Gazette that eventually experts would "pinpoint the precise beginning of the decline and fall of the Dallas Cowboys' empire" as the signing of Deion Sanders.

Although many players loved Jones, who had been reviled when he first arrived (both Irvin and Smith would choose him to be their presenter when they were inducted into the Hall of Fame), the team was in constant turmoil, and Aikman and Switzer never got along, rarely speaking to each other outside of games. Still, for one last glorious season, they were so good that it didn't matter. In a battle to become the first team to win five Super Bowls, the Cowboys beat the Steelers, 27–17, in Super Bowl XXX and became the undisputed kings of the 1990s.

Then their reign was over, hollowed out at the core. Less than two months after the big game, Irvin was busted in a room with cocaine, marijuana, and a pair of prostitutes. It was a sign of the times. The team finished first again in 1996 but was only 10-6, with the 25th best offense in the league. They were bounced from the playoffs in the divisional round. Stumbling to 6-10 the following season, the Cowboys' dominance appeared to be over.

Still, the dominance they had achieved in those four seasons at the top was remarkable, especially as free agency changed the game on them. Some look back in regret at the opportunities lost in the push-and-pull between Johnson and Jones, but this was one team that, while it lasted, thrived on the conflict. As Aikman later said, "I don't believe our team was anywhere near finished doing what we could have done."

Cowboys head coach Jimmy Johnson, right, talks with running back Emmitt Smith. (AP Photo/Ron Heflin)

3 | THE 1980s 49ERS

The San Francisco 49ers had plenty of weapons as they amassed four Super Bowls in the 1980s, but ultimately the 49ers were all about Joe Cool.

Coach Bill Walsh was, of course, the foundation of it all, with his keen eye for drafting talent and his "West Coast Offense" in which short, precise passes often replaced handoffs. But he wasn't there for the entire run, retiring after the team's third Super Bowl win. (The fourth was coached by George Seifert.)

Dwight Clark made "the Catch" that propelled San Francisco to its first title, but he was out of football for the team's two final Super Bowls of the decade.

Roger Craig was the first running back to gain 1,000 yards each rushing and receiving in a single season, the only one to lead the league in catches, and the only one to have 100 yards receiving in a Super Bowl. But he didn't arrive until 1983, after the first trophy had been secured.

Jerry Rice is considered the greatest wide receiver ever, with accomplishments too numer-ous to list here. But the man who was just the third receiver to win a Super Bowl MVP played on only two of the 49ers championship squads of the 1980s. (He later won a third crown with the 49ers in 1994, with Steve Young at quarterback.)

The defense, which was routinely at or near the top of the league, had three players—Eric Wright, Keena Turner, and Hall of Fame cornerback/safety Ronnie Lott—who started in all four Super Bowls, but the team was still finally about that guy at quarterback.

Barely over six feet tall, Joe Montana seemed to lack the build and even the powerful arm of a prototypical NFL quarterback. He had, accord-ing to Walsh, "this inherent, instinctive" flair for finding the receiver on his route before he was even open and then throwing a perfectly timed, precisely placed pass. That allowed him to amass a career passer rating of 92.3, which is second among retired players. (Ironically, he trails only his former backup, Steve Young.) He is also the game's only three-time Super Bowl MVP.

49ers wide receiver Jerry Rice (80) runs upfield. (AP Photo/ Greg Trott)

49ers quarterback Joe Montana (16) is chased by Philadelphia Eagles defenders. (AP Photo/Rusty Kennedy)

Montana was always grateful to Walsh for giving a "189-pound skinny-legged quarterback" a shot, but Lott has said that the team was grateful that success early in his career didn't change his team-oriented focus. "He could have spun away from us," Lott said at the end of the 1980s. But "he hasn't changed a bit since 1981. He's extraordinary but ordinary. . . . He's got to be the most unselfish player in the history of the game."

One way to judge Montana's cool under pressure is this: in the NFL, home-field advantage is usually critical, but the 49ers of 1981 to 1989 posted a better road record than every other team's home record. They were helped by an imposing defense and owner Eddie DeBartolo Jr.—who gave his players two seats per person on chartered flights and solo hotel rooms with extra days in town to acclimate. "Eddie was a great guy," Pro Bowl offensive lineman Randy Cross said. "We kept flying DC-10s, and we kept wearing people out." But all that couldn't have been done without an unflappable field general.

In the biggest games, of course, Montana was at his best. After that remarkable pass to Clark to complete their comeback win against Dallas in 1981, the team beat Cincinnati in Super Bowl XVI—Montana completed a flea-flicker-reverse for 14 yards in leading his team to a touchdown on his first Super Bowl drive, then set a record with a 92-yard touchdown drive soon after. By halftime, the 49ers had a 20–0 lead, the biggest margin in history; they'd hold on to win their first crown ever.

In 1984, San Francisco roared through a 15-1 season, averaging almost 30 points a game. But in Super Bowl XIX, they faced Miami's Dan Marino, who had broken just about every passing record that season; the Dolphins had averaged 32.1 points per game.

Irritated by the media's focus on Miami, Walsh sneered at one point, "This week we are playing against the greatest passer of all time, as I understand it." But the 49ers defense shut Marino down almost completely while Montana threw for three touchdowns and ran for one in a 38–16 blowout.

49ers center Randy Cross (51) blocks Patriots linebacker Steve Nelson (57) during the NFL Pro Bowl in 1985. (AP Photo/NFL Photos)

49ers safety Ronnie Lott (42) waits for the snap. (AP Photo/Jack Smith)

"When you heard all week, 'Miami, Miami, Miami,' you had to think, 'Hey, what about us,'" Montana said after the game.

After three subpar playoff appearances, the 49ers returned to form in 1988 after Walsh settled a quarterback rivalry between Montana and Young—having Young on the bench seemed to spark Montana to even greater heights. Rice won the Super Bowl MVP that season thanks to his record 215 yards receiving, but it was in this game that Montana—who passed for 357 yards—sealed his reputation with a stirring 92-yard drive at the end of the game with his team trailing Cincinnati, 16–13. "Somebody came over to me on the bench and said, 'We're in good shape,'" said Bengals receiver Cris Collinsworth later. "I asked him if number 16 was still on the field. I think I would have been more surprised if Joe Montana did not score that TD. He is not human out there."

In his first season under Seifert, Montana showed that he could make the offense work without Walsh—he set a record (since broken) with a passer rating of 112.4 and completed an astonishing 70.2 percent of his passes, which was then the second-highest mark ever. "Joe Montana was a surgeon," said Dan Reeves, coach of the Denver Broncos, who faced the 49ers in the Super Bowl. There were no close calls in that postseason—the 49ers won their three games by 126–26, and the team's 55–10 win against Denver was the biggest rout in Super Bowl history, a fitting grand finale for the team of the 1980s.

Even though that last game wasn't close, if it had been, few would have doubted that San Francisco would find a way to win. Walsh summed it up best: "When the game is on the line, and you need someone to go in there and win it right now, I would rather have Joe Montana as my quarterback than anyone else who ever played the game."

San Francisco's Roger Craig takes to the air. (AP Photo/ Paul Sakuma)

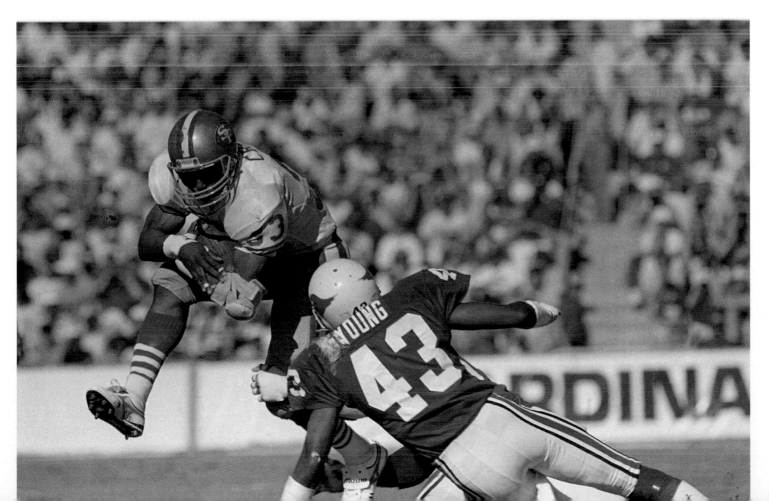

4 | THE 1970s STEELERS

Steelers head coach Chuck Noll speaks with quarterback Terry Bradshaw on the bench. (AP Photo/ Gene Puskar)

The football sails into the arms of Pittsburgh's Lynn Swann (88) in the AFC championship game in 1979 against the Houston Oilers. (AP Photo/ R. C. Greenawalt)

The Pittsburgh Steelers of the 1970s produced what many think is the greatest play in NFL history during the playoffs in 1972—Terry Bradshaw to Franco Harris (off Jack Tatum), immortalized as "the Immaculate Reception."

They also had the single greatest draft in NFL history in 1974, when they picked up four future Hall of Famers: Lynn Swann, John Stallworth, Jack Lambert, and Mike Webster. And they assembled the greatest collection of talent ever on one team, with nine eventual Hall of Famers plus an annual assortment of Pro Bowlers. "The Steelers had the best grouping of players in the history of the game," said Bill Walsh, who coached the 49ers dynasty. "No question about it."

They even had the greatest sports-related TV commercial ever, thanks to "Mean Joe" Greene's "Hey, kid, . . . catch" ad for Coca-Cola.

But none of that would have added up to much if not for the bottom line: the Steelers won it all and then did it again, and again, and again, winning four Super Bowls in six years—and doing it during an era of great teams like the Dallas Cowboys, Oakland Raiders, Minnesota Vikings, and Miami Dolphins.

Hall of Fame cornerback Mel Blount credits the man with the keen eye for talent who oversaw those drafts and pushed his players hard. "They talk about the Vince Lombardi Era, but I think the Chuck Noll Era is even greater," he said. Noll was tough on his players but enjoyed the role of teacher. And in the media, he shifted attention and praise away from himself and toward his players.

Defense was the soul of the Steelers, with Greene and Lambert setting the intimidating tone.

"Yes, I get satisfaction out of hitting a guy and seeing him lay there a while," said Lambert, whom some considered the meaner of the two.

"The Steel Curtain" initially referred to the front four of Greene, L. C. Greenwood, Dwight White, and Ernie Holmes (they made the cover of *Time* magazine) but eventually encompassed the whole defense, including Lambert, perennial Pro Bowler Andy Russell, Hall of Famer Jack Ham at linebacker, and Blount leading the secondary.

The NFL began to give out a Defensive Player of the Year Award in 1971; in a five-year span starting the following year, Greene won it twice and Lambert and Blount once each. Of Greene, Russell once said, "Joe was like a one-man army. . . . I caught myself applauding a couple times."

Jim Otto, a Hall of Fame center for Pittsburgh's rival Oakland Raiders, once said of facing Greene, "You came out hurting all over, and what didn't hurt didn't work."

But the entire defensive unit was ferocious and relentless—*Sports Illustrated* called it "the most

A pass to Oscar Roan of the Cleveland Browns is broken up in the end zone by the Steelers' Mel Blount. (AP Photo/R. C. Greenawalt)

Members of Pittsburgh's "Steel Curtain" defense react as Vikings quarterback Fran Tarkenton recovers his own fumble in the end zone for a safety in the second quarter of Super Bowl IX. (AP Photo/ Charlie Kelly)

destructive force in football." In their first Super Bowl win, 16–6 over Minnesota, the Steelers didn't allow a score (the Vikings touchdown came on a blocked punt) and yielded a mere 119 yards of total offense even though Lambert and Russell missed much of the second half with injuries.

The following year, when Pittsburgh repeated as champions, Greenwood sacked Dallas quarterback Roger Staubach on the Cowboys' first play, and safety Glen Edwards intercepted Staubach in the end zone on their last play, preserving a 21–17 win.

But Pittsburgh really did have it all (including "the Terrible Towel," the symbol of their fans' ardent support, which debuted in 1975). As the league changed the rules to allow for more offense—in large part because of the Steel Curtain—the Steelers simply scored more, winning their last two Super Bowls by 35–31 and 31–19.

At quarterback, Bradshaw took a while to de-

velop and often seemed at odds with coach Chuck Noll, but he made the big plays when they counted most—a task made easier by the speed, strength, and athleticism of Swann and Stallworth and a running game powered by the indomitable Harris.

Harris powered past Minnesota for 158 yards in 1975 and became just the second running back to be named Super Bowl MVP. Swann became the first receiver to win a Super Bowl MVP thanks to his four catches (some seemingly impossible) for 161 yards the following year. Bradshaw was the first player to win the award twice. And his second one was due in large part to Stallworth, who caught three passes for 121 yards, including a 73-yard touchdown in the Steelers' comeback over the Rams in Super Bowl XIV for their final ring.

Chuck Noll's motto as a coach was: "Whatever it takes." In the 1970s, the Steelers clearly had that . . . and more.

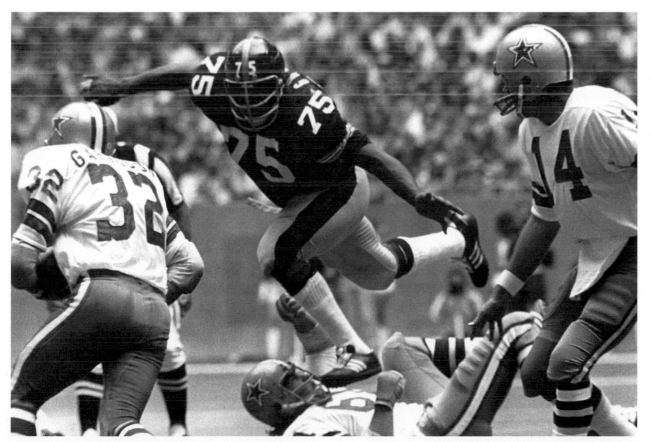

Steelers left tackle Joe Greene (75) takes a shortcut across Dallas Cowboys guard Blaine Nye (61) to put a sudden halt to the forward progress of Cowboys fullback Walt Garrison (32). (AP Photo/ Ferd Kaufman, File)

5 | THE 1960s PACKERS

Green Bay quarterback Bart Starr (15). (AP Photo)

Packers coach Vince Lombardi, with assistant coach Phil Bengtson, ride the practice blocking skid at the Packers' training camp. (AP Photo)

In 1961, Green Bay merchants, to boost pride in the city, turned to the Packers' six NFL titles and started calling their home "Titletown." Yet it was an odd moniker for a team that hadn't won an NFL championship since 1944 and was fresh off a loss in the 1960 championship game. Green Bay coach Vince Lombardi didn't like the presumptuousness of the nickname. But he, more than anyone else, made it come true.

Fourteen NFL teams have won back-to-back championships since 1940, and seven of those took home three crowns in a decade, with four coming out on top four times in 10 years. But only one team managed to win not only three straight championships but five titles within a decade, and that was Vince Lombardi's Packers. *Sports Illustrated* called the Packers "those against whom all others

are measured," saying that the team "has the elusive quality of character—a willingness to play as well as possible for as long as necessary." Twenty years later, the magazine returned to that dynasty and called Green Bay "a team for all time."

Lombardi could not abide defeat and would always push his players to redouble their efforts in their quest for a title. "If you can accept losing," he famously once said, "you can't win."

The Green Bay Packers of 1958 had seen just one winning season in a decade. They finished 1-10-1, last in both points scored and points allowed. That would have been bad for any team, but it was unheard of for one with six future Hall of Famers playing regularly—Bart Starr, Paul Hornung, Jim Taylor, Forrest Gregg, Ray Nitschke, and Jim Ringo. Jerry Kramer and Max McGee, two other crucial components of the dynasty to come, were also on that team. The problem was the coach, Scooter McLean, who was more likely to be found playing cards with his players the night before the game than going over Xs and Os with them.

For 1959, the Packers hired Lombardi—who had proved to be a wizard as the offensive coordinator for the New York Giants. He was made coach and general manager, to which he added one more informal title . . . drill sergeant.

"Lombardi got our attention immediately," Paul Hornung once wrote. "He told us if we didn't give him 100 percent all the time, our butts would be out of Green Bay. He laid down his rules right away. That's what all of us needed. . . . He was tough, tougher than any coach I had ever known."

Lombardi worked his men almost unbearably hard, breaking the bad habits from years of losing. Lombardi likened the game of football to life itself, believing that "it requires perseverance, self-denial,

hard work, sacrifice, dedication, and respect for authority." "We had the core of a good football team, but what we lacked was leadership," Starr said. "He brought that the day he walked in the front door. We were much better organized and we were much better prepared because of his leadership and teaching."

Lombardi instilled in his players a will to win plus an emphasis on fundamentals, best seen in his power sweep—his men could run this simple, straightforward play so well that other teams couldn't stop it even when they knew it was coming. "That sweep worked because everyone on that team did their job," said Don McCafferty, who was an assistant coach for Baltimore. "It was merely execution—and the defenses were the ones to get executed."

By 1960 the Packers had the league's second-best offense and second-best defense and were in the NFL championship. But they lost, 17–13, to Philadelphia after Lombardi went for broke on fourth down twice instead of settling for field goals. Afterward he took responsibility and vowed to his men that they would never lose another championship game. He was right.

The 1961 championship was particularly satisfying for Lombardi, not just because it was the first but because the Packers crushed the New York Giants, 37–0.

Lombardi, a Brooklyn native, had once said that he wanted the Giants' head coaching job "worse than anything in the world." "He felt he had earned the right to be a head coach long before that, so when it became a reality, he wanted to leave no doubt," defensive end Willie Davis recalled.

Packers fullback Jim Taylor (31) runs upfield. (AP Photo/ NFL Photos)

"There was an incredible driving force behind him, and it was so obvious before the Giants game. It was like he wanted the Giants wiped out."

The 1962 team was even stronger, perhaps the best Green Bay team of all. The Packers raced out to a 10-0 start, with eight wins by at least 11 points, and finished 13-1—a record that no Green Bay team has matched since. They won their first four games by 109–14, and their final point differential of 19.1 points per game was the best since the Chicago Bears of 1942 and would not be topped until the New England Patriots of 2007.

"This was probably our strongest team overall," Jerry Kramer said. "Jim and Paul were still strong and young, and Bart had come of age. And I think we all were cohesive, all strong, all full of it, and all hungry."

Despite losing Hornung to injuries for five games, the Packers again scored the most points in the league, averaging almost 30 per game. Starr and Taylor reached new levels of play: Starr led the league in completion percentage and passer rating for the first time, a feat he would repeat in 1964 and 1966.

"Bart did not have the strongest of arms," Hornung said, but he had what counted more: accuracy within 40 yards and a vision of the game and the field. "I played with Bart for nine years, and I'll guarantee you he never made 10 mental mistakes the whole time."

Taylor, who had gained 1,101 yards in 1960 and 1,307 the next year, gained 1,474 in 1962, becoming the only person ever to gain more yards in a season than Jim Brown. He also led the league with 19 rushing touchdowns as the Packers set an NFL record with 36 rushing touchdowns (which hasn't been broken even in the modern 16-game seasons).

The defense, with future Hall of Famers Nitschke, Willie Wood, Willie Davis, and Herb Adderly, had its best season, allowing less than 11 points per game, the best in the NFL. The team had six games in which it held opponents to single digits, including two 49–0 shutouts. The most awe-inspiring was their decimation of Philadelphia: the Packers gained 628 yards while holding the Eagles to a mere 54, one of the most lopsided totals in history. And in the championship rematch against New York, Green Bay's defense throttled the Giants: the Packers prevailed, 16–7, the only New York score came on a blocked punt, and Nitschke was named MVP. But the most memorable win was a 9–7 triumph over Detroit, a last-minute comeback spurred by an Adderly interception. This game was the focal point of *Run to Daylight*, a book "written" by Lombardi about a week's preparation for an NFL game. (The book was actually penned by legendary sportswriter W. C. Heinz.) In it, Lombardi acknowledged that winning is "like a habit-forming drug. . . . Once you have sampled it you are hooked." The instant classic helped mythologize Lombardi and his Packers even more than their second championship did.

The team was stunned when Paul Hornung was caught gambling on football and suspended in 1963. The result was that Green Bay "fell" to 11-2-1, finishing second to the 11-1-2 Bears, the only team to beat them. The following year was a genuine struggle — the team started just 3-4, losing three times by three points or less. They rallied to finish 8-5-1, but Lombardi was dissatisfied and ready to shake things up.

In 1965 he brought in Don Chandler to kick and Carroll Dale at flanker. Lombardi even challenged the entire team's commitment during a meeting. "I'm the only one that puts his blood and guts and his heart in the game," he shouted, in a vintage Lombardi challenge. "You're nothing! I'm the only guy that gives a damn if we win or lose." Angered, the players shouted back, affirming that they had gotten the message. He even benched Hornung for a game when he was struggling. (Hornung scored five touchdowns the very next week.) The offense was never fully in sync — Starr had a down year, while Taylor and McGee began precipitous declines — and finished just eighth in points scored. Yet there were always enough points for a win:

from 1961 to 1967, the Packers were first or second in points allowed every year except one (when they were third), and they took home the first of their three straight titles.

"By 1965, and in the two years after that too, things had evened out a lot," said receiver Boyd Dowler. "There were four or five other teams with comparable personnel. They could have won it. The point is, they didn't. We won it, and I know now it was the motivation the man gave us that did it."

The next two seasons were even more impressive. For starters, the team had to beat the Dallas Cowboys to win the NFL championship both years — the first time by intercepting a game-tying pass in the end zone, and the second on Starr's quarterback sneak. That Ice Bowl win reinforced the notion that a Packers win was inevitable, that their will was just too strong.

"The discipline and conditioning programs they went through, the punishment and the suffering, they all tend to develop character," Cowboys coach Tom Landry said later. "Vince developed a lot of character in his players, character that a lot of them probably never would have had without the leadership and discipline he developed in them."

In 1966 and 1967, because the NFL had agreed to merge with the AFL, Green Bay had to win the "World Championship Game" against the best AFL team. Both times the Packers dominated their foe, beating Kansas City, 35–10, and Oakland, 33–14, and reinforced a belief that the NFL was superior.

But it wasn't the NFL that was superior — as the Jets would show the following year against Baltimore — it was the Packers. During their reign, the team went 74-20-4 in the regular season. They also went 5-0 in NFL championships and 2-0 in NFL-AFL championships. And it started with their coach, which explains why Super Bowl victors now take home the Vince Lombardi Trophy. It is a name synonymous with winning.

Rams running back Dick Bass (22) is stopped by Green Bay linebacker Ray Nitschke (66) and safety Willie Wood (24). (AP Photo/ NFL Photos)

6 | THE 1950s BROWNS

The defining moment of the Cleveland Browns' reign as the NFL team of the 1950s came, oddly enough, in their very first NFL game.

The Browns began playing in 1946 in the All-America Football Conference, a league designed to challenge the NFL. They had everything a great team needed: coach Paul Brown's meticulous professionalism and superior recruiting skills, quarterback "Automatic" Otto Graham's poise and consistency, Lou "The Toe" Groza's deadly kicking, and a hard-hitting defense that gave up the fewest points in the AAFC every season. Graham's favorite passing targets were stars Dante Lavelli, Mac Speedie, and Dub Jones, who ran Brown's comeback pass patterns with precise, sharp angles. The Browns were also integrated from day one, unlike most AAFC and especially NFL teams, signing fullback Marion Motley and defensive lineman Bill Willis, both of whom had Hall of Fame careers.

The Browns shredded their AAFC competition, winning four straight titles and losing only four games overall. Every year, Cleveland challenged the NFL champion to a game but was rudely dismissed. When the league folded, Cleveland was one of three teams invited into the NFL. There, however, they had to prove themselves all over again as the NFL establishment dismissed the AAFC as strictly minor league.

The Browns made their NFL debut in 1950 in Philadelphia against the defending NFL champion Eagles. "We had waited four years for this game," Lavelli said.

The press called it "the World Series of Pro Football." Skeptics salivated at the thought of the Browns getting their comeuppance before 70,000 screaming fans. "The worst team in our league could beat the best team in theirs," Washington owner George Preston Marshall sneered.

"We were playing for our honor," Lavelli said. The game wasn't even close. But it wasn't what the NFL expected. After falling behind 3–0, Graham threw a 59-yard bomb to Jones; he went on to pass for 346 yards, and the defense, anchored by Willis and another AAFC refugee, Len Ford, shut down the Eagles as the newcomers crushed the champions, 35–10. Afterward, NFL commissioner Bert Bell called them "the best-coached football team I've ever seen."

By the end of the year, it was the Browns who were NFL champions, edging the Los Angeles Rams in the title game and removing all doubt about their qualifications.

The offense began a gradual transition over the next few years—it lost receiver Mac Speedie after 1952, the last productive season for Motley was 1953, and for Jones and Lavelli it was 1954—but three things in Cleveland remained constant: Otto Graham, Paul Brown, and the top defense in the nation.

The Browns finished that first NFL season in 1950 with the second-best defense. That would happen just one more time between 1951 and 1957—for the rest of their reign, the Browns defense was the absolute best. And even though they lost three straight NFL championships starting in 1951—including two to the Detroit Lions—they snatched the crown back from the Lions in 1954 and defended their title in 1955. After Graham retired, the Browns stumbled in 1956, but they drafted running back Jim Brown, who brought them back to the championship game in 1957.

If you count the AAFC years, the Browns appeared in 10 straight championship games, winning seven. Even if you discard those early years—as the NFL does—the Browns of the 1950s showed that the question wasn't whether they were good enough for the NFL, but whether the NFL was good enough for them.

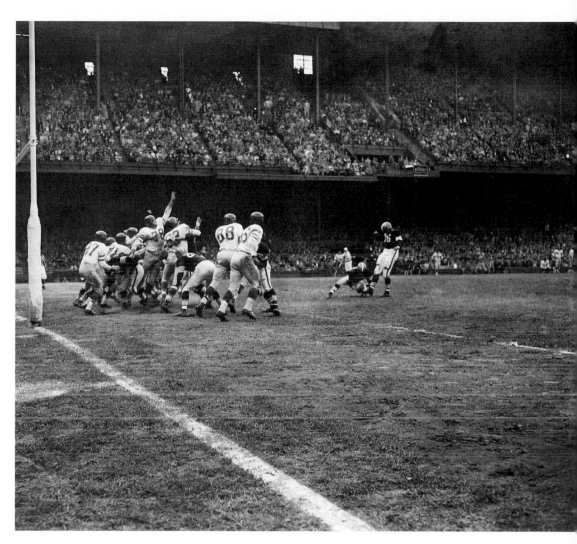

The Browns' Mac Speedie carries the ball for a 19-yard gain in a 1950 game against the Eagles. (AP Photo)

Browns receiver Dante "Gluefingers" Lavelli (56). (AP Photo/File)

Lou Groza of the Cleveland Browns kicks an extra point, his sixth of the day, in a 1952 game against the Philadelphia Eagles. Tom James does the holding. (AP Photo)

7 | THE 1940s BEARS

The Redskins' Jimmy Johnstone (31) is tackled by the Bears' Sid Luckman. Also converging on Johnstone in the 1940 NFL championship game are Bears Joe Stydahar (13), Bill Osmanski (9), John Siegal (6), Dan Fortmann (21), and George McAfee (5). (AP Photo)

George Halas was ready to start another revolution. Halas had been present at the NFL's birth in 1920, then played for and coached the team that would become the Chicago Bears from its inception, leading the Bears to their first championship in 1921 and eventually becoming sole owner of the team too. In the 1930s, he had pushed for a number of rule changes to favor the passing game and the invention of the NFL championship game. Then he had coached the Bears to victory in the first title tilt.

But in 1938, offensive and defensive legend Bronislaw "Bronko" Nagurski quit over a salary dispute with Halas, and the Bears went just 6-5-1, their worst record in a decade. So Halas, working with his friend the University of Chicago coach Clark Shaughnessy, created a T-formation offense that would transform the game. Quarterbacks took the snap from under the center—snaps previously went to a running back—and new blocking patterns, men in motion, and option plays created far more choices and chances to deceive the defense and opened up possibilities for an explosive passing game.

Halas would need a smart and talented quarterback, however, one who could understand and exploit the new system. Columbia University's star halfback Sid Luckman was his choice. "Sid wasn't built for quarterback," Halas said later. "He was stocky, not fast, and not a great passer in the old tradition. But he was smart, and he was dedicated."

Chicago had the sixth draft pick and didn't think Luckman would last that long. So Halas made a trade with Pittsburgh to also give the Bears the second pick, which Halas used to snare Luckman. However, Luckman then told Halas that he wasn't planning on playing pro football. "My plans are to

enter the trucking business with my brothers," he said.

Halas explained the new offense to Luckman and how well suited he would be to this system. That sales pitch, plus a lucrative $5,000 contract, persuaded the quarterback. Luckman was erratic early in 1939, but after being shut out against Detroit, the Bears won their last four.

But they were not yet a complete team. They had finished just fifth in defense in 1939, and Halas knew where to look for a remedy. Hunk Anderson, who played for Knute Rockne at Notre Dame and replaced Rockne after his death, had joined the NFL in 1939 as coach of the Detroit Lions. He introduced new wrinkles like linebacker and safety blitzes, and when the Bears faced the Lions, Detroit had brutalized Chicago. Having seen what Anderson could do, Halas hired him away. Using established Bears like George Musso, Joe Stydahar, and Dan Fortmann, along with newcomers like "Bulldog" Turner and later Ed Sprinkle, Anderson created the "Monsters of the Midway" defense that terrorized the NFL throughout the 1940s.

After Halas also drafted Turner and end Ken Kavanaugh and traded for another first-round pick, speedy running back George McAfee, he had built a team that could implement all of these innovative tactics. The Bears had a formidable ground game, a superstar at quarterback, a big-play threat in McAfee (who returned a kick 93 yards for a touchdown in his debut), and future Hall of Famers on the offensive and defensive lines.

The Bears' 1940 championship was one of the most famous blowouts in any sport, a 73–0 shellacking of the Washington Redskins. The next year, they overwhelmed opponents by an average score of 36–13 to finish 10-1. Their sole loss was to

Bears quarterback Sid Luckman (42). (AP Photo)

Green Bay, which was also 10-1. In the league's first tiebreaker playoff game, the Bears gained 277 yards rushing and forced four turnovers to easily avenge themselves, 33–14. In the title game, the Monsters took the ball away five times as Chicago cruised, 37–9. Astonishingly, the Bears were even better in 1942. Although Halas left after five games to join the Navy and stars like McAfee and Bill Osmanski also left for World War II, the Bears had enough talent—including Luckman—to win 11 straight, averaging 34 points to their opponents' eight. (They allowed just 14 points over the last six games.) But Washington got payback in the championship, intercepting three passes and eking out a 14–6 win.

The next season saw even more players depart

for military service, but it also produced two of the NFL's most storied players. On November 14, the Bears traveled to New York, where Luckman—a Brooklyn native—was feted with Sid Luckman Day at the Polo Grounds. Luckman had a sore shoulder and needed a Novocain shot just to play, but play he did. Two weeks after his rival, Washington's Sammy Baugh, set a record with six touchdown passes, Luckman did one better, hurling seven TDs and setting another mark with 453 yards passing.

But Luckman was hit by the grippe, and after 24 straight regular-season games without a loss, the Bears went down against the hated Redskins. To clinch their division and have another shot at Washington in the NFL championship, the Bears needed a win against the crosstown Cardinals in the finale. Before the season, Hunk Anderson had persuaded Bronko Nagurski to come out of retirement and fill out the depleted roster. The creaky and achy 35-year-old played well on the line, but now he went to Anderson and asked to be reinstated at fullback. The coach knew, however, that he would have to use Nagurski sparingly. Fortunately, the Cardinals were both awful and even more shorthanded than the Bears—they were winless that season. Unfortunately, they picked this game to play their best football. The Cardinals took a 24–14 lead into the fourth quarter. Finally, with snow starting to fall, Anderson turned to Nagurski. The Bronk blasted through the Cardinals defense, dragging defenders with him, refusing to go down. He carried five straight times for 31 yards. From the Cardinal 20, he crashed 19 yards, carrying half the opposing defense on his back by the end. The entire Cardinal squad tried to stop him at the 1-yard line but failed. On the next drive, Nagurski did it again, including gains of 12 on a fourth-and-4 and three on a fourth-and-1. The crowd, which had awaited their savior all afternoon, went berserk as the Bears won, 35–24.

These games were the stuff of legend, but it took the total demolition of Washington in the championship to complete the saga. The defense created six turnovers, Luckman threw for five touchdowns, and in his final game ever Nagurski ran for one more. The Bears won, 41–21. For the third time in four years, they were the best.

Too many players were gone in the next two years as the entire league fell into minor disarray, but after the war Halas and his men came home for one last hurrah: in 1946 the team beat the Giants in the NFL championship, 24–14.

Bears player/coach George Halas in 1933. (AP Photo)

8 | THE 1930s GIANTS

For 50 years, one genuine dynasty has emerged each decade, putting its unique stamp on that decade. But after the NFL introduced its championship game in 1933, three teams—the Green Bay Packers, the Chicago Bears, and the New York Giants—shared the throne for that first decade.

The Packers, who had compiled the league's best record in 1930 and 1931, played in three and won two of the first seven title games. The Bears had the best record in 1932 and won the first championship. Still, it was the Giants who staked the strongest claim, reaching the new championship five times and becoming the first team to win it twice.

The Giants had made their great defensive lineman Steve Owen their coach in 1931; the 5'11", 230-pound sparkplug had captained the team since it went 11-1-1 and yielded just 20 points in 1927. (Owen never signed a coaching contract, but his handshake agreement with the Mara family kept him in place until 1953.) Owen coached conservatively, emphasizing defense and often taking the field goal rather than risking more to go for a touchdown. "Football is a game played down in the dirt, and it always will be," he once said. "There's no use getting fancy about it."

Yet he was also an innovator, ahead of his time in stunting linemen and blitzing linebackers and safeties in the days before it was called "the blitz." He also utilized two different units in an era when teams ran most players ragged for the full 60 minutes. He created the A-formation offense, which split the linemen and realigned the backfield to create a strong running game up the middle. He would eventually adapt and switch to the T formation popularized in 1940 by the Bears.

Owen's team was filled with tough, smart, and talented players like future Hall of Famers halfback Ken Strong, tight end Red Badgro, center Mel Hein, and fullback Tuffy Leemans.

For 1933, the team got an infusion of new talent, including rookies Harry Newman and Kink Richards, plus Strong, the former New York University star who came over from the Staten Island Stapletons after they folded. After a 4-3 start, they reeled off seven straight wins on the backs of the defense (after yielding 68 points in the first seven games, the Giants defense allowed just 33 in the final seven) and an offense led by Strong, who passed, ran for, and caught seven touchdowns; Richards, who had seven touchdowns running and receiving; and Newman, who led the league in passing yards and touchdowns.

In the first NFL championship game, the Giants took the Bears to the wire—there were six lead changes before the Bears prevailed, 23–21. The Giants got revenge in 1934, beating the Bears, 30–13, in the famous "Sneakers Game": the Giants won that game on the frozen Polo Grounds turf because they shrewdly wore sneakers, gaining superior footing.

The 1935 team posted the league's best defense, allowing just 84 points and notching four shutouts; Ed Danowski, a second-year man from Fordham University, took over the offense and led the league in passing yardage and touchdowns, and rookie Tod Goodwin led the league in receptions and yards per catch. The Giants reached the championship again, but fell to the Detroit Lions, who blew open a 13–7 game with two late touchdowns.

The New York Giants' Mel Hein in 1939. (AP Photo)

A crowd of 57,461 at the Polo Grounds in New York City in 1938. (AP Photo)

It took two years to get back to the championship, but by 1938 Owen had brought in enough new talent to support Hein and Danowski that the Giants dominated their division—they were 8-2-1 and finished first in the league in defense and second in offense. Danowski led the league in completions, and additions Tuffy Leemans and Hank Soar both were near the top in all-purpose yards. The Giants faced off against the Packers in the championship, with the winner heading for the history books as the first team to win two championships. Before 48,000 fans at the Polo Grounds, the Giants asserted themselves in a fierce battle; trailing 17–16 in the fourth quarter, Danowski and Soar connected for a 23-yard touchdown pass that gave New York the title. Both teams returned in 1939, and the Packers won that matchup, 31–16. Although Green Bay ended the decade on a high note, the 1930s ultimately belonged to the Giants.

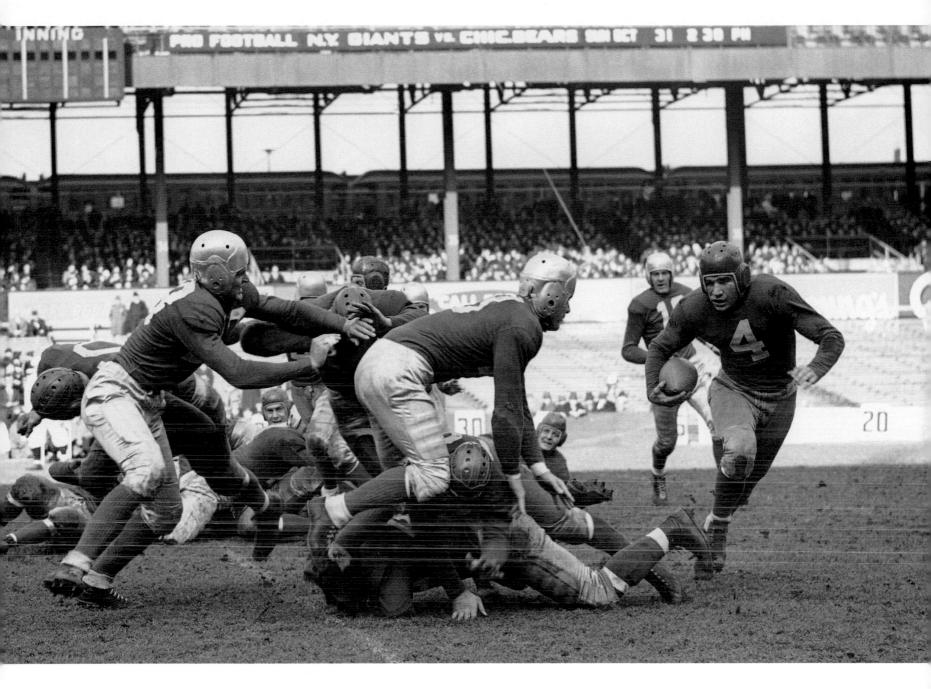

New York Giants halfback Tuffy Leemans (4) breaks away for a four-yard gain against the Brooklyn Dodgers in a 1937 game at the Polo Grounds. (AP Photo)

9 | THE 1920s BULLDOGS

Canton, Ohio, is the birthplace of the NFL. It is also the birthplace of an NFL dynasty.

The league, initially called the American Professional Football Association, started there in 1920 because Jim Thorpe, the world's most famous athlete, had transformed the Canton Bulldogs into a football powerhouse in the previous decade.

But Thorpe left the Bulldogs after 1920, and the team managed just a 5-2-3 record the following season. To turn things around, owner Ralph Hay hijacked Guy Chamberlin, the left end and budding star, from George Halas in Chicago. In an autobiographical article published in the *Saturday Evening Post* on November 23, 1957, Halas recalled that "Chamberlin was the best 2-way end I've ever seen. He was a tremendous tackler on defense and a triple-threat performer on offense."

Hay was impressed with how Chamberlin had run back an interception 70 yards for a touchdown to beat rival Buffalo in the season's decisive game. Hay made Chamberlin not just the star but the coach. The newcomer cleaned house, keeping just five players from the previous year, including tackle Pete Henry; he also brought in another tackle, Link Lyman, from his alma mater, the University of Nebraska.

In 1922 the APFA became the NFL, and the Bulldogs took over. The early days of the NFL were built around defenses. The Bulldogs didn't just win games—they dominated them, crushing opposing offenses without mercy. They won seven games by

at least two touchdowns and were scored upon in just three games, allowing a mere 15 points overall to finish 10-0-2. (The ties were scoreless.) The offense, led by Chamberlin, was second overall with 184 points. In one of the few close calls, the team trailed the Chicago Cardinals, 3–0, in the fourth quarter when Chamberlin took over; after blocking a punt to set up one touchdown, he ran back two interceptions for scores and a 20–3 final. There was no title game back then. With the first-place team simply declared the champion, the Bulldogs bested Halas's 9-3 Bears for the top spot.

Impossibly enough, the team was even better in 1923. Three players blossomed—two lesser players from the previous season, Lou Smyth and Doc Elliott, along with rookie Ben Jones—with each scoring at least six rushing touchdowns. Their fearsome ground game helped the Bulldogs churn out a league-best 246 points (the Cardinals were next with only 161), while the defense remained invincible, allowing just 19 points—and 10 of those came in a game where the Bulldogs scored 46 against the Cleveland Indians. Again, the 11-0-1 team outpaced the 9-2-1 Bears for the NFL crown.

But the team wasn't scoring financially. After 1922, Hay sold the Bulldogs to a group of local businessmen. Their championship payroll in 1923 lost money, so they sold the team for $2,500 to Samuel Deutsch, a Cleveland jeweler and boxing promoter who also owned a minor league baseball team and had bought the Cleveland Indians before that

Jim Thorpe, one of the world's most famous athletes, playing halfback for the Canton Bulldogs in the early 1920s. (AP Photo/NFL Photos)

season. Deutsch took the Bulldogs' name and the best players—including Lyman, Jones, and Elliott—to Cleveland, where he again installed Chamberlin as coach. The Bulldogs, led by Elliott, outscored everyone else with 229 points, and their 7-1-1 record was enough to leave the Bears in second place once more.

But money woes broke up the dynasty: Deutsch sold the Bulldogs franchise back to Canton but kept another version in Cleveland; the key players scattered to other teams; and both Bulldogs teams failed and soon folded. The central figure, Chamberlin, coached the Frankford Yellow Jackets, and

in 1926 he led his team to a 14-1-2 record and his fifth and final championship as a player or coach of the decade.

Four decades later, from 1963 to 1965, the Bulldogs stars—Henry, Lyman, and Chamberlin—would be reunited when each of them was elected to the Pro Football Hall of Fame, which the NFL had placed in Canton. Chamberlin credited his team members, calling William "Link" Lyman and Wilbur "Pete" Henry "the two greatest tackles ever to play the pros," and he further noted, "Lots of fans said they were responsible for our success, and they were about right."

The 1922 Canton Bulldogs. (AP Photo/ Pro Football Hall of Fame)

Canton tackle William
"Link" Lyman. (AP
Photo/Pro Football
Hall of Fame)

1 | SINGLE–SEASON GREATNESS

In the Super Bowl era, 28 teams have gone 14-2 or 15-1 or been undefeated in the regular season. Yet just 11 of those also won the Super Bowl. The three dynasties —the 1970s Steelers, the 1980s 49ers, and the 2000s Patriots—account for five of those wins. The other half-dozen teams may not have had such long runs, but their singular seasons are still worth celebrating.

Miami Dolphins coach Don Shula lets out a celebratory roar as the gun sounds. Shula coached the 1972 Dolphins to a 17-0 record, still the only perfect season in NFL history. (AP Photo/File)

THE 1972 MIAMI DOLPHINS

Some NFL pundits dismiss the 1972 Dolphins as over-rated, pointing to their absurdly easy schedule—only two of their foes had a winning record (both were just 8-6). That's true, but it also doesn't matter.

Nor, ultimately, does it matter that the Dolphins, despite injuries that sidelined quarterback Bob Griese, scored the most points in the NFL while their "No-Name Defense" allowed the fewest. And we can discount the Dolphins' six Hall of Fame players—Griese, Larry Csonka, Paul Warfield, Larry Little, Jim Langer, and Nick Buoniconti—plus Don Shula at coach, as well as their trips to the Super Bowl both the season before and the season after this one.

All that matters is their final record: 14-0 in the regular season, 3-0 in the postseason. No other NFL team has ever done that, before or since.

The 1934 and 1942 Bears and the 2007 Patriots all went undefeated in the regular season but lost their title game. "If we had lost the Super Bowl, everything else we had accomplished would have been wasted," Shula later said, especially since he had heard the "choker" label after the Dolphins' Super Bowl loss the previous season. The Washington Redskins were actually favored for this Super Bowl. As Shula later said, it "wasn't the best game we played that season, but it was the one in which we faced the most pressure and the one in which our guys showed how tough and dedicated they were."

THE 1985 CHICAGO BEARS

The 1985 Chicago Bears were the best team in NFL history according to an ESPN.com poll, and the second-best Super Bowl team in history according to NFL Network's 2006 *America's Game* series. They were a great show. They had "The Super Bowl Shuffle" (taped halfway through the season), quarterback Jim McMahon's attitude and headbands, and William

"The Refrigerator" Perry, the outsized defensive lineman who fancied himself a running back. But the Bears, coached by Mike Ditka, also had outsized talent across the board, from legendary running back Walter Payton to the men manning the famed "46" defense — Mike Singletary, Richard Dent, Dan Hampton, Wilber Marshall, and Steve McMichael. (The "46" was an aggressive attack that brought extra force to the line of scrimmage almost constantly.)

The Bears went 15-1 during the regular season, but these weren't ordinary wins. They won five times by at least 20 points; in six games against teams that finished with at least 10 wins, the Bears went 5-1, outscoring their best foes 178-71.

Then they stepped up their game in the playoffs. Facing the best the NFL had to offer, Chicago shut out two straight foes, then only allowed a touchdown in the final quarter of the Super Bowl, a 46-10 thrashing of New England. From beginning to end, it was perhaps the most dominating season the NFL has ever seen.

New England coach Raymond Berry, a Hall of Fame wide receiver, put the Bears defense among the three best ever. "Their front seven compared very well to the great Steeler front, which is saying a lot," he said.

Or as New England guard Ron Wooten aptly put it after the Super Bowl, "It kind of felt like we were the team that the Globetrotters play all the time."

THE 1976 RAIDERS

Throughout most of the 1970s, the Oakland Raiders, despite their great talent and winning records, played in the shadow of the Miami Dolphins and then the Pittsburgh Steelers. But 1976 was finally Oakland's year.

The offensive line, anchored by Art Shell and Gene Upshaw, always gave Ken Stabler enough time to find Cliff Branch, Fred Biletnikoff, or Dave Casper with his passes. And coach John Madden reacted on the fly when injuries damaged his defense (leading to the team's only loss, a 48-17 rout by New England): he ditched his 4-3 defense and switched to a 3-4 setup. The team then allowed more than 20 points just once in its last 10 wins.

In the playoffs, the team stopped New England, thanks to a bootleg by Stabler with 10 seconds left. Then, in the AFC championship, they avenged two years of postseason losses by beating Pittsburgh, scoring 24 points off a Steel Curtain defense team that had allowed 9.9 points per game. They repeated that performance in the Super Bowl with a 32-14 rout of the Minnesota Vikings and their famed "Purple People Eaters" defense. "The toughest part was getting to the Super Bowl," Shell said later. "Once you got there, it was easy because we knew how to win."

THE 1991 REDSKINS

Any quarterback would have killed to play for the 1991 Washington Redskins, which had one of the most dominating offensive lines known to man. "The Hogs" were Jim Lachey, Raleigh McKenzie, Jeff Bostic, Mark Schlereth, and Joe Jacoby. Without them, Washington—a team largely devoid of superstars on offense and defense—would have merely been very good. With them, they were unstoppable.

Mark Rypien was the lucky recipient of this protection—he was sacked just nine times (while the Redskins defense delivered 50 sacks to opposing QBs)—and he made the most of it. With so much time in the backfield, he led the league with 14.3 yards per pass completion and 14 touchdown bombs of at least 25 yards.

Running backs Earnest Byner (fifth in rushing yards) and Ricky Ervins (fourth in yards per carry) also benefited from the Hogs' awesome performance as the 'Skins averaged 30.3 points per game. Meanwhile, the defense yielded just 14 per game; the team won its first game 45–0, the third by 34–0, and the fifth by 23–0.

But beyond the offensive line, much of the credit must go to coach Joe Gibbs, who would win his third Super Bowl—and become the only coach to do so with three different quarterbacks. Gibbs was always looking ahead, and late in the season, instead of coasting to the finish line, he added a no-huddle offense that initially challenged his players but ultimately helped them beat Buffalo in the Super Bowl.

"I never enjoyed coaching a team more," Gibbs said, adding that it was the team's cohesiveness more than the collection of awesome talent that won. "I really believe it was a well-balanced team with great team chemistry."

THE 1986 GIANTS

The 1986 New York Giants are often overlooked in discussions of great teams—partly because of the huge shadow cast in football by the 1985 Chicago Bears and partly because of the huge shadow cast in New York by the 1986 Mets, one of baseball's legendary teams.

But the Giants went 14-2 and beat strong competition, including the 12-4 Redskins twice and the 10-5-1 49ers. In the postseason, they routed San Francisco, 49–3, and shut out Washington, 17–0. Then, against Denver and its rising star, quarterback John Elway, New York quarterback Phil Simms produced one of the greatest performances in Super Bowl history, going 22-25 for 268 yards and three touchdowns, with a passer rating of 150.9.

Still, the team was also, by and large, lacking in outsized talent, especially on offense—nearly every Super Bowl winner has at least one Hall of Famer at quarterback, running back, or wide receiver. The Giants did not.

But make no mistake, this was a team of giants, especially when it came to defense. The coach was Bill Parcells, who had turned around a disastrous franchise that seemed synonymous with losing. Parcells preached ball control and defense; his players respected and even feared him . . . and routinely snuck up on him at the end of each win that glorious

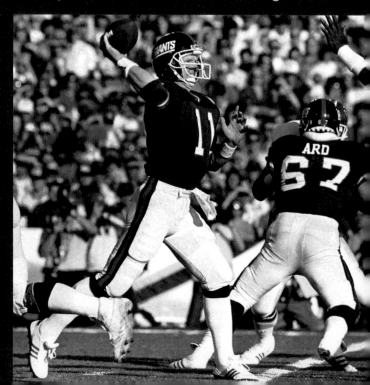

season to dump Gatorade on him. (Doing it in the Super Bowl created an annual tradition that other teams have followed.)

Parcells's defensive coordinator was Bill Belichick, who would later mastermind the New England Patriots dynasty. The unit featured Hall of Famer Harry Carson and Pro Bowlers Leonard Marshall and Jim Burt.

But there was no doubt that the team revolved around Lawrence Taylor. In 1986, LT became just the second defensive player and the only linebacker in history to win the NFL's MVP Award. "He was the only defensive player I can remember who we had to design our game plan around," recalled Joe Theismann, who suffered a horrifying broken leg after a Taylor tackle.

Lightning quick, fierce, and strong, the mercurial Taylor led the league with 20.5 sacks (then the second-highest tally ever) and seemed omnipresent on every play.

"He was the catalyst," Parcells said. "He inspired the other players, he inspired the other coaches, he inspired me."

Broncos running back Terrell Davis (30). (AP Photo/Elise Amendola)

THE 1998 BRONCOS

For the first 13 weeks of the 1998 season, the defending champion Denver Broncos looked more than just unstoppable—they looked flawless. They were 13-0, and they had scored at least 30 points in 10 of those wins while allowing fewer than 20 points in eight of them.

At the age of 38, John Elway was en route to posting his best quarterback passer rating ever at 93.0. When he missed four games with injuries, backup Bubby Brister improved on that with a 99.0 rating. Terrell Davis became just the fourth player to rush for 2,000 yards, and he also led the league in touchdowns with 21 and set an NFL record by averaging 5.1 yards per carry.

But when Mike Shanahan's team lost to the Giants and Dolphins, questions started bubbling up. Would the Broncos go flat, finishing just short, the way so many teams with great records had done? The answer, in short, was no. They finished the season with a win and then avenged that loss to Miami with a 38–3 beat-ing. After besting the Jets in the AFC championship, they went to the Super Bowl against Atlanta, coached by Dan Reeves, who had coached Elway early in the quarterback's career and fired Shanahan as offensive coordinator.

Shanahan and Elway executed their game plan perfectly: the quarterback threw for 336 yards, including an 80-yard touchdown pass, and ran for one more in a 34–19 rout. It would be Elway's final game.

"I never thought it could get any better than last year, but just look at this," he said right after the game. Later he would say, "I was so lucky to walk away with two Super Bowls and know that the last year was positive."

THE NFL CHAMPIONSHIPS

The only yardstick for success our society has is being a champion. No one remembers anything else.
— John Madden, NFL coach

1 | 1958: "THE GREATEST GAME EVER PLAYED"

Frank Gifford at a Giants workout on September 9, 1958, in New York. (AP Photo/Rooney)

The Colts' Lenny Moore (24) gets a good block on the Giants' Emlen Tunnell (45), and Johnny Unitas (19) is at right, along with the Giants' Jim Patton (20), as Colts fullback Alan Ameche advances through a big opening to score the winning touchdown. (AP Photo)

"The Greatest Game Ever Played" wasn't even sold out. The New York Giants and Baltimore Colts played flawed and sometimes outright sloppy football, with seven turnovers. But the nickname was well earned, in part because of the excruciating drama—it was the NFL's first sudden-death overtime game ever—and no other game, with the possible exception of Super Bowl III, did more to shape the future of the sport. "That game is the reason why pro football is what it is today," Baltimore quarterback Johnny Unitas said forty years later.

The 1958 NFL championship starred the glamorous New York Giants, who had become the golden boys of Madison Avenue after their 1956 championship, with players like Frank Gifford and Sam Huff

landing endorsements. They had the league's best defense geared up for the game against the gritty Baltimore Colts, who had the league's best offense. The focal point would be Colts quarterback Johnny Unitas, who had been rejected by his first college choice (Notre Dame) for being too scrawny, who was cut by his first pro team (Pittsburgh) for not seeming bright enough, who was a disaster in his rookie season (his first pass was intercepted and he fumbled his first handoff), and who, after an MVP season in 1957, was hospitalized with broken ribs and a punctured lung midway through 1958. But in this game, playing for his first championship, he would emerge as the quintessential modern quarterback.

This championship game was not just about the on-field action. Coming at a time when football was gaining popularity, it marked the start of the sport's long and fruitful marriage with television, which was undergoing a growth spurt of its own. The 45 million Americans who watched on 11 million sets helped pave the way for the NFL as "America's Game." (Ironically, the game was blacked out in New York because commissioner Bert Bell insisted that people should not get for free what they could pay to see at the stadium.)

Despite his cool persona, Unitas later admitted that his team was "a little intimidated" by the vaunted Giants and Yankee Stadium. He fumbled on his first series and was intercepted soon after. But in the second quarter the Colts recovered two

Frank Gifford fumbles, and Unitas converted both into touchdowns for a 14–3 halftime lead.

In the third quarter, the Colts reached New York's 3-yard line with a chance to put the game away. But the tenacious Giants kept the Colts at bay. On fourth down, amid the Yankee Stadium din, fullback Alan Ameche misheard the call for a full-back option pass and ran a sweep; Giant Cliff Livingston nailed him at the 5-yard line. Inspired, the Giants clicked on offense. Charlie Conerly hit Kyle Rote with a 27-yard pass that he carried for another 35 to Baltimore's 25—where he was drilled so hard that he fumbled, but running back Alex Webster, who had shrewdly trailed the play, grabbed the ball and raced to Baltimore's 1, setting up a touchdown. Early in the fourth quarter, Conerly led another long drive. After two passes netted 63 yards, he exploited something revealed in the Polaroid photos that owner Wellington Mara had taken from the press box during the first half. The Colts' secondary was shifting to the strong side, so Conerly passed to Gifford on the weak side; Gifford lugged corner-back Milt Davis with him into the end zone, and the Giants had a 17–14 lead.

With mist settling over the field, Baltimore missed a field goal, and after Unitas was sacked twice on the next drive, the clock was ticking loudly on the Giants' behalf. With less than two and a half minutes remaining—just around the time Conerly was voted most valuable player in the press box—the Giants faced third-and-less-than-4 near midfield. A first down might clinch the championship. Gifford swept outside, then cut back toward a hole. Baltimore lineman Gino Marchetti grabbed him with a desperate, off-balance lunge, but Gifford appeared to have gained just enough.

Suddenly, a howl tore through the cluster of players, distracting everyone. Baltimore's 288-pound "Big Daddy" Lipscomb had accidentally landed on Marchetti, shattering his right leg above the ankle. After Marchetti was carted off, the ref marked—*mismarked*, according to the outraged Giants—the ball inches shy of the first down. The Giants wanted to run the ball at Marchetti's replacement on fourth down, but New York coach Jim Lee Howell elected to punt. "We only needed four inches," said guard Jack Stroud later. "We would have run through a brick wall at that point."

Still, the punt shoved Baltimore back to its 14, and as Raymond Berry later observed, "the goal-posts looked like they were in Baltimore." Unitas was undeterred, even after two incomplete passes; calling audibles on almost every down, he made decisions with a confidence that presumed inevitable success. On third-and-10, he stunned the Giants by switching to the run and Lenny Moore burst forth for 11. After two more incompletions, Unitas hit Berry—the slow guy, the one with the contact lenses and the two different shoes to compensate for having one leg shorter than the other—for 25. With the Giants fearful of Moore as a deep threat, Unitas kept going back to Berry, for 15 and then 22 yards. Unitas brought the Colts to New York's 13. With seven seconds left, Steve Myhra nailed the field goal, and the game was tied.

At first, nobody was sure what would happen—tie games just ended that way, but you couldn't have a championship end in a tie. Unitas

later said that most of the players didn't even know about sudden-death overtime—there was a rule on the books about it, but it had only been implemented in an exhibition game.

The Giants won the toss but had to punt. The Colts started at their 20, and again Unitas demonstrated his mastery, mixing short and midrange passes with runs. After a pass to Berry worked for 21 yards, Unitas called the play again. But when he noticed linebacker Sam Huff shifting to help out, he audibled a fullback trap for Ameche, who barreled for 23 yards. Then, with the Giants off balance, he went back to Berry, who would catch 178 of Unitas's 349 passing yards and who caught this one near the 8.

That's when disaster struck. Not for the Colts but for pro football and television. Excited Colts fans in the stands had accidentally dislodged a power cable, and sets across America went dark. After a brief time-out, the Colts were about to go when a man raced onto the field; the fans cheered while the police chased him. The press reported it as a drunkard's stunt, but in fact it was a strategic ploy: Stan Rotkiewicz, an NBC business manager doubling as a statistician on the sidelines, improvised the desperation down-and-out pattern to buy precious moments for engineers working to repair the cable.

The move worked—fans missed a one-yard rushing play, but the picture was restored in time for the nation to see the final two glorious plays. During that time-out, coach Weeb Ewbank told Unitas to keep the ball on the ground and settle for a field goal. But Unitas floated a seemingly dangerous cross-field pass into the flat where an interception would yield a long, possibly fatal runback. Unitas downplayed the risks later: "When you know what you're doing, you don't get intercepted," he said, explaining that he had seen the Giants overshifting against Berry. The quarterback's confidence in himself was justified as Jim Mutscheller snared the pass and brought Baltimore to the 1.

On the final play, Unitas crossed up the Giants once more. He handed off to Ameche as expected,

but ran the play away from Jim Parker, Baltimore's best blocker. When Ameche poured through an enormous hole, Baltimore had won, 23–17.

As bitter as the loss was, Giants owner Tim Mara appreciated what the game meant for football, saying, "We're gonna sell out next year." And they did—the NFL as a whole always averaged at least 40,000 per game from then on, while a new commissioner, Pete Rozelle, came in and replaced small-time local television deals with a national TV contract, which eventually led to billions of dollars in contracts and a network all their own. After the game, in New York's *Daily News*, Gene Ward wrote, "In years to come when our children's children are listening to stories about football, they'll be told about the greatest game ever played—the one between the Giants and Colts for the 1958 NFL Championship."

He was right.

Ameche is carried off the field by his teammates and Colts fans after scoring the winning touchdown. (AP Photo/ NFL Photos)

2 | 1934: "THE SNEAKERS GAME"

When the NFL started playing its championship games in 1933, college football still ruled the gridiron. The first championship in Chicago was a success, but it was the second title game—a repeat of New York versus Chicago—that became the first NFL game for the ages, helping to give pro football some folklore of its own.

The 1934 championship was held at the Polo Grounds in Manhattan, which drew the New York and national press. The expected blowout by heavily favored Chicago—they had gone 13-0, outscoring foes 286–86—might have dampened the media's enthusiasm, but instead they saw a hard-fought game that turned on a behind-the-scenes twist, one the writers used to mythologize this championship as "the Sneakers Game."

The temperature was barely in double digits on December 9 when Jack Mara, team president and son of owner Tim Mara, inspected the field and saw that it was better suited for hockey than football. The tarpaulin was frozen onto the field. Mara called coach Steve Owen, who informed his players about the disastrous conditions. On a frozen field with no soft grass to plunge into, their cleats would offer little traction. "Why don't we wear sneakers?" asked captain Ray Flaherty, who had done that in a game at Gonzaga University in 1925 with great success.

Finding sneakers on a Sunday morning in 1934 was perhaps a tougher challenge than shutting down the Bears. Owen, Flaherty, and tackle Bill Morgan hit the phones, but every sporting goods store was closed. Owen also called running back Ken Strong at home in Queens, since Strong had an off-season job with a sporting goods firm, but had no luck. Dejected, Owen and his men headed to the Polo Grounds, where they saw Abe Cohen waiting for them in the locker room.

Abe Cohen was five feet tall and 140 pounds; he was a tailor, not a football player. He never played a down of pro football, yet he loved the game so much that in addition to tailoring Manhattan College's uniforms, he volunteered on game days to help the Giants' trainers. When Owen learned that Cohen had a key to Manhattan College's supply room, he realized that he had found his hero. Owen sent the little man off in search of a taxi to the school.

Unfortunately, getting to Manhattan College at 242nd Street takes time even on days when the streets aren't slick with ice. On this day, Cohen was gone a while. The Giants got an early field goal, but the Bears, with their bigger, stronger line, shoved the Giants around—running back Ken Strong was temporarily knocked out of the game by 246-pound Link Lyman—and Chicago headed into halftime with a 10–3 lead, leaving the Giants mentally and physically worn down.

But—cue the trumpets—that was when Cohen arrived. He had scrounged up nine pairs of sneakers. (According to Wellington Mara, Cohen may not have had the key and may have broken in to get the crucial footwear.) Both teams had worn their cleats down practically to nubs on the hard surface, but not all the Giants players embraced the new equipment immediately. However, once they saw Strong, who had returned for the second half, moving around well, they were convinced. When Chicago coach George Halas learned of the switch, he hollered, "This ain't goddamned basketball," and urged the referee to make the Giants put their cleats back on. Finally, he urged his men, "Step on their feet," but the Bears couldn't keep their footing well enough to do that.

"We were helpless," Bears star Bronko Nagurski recalled. "We had to mince about. We were down more than we were up."

Trailing 13–3, the Giants soon realized they could make sharper cuts that left the Bears slipping and sliding. Strong executed an off-tackle run for a 42-yard touchdown, then pulled off another touchdown on a reverse—a call that would have been unthinkable had the team still been in cleats. When they were down 17–13, the Bears turned to Nagurski, who carried the ball seven times for 37 yards down to the Giants' 35. But the Giants stopped him on fourth-and-1. Then they added two more touchdowns for a 30–13 rout. Call that icing on the cake.

"If they'd had new cleats in the second half, they would have walloped us," Strong said afterward.

The fans, reacting like a college crowd, flooded the field and tore down a goalpost. Their Giants stood tall that day, but no one loomed larger than the smallest man in the locker room. In the *New York American*, Lewis Burton wrote, "To the heroes of antiquity, to the Greek who raced across the Marathon plain, and to Paul Revere, add now the name of Abe Cohen."

Nagurski is tackled by the Giants' Mel Hein during the 1934 "Sneakers Game." (AP Photo/Pro Football Hall of Fame)

3 | 1950: RAMS VS. BROWNS

Rams halfback Paul Younger tackles Cleveland's Marion Motley (76) as halfback Dub Jones (86), running interference for Motley, comes up too late to put a block on Younger in the 1950 NFL championship game. (AP Photo)

In 1950 the Rams had been playing in Los Angeles for four years—they had fled Cleveland after winning the 1945 championship to avoid competing with a new team, called the Browns, in the upstart All-America Football Conference. But for the 1950 championship they had to return to Cleveland to prove themselves all over again.

The NFL had absorbed the formidable Browns (winners of four straight AAFC championships) prior to the season, and the team had shocked NFL skeptics by going 10-2 and beating the New York Giants in a playoff to reach the championship. The teams hadn't met during the season, but Cleveland coach Paul Brown knew that despite his 10-2 record, a loss would invalidate their four AAFC titles.

Christmas Eve in Cleveland was freezing, with 30-mile-per-hour winds, but the players often seemed not to notice—the offenses dominated much of the day with a mix of methodical drives and big plays, although each team's defense stepped up to force turnovers at crucial moments.

The Rams, who set a record that still stands by averaging 38.8 points per game that season, set the tone on the first play from scrimmage at their own 18. They had noticed that the Browns right linebacker would double-team a wide receiver if the halfback stayed in to block. So halfback Glenn Davis waited in the backfield at the start of the play before slipping downfield unguarded. He caught Bob Waterfield's pass at the 45 and raced in for an 82-yard touchdown. Was the jig finally up for the Browns?

Cleveland quarterback Otto Graham answered with a resounding no, firing a 31-yard touchdown pass to tie the game. At halftime, Los Angeles was clinging to a 14–13 lead, but that didn't last long. In the third quarter, Paul Brown began sending

his running backs on pass patterns, forcing Los Angeles into single coverage on Dante Lavelli, who had already caught a 35-yard touchdown. Soon, Graham and Lavelli connected on a 39-yard bomb for a 20–14 lead. But the Rams threw Cleveland off balance by switching to their running game, which yielded a touchdown, a Cleveland fumble, and a 28–20 Rams lead.

On the next drive, Graham connected with Lavelli eight times, and Brown went for broke on three fourth-down plays. After Cleveland scored to make it 28–27, the Browns had a chance to take the lead after an interception and a drive to the Rams' 24. But Graham was hit hard and fumbled the ball away with just 3:16 left.

"I wanted to die right there," Graham said after the game. That feeling never went away. Decades later, he would say, "Honestly, I was more devastated at that moment than I was a few years ago when the doctor told me I had cancer." But on the sideline, Brown told his distraught star, "We'll get the ball back for you and win this thing yet."

Brown, as usual, was right. With 1:50 left, the Browns, with no time-outs, got the ball on the 34. Graham scrambled and mixed in short and long passes to bring his team to the Rams' 11. Then they brought in kicker Lou Groza.

Groza said afterward that he wasn't nervous—"I was just thinking of fundamentals . . . I didn't want to make any mistakes"—but all of Cleveland held its breath until his kick split the uprights for a 30–28 lead.

Thousands of fans, delirious with joy, raced onto the field. But there was still time left on the clock, and police had to be called to clear the fans off. Los Angeles ran the kickoff back to their 47. With time for one last desperation heave, the Rams

Lou "The Toe" Groza kicks a field goal to put the Browns ahead of the Los Angeles Rams, 30–28, in the NFL championship game. (AP Photo/CSU/Cleveland Press Archives)

went with their other quarterback, Norm Van Brocklin, who had a stronger arm than Waterfield. Van Brocklin saw Davis deep and fired the ball to the 5-yard line. Defensive back Warren Lahr got there first, however, and came down with the ball . . . but Davis never gave up, and as he tried to wrestle the ball away the two men fell into the end zone. If Davis had possession, the Rams would win.

"It was terrible," Graham said. "We didn't know for several seconds what the referee was going to call."

But there would not be one last lead change—the referee ruled the ball dead at the 5. The fans swarmed the players, tearing at their jerseys. They tore down the goalposts. And they weren't the only ones celebrating—even Brown, normally cool and collected, couldn't stop shouting in the locker room. "There never was a game like this one," he declared.

For the fifth year in a row, the Browns were league champions. But this time they were champions of all of football.

Groza (center) hugs the shoe that kicked the game-winning field goal. Just as affectionate over the shoe are coach Paul Brown (left) and Browns owner Mickey McBride (right). (AP Photo)

4 | 1938: GIANTS VS. PACKERS

The Giants' Mel Hein receives a watch from Joseph Carr, president of the National Pro Football League, for being chosen as the game's most valuable player. (AP Photo)

The Packers' Clarke Hinkle was halted by the Giants only two feet short of a touchdown in the second quarter of the 1938 championship game. Other players shown are Bud Svendsen (53) and Cecil Isbell (17) of the Packers and Bill Lee (40) of the Giants. (AP Photo)

All those clichés and exaggerations about how the game was rougher and tougher in the good old days? Well, if the 1938 NFL championship game at the Polo Grounds is any indication, they're all true. This was a brutal battle between the New York Giants and the Green Bay Packers—both teams were vying to become the first to win two championship games, and neither spared any effort.

The Giants took the worst of the blows but made it worth the pain. Giant offensive lineman Johnny Dell Isola left on a stretcher with a spinal concussion that was nearly a fractured vertebra; running back Ward Cuff departed with his sternum possibly fractured but returned; running back Leland Shaffer stayed in with a broken bone in his leg; and NFL MVP and Giant leader Mel Hein was temporarily knocked out with a broken nose and a concussion. Green Bay's lone injury was to its unstoppable wideout Don Huston, who missed much of the second half with an injured knee. Both sides resorted to fists to make their point at various times. "This was the gridiron sport at its primitive best," Arthur Daley wrote in the next day's *New York Times.*

The Packers were defending champions and had the league's best offense, but the Giants' Hein devised what essentially was a rope-a-dope strategy: he called plays to allow plenty of short yardage gains in hopes of avoiding Green Bay's knockout plays.

The Giants couldn't completely contain Green Bay—the Packers would amass 378 yards (to the Giants' 212), including a 40-yard touchdown pass, a 66-yard breakaway off a screen, and a 34-yard run—but they slowed Green Bay down and made several big plays that proved critical.

The Giants scored first, thanks to future coach Jim Lee Howell—he blocked one punt to set up a field goal and then scooped up a loose ball after another blocked punt to set up a touchdown for a 9–0 lead. After Green Bay closed to 9–7, Hein recovered a fumble to set up another score. But the Packers closed to 16–14 by halftime.

Green Bay seized a 17–16 lead in the third quarter, but the Giants responded by mounting their first sustained drive of the game. Most of the credit went to Hank Soar, who would later have a second career as a baseball umpire. (He umped first base in Don Larsen's perfect game.) Soar rushed five times and caught one pass as the team marched 39 yards to the Packers' 23. On the next play, Soar was double-teamed, but quarterback Ed Danowski went back to him once more, with a risky pass near the 6. Soar hauled it in and, with Clarke Hinkle clinging to his leg and trying to drag him down, lugged his way into the end zone.

New York had a 23–17 lead, but there was a full quarter to play. Green Bay marched to the Giants' 40 or beyond three times. But the Giant defense cut them down with two big plays—an interception inside New York's 30 and a fumble recovery—and on the final drive time simply ran out.

In a game that Daley described as a struggle of such "magnificent stature" that it "delved into the realm of fiction," the Giants defense had held on for a 23–17 win. With two championships and four title games in six years, the Giants could unofficially but proudly claim the crown of the NFL's first modern dynasty.

5 | 1960: LOMBARDI'S FIRST — AND LAST — PLAYOFF LOSS

Eagles center-linebacker Chuck Bednarik (60), quarterback Norm Van Brocklin (11), and fullback Ted Dean (35) congratulate head coach Buck Shaw following the victory over Green Bay. (AP Photo/NFL Photos)

In 1960 the Green Bay Packers were the team of the future. They had a relatively new coach, a former offensive assistant for the New York Giants who had hung around waiting for the head coach's job before finally getting impatient and leaving his hometown team for the relative obscurity of Wisconsin. This unknown, Vince Lombardi, had put together a team that was almost entirely 26 or younger and that featured nine future Hall of Famers—including Bart Starr, Jim Taylor, and Paul Hornung on offense and Ray Nitschke and Willie Davis on defense.

By contrast, the Philadelphia Eagles were a team running out of time. They knew that this was their last shot at glory, given how old their key players were. In fact, their two biggest stars, Norm Van Brocklin and Chuck Bednarik, had been around since 1949, which was the last time the Eagles had won an NFL championship. Van Brocklin was a Navy veteran and a rookie quarterback for the losing Los Angeles Rams in that 1949 game. He had been a nine-time Pro Bowler and had finished in the

top four in passing yards every year since 1950; he had even set a single-game record—throwing for 554 yards in a 1951 game—that still stands. And on his way to becoming the league MVP for 1960, he had guided an Eagles offense that lacked a running attack. (They had the league's second-worst ground game.)

Chuck Bednarik had accomplished more before his 25th birthday than most men do in a lifetime—he had been a baseball and basketball star in high school, then flew more than 30 bombing missions (and 50 overall) as a gunner in the Army Air Corps during World War II, earning an Air Medal. Returning home, he went to the University of Pennsylvania, where he became a two-time All-American at center and received the Maxwell Football Club Award for best defensive player of the year as a linebacker. He continued playing both sides of the ball as a pro—through 1956, he was acclaimed as a center but most feared as a linebacker, where he was a perennial All-Pro. After his rookie year, he missed just one game. He retired after 1959 but later came out of retirement because he needed the money after having a fifth child.

Bednarik earned every cent of his salary in 1960. He came back as a center, which was less demanding than linebacker. But when the team lost a linebacker to injury, Bednarik stepped up again. He played relentlessly and gained lasting infamy on a game-winning play against the New York Giants with his hit on Frank Gifford, which caused a fumble and knocked Gifford clean out of football with a severe concussion for the rest of the season and all of 1961.

Van Brocklin had his team loose and laughing in the locker room before the Eagles-Packers game, but the offense came out almost too relaxed—its carelessness nearly cost them the game in the opening minutes. On the first play, the quarterback lateraled to Bill Barnes, but the ball bounced off Barnes's hands to Packer Bill Quinlan at Philadelphia's 14. But the Eagles defense stood tough, and when Lombardi opted to go for it on fourth down, the effort failed. Barnes then fumbled on the Eagles' 22, but again the Packers got nowhere. This time they kicked a field goal for a 3–0 lead. Green Bay would fall just short throughout the game—despite rolling for 401 yards and 22 first downs (compared to 296 and 13 for Philadelphia), they almost always ended up with a field goal or nothing at all, as Lombardi repeatedly went for the first on fourth down and failed.

The Eagles, thanks to Van Brocklin's 35-yard touchdown pass to Tommy McDonald, took a 10–6 lead into the half. Then, in the third quarter, Bednarik knocked Hornung out of the game. "It was just a good, hard shot by a great player," Hornung said later, though the pinched nerve in his shoulder would remain a chronic problem.

The Packers rallied in the fourth when Max McGee faked a punt and ran for 35 yards on fourth down to set up a touchdown, but the Eagles retaliated with a score of their own for a 17–13 lead.

The next Packer drive ended when McGee fumbled and the omnipresent Bednarik was there to grab the ball. Time clicked on, and suddenly it was last call for the Packers. Sixty-three yards from the end zone, with 80 seconds left to play, Starr methodically began to move his team to the Eagles' 22. The Packers had time left for one, perhaps two plays, so Starr looked to throw deep. The Eagles secondary had shut down the end zone, so he went underneath to fullback Jim Taylor, who caught the ball just past the line, then barreled his

way inside the 10. Bobby Jackson made an initial hit, but not surprisingly, it was Bednarik who came over to throw Taylor to the ground and finish off the play. Then he sat on the wriggling Packer as time ran out. "You can get up now, Jim," Bednarik finally said after the clock reached 0:00. "This game is over."

Lombardi blamed himself afterward for not taking those two early field goals. "We will never let this happen again," he told his team. "We will never be defeated in a championship game again." The "Lombardi Packers," of course, would go on to win five NFL titles and two Super Bowls.

The Eagles never won another championship. And looking back, Bednarik, who had played 139 of the 142 plays in the 1960 game, later marveled that they had won it. "It was a great achievement because man for man, we weren't that good. I still don't know how we did it."

Eagles fullback Ted Dean (35) runs wide left behind strong blocking from guard Jerry Huth (65) in the 1960 NFL championship game. (AP Photo/NFL Photos)

6 | 1933: THE NFL'S FIRST CHAMPIONSHIP GAME

The "national holiday" that is the Super Bowl owes its existence to its forefather, the NFL championship, a game that was played with less pomp and circumstance but an equal amount of intensity. The title game was improvised out of happenstance, yet from the very beginning it provided the kind of drama the NFL needed to build a following.

In the league's early days, the NFL champion was determined by winning percentage. But the 1932 season produced a mess. The Green Bay Packers finished 10-3-1, but because the NFL didn't count ties, both the Chicago Bears (6-1-4) and the Portsmouth Spartans (6-1-6) had a higher winning percentage. To break their tie, the NFL decided to hold an extra game in Chicago that would count toward the standings. Although it was so cold that the game had to be played indoors in Chicago Stadium on a makeshift 80-yard field (the Bears won, 9–0, dropping the Spartans to third place), the NFL liked the solution so much that it split the league into two divisions and created the NFL championship to be held each December after the season ended.

Only a Hollywood scriptwriter could have conceived the wild finish of the very first championship, held in 1933 at Chicago's Wrigley Field. The game matched the New York Giants, whose 244 points scored was 74 more than the second-highest team (Green Bay), against the Chicago Bears, who had allowed just 6.3 points per game.

To counter the Bears' vaunted defense, the Giants relied on innovation and improvisation. And it almost worked.

In the first quarter, the Giants had all six linemen line up to the right of center Mel Hein, making him an eligible receiver. Quarterback Harry Newman took the snap, but surreptitiously slid the ball right back to Hein, who slipped it into his jersey and casually sauntered downfield while Newman dropped back to "pass," then faked a fumble. Most of the Bears fell for it, but 12 yards downfield Hein got excited too soon and broke into a run without waiting for his blockers. Bear safety Carl Brumbaugh figured it out and caught up to the big man at Chicago's 15. The Giants failed to score.

But after Newman later connected on a 29-yarder to end Red Badgro, the team went into halftime with a 7–6 lead. After the lead seesawed in the third quarter and the Bears again found themselves behind, 14–9, they turned to star back Bronko Nagurski. "The only way to stop Nagurski is to shoot the son of a bitch before he leaves the dressing room," New York coach Steve Owen said before the game. Now Nagurski carried on nine straight plays, single-handedly moving Chicago down to the New York 16. The next play looked like more Nagurski smash-mouth football, but then he stopped short, jumped in the air, and threw a pass to Bill Karr in the end zone.

Newman then completed two passes totaling 51 yards to end Ray Flaherty. After Strong rushed for 15, the Giants ad-libbed a play that's used to this day. Strong, running wide on a reverse, realized he was trapped and lateraled the ball back to Newman, who passed it to him in the end zone for a touchdown. That improvisational play is now known as the flea-flicker.

But with three minutes remaining, Chicago supplied more of its own razzle-dazzle. Nagurski faked another run and flipped a pass to Bill Hewitt, who ran five yards, then lateraled to Karr for a 36-yard touchdown and a 23–21 lead.

On the game's final play, Newman fired to Red Badgro, who grabbed the ball and turned upfield, set to lateral to the open Dale Burnett. But Red Grange, one of the greatest players of all time, anticipated the Giants' move. Nearing the end of his career, Grange had lost much of his remarkable speed but none of his smarts—instead of going for the sure tackle at the legs, he wrapped his arms around the Giant, preventing the lateral. When Grange dragged Badgro down, the first championship belonged to Chicago, but he also paved the path for the legendary players and climactic plays that would follow in the NFL championships and then the Super Bowl.

Bears end Bill Hewitt (56) laterals the football to Billy Karr (22) for the winning touchdown. (AP Photo/Pro Football Hall of Fame)

7 | 1940: THE MOST ONE-SIDED VICTORY IN NFL HISTORY

The scoreboard above the crowd shows the Chicago Bears leading 60–0 early in the fourth quarter. (AP Photo)

George Preston Marshall never should have opened his mouth. When Marshall's Washington Redskins beat the Chicago Bears, 7–3, after a disputed call in November 1940, the Redskins owner called the Bears "crybabies" and "quitters."

In early December, the Bears journeyed back to Washington for a rematch, but this game was for the NFL championship. The Bears owner/coach George Halas gave his players newspaper clippings of Marshall's insults, telling them, "Gentlemen, this is what George Preston Marshall thinks of you. I think you're a great football team, the greatest ever assembled. Go out on the field and prove it."

Less than one minute into the game, Chicago, running from its innovative "man-in-motion" T formation, which put the quarterback under the center, gave its first retort. Bill Osmanski took a handoff from quarterback Sid Luckman and ran around the left end 68 yards for a touchdown.

Washington returned the kickoff 56 yards to Chicago's 40, and two plays later quarterback "Slingin' Sammy" Baugh fired a pass to wide open Charley Malone near the end zone. But the ball bounced off his hands, and the Redskins missed the field goal attempt.

The Redskins would get inside the Bears' 20 three times that afternoon, but they never managed to score. The Bears, by contrast, never stopped scoring. They produced two more touchdown runs of more than 40 yards, a 30-yard pass, and three interceptions (out of eight total) run back for touchdowns. (In the misleading statistics column: the Bears pulled off so many big plays that the Redskins actually finished with more first downs, 18–17.)

The score was 28–0 at halftime, and though Halas told his team, "We can't let up," as the score mounted Halas "had a stunned look on his face at what we were doing," according to third-string quarterback Sollie Sherman.

Halas had gone to his backup quarterback, Bob Snyder, in the third quarter and was giving anyone who asked a chance to kick extra points. But with the score 60–0, he put in the little-used Sherman, whose two-year career ended after this game when he got married and found that he needed to earn more money than he could playing pro football. Sherman led his team to yet another touchdown, even though passing was difficult because the Bears had kicked so many extra points into the stands that the refs were using a nonregulation ball that felt "too big and inflated, like a beach ball." After the score, the refs told him that there were no more footballs left so he shouldn't kick the extra point. Instead, the Bears lined up as if to kick, Sherman—as the holder—took the snap, got up, and passed into the end zone to make it 67–0. Sherman was then replaced by fourth-stringer George McAfee, who led another drive but missed his point-after pass.

The final score was 73–0, the greatest rout in the history of sports championships. Afterward, someone asked Baugh if he felt that things might have turned out differently had Malone caught his pass to tie the game and stop the Bears' momentum in the opening moments. "Sure," he quipped. "It would have been 73–7."

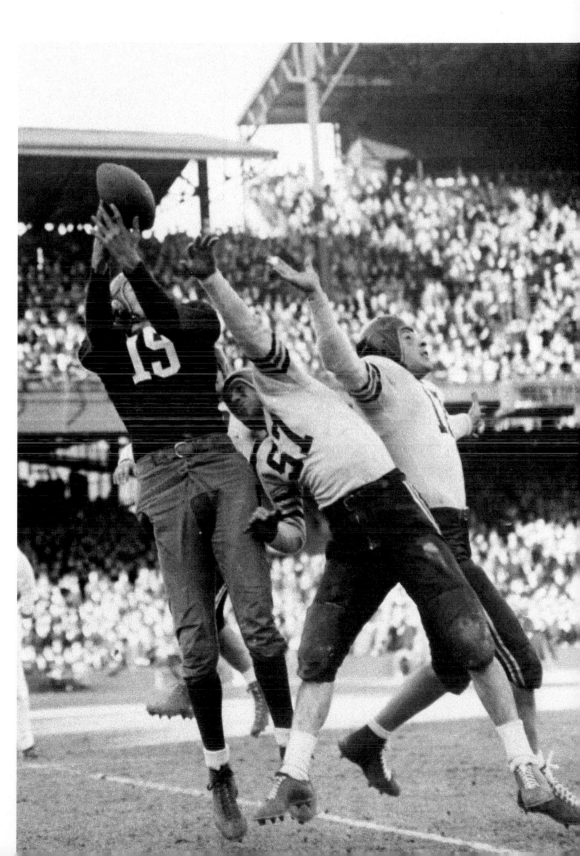

Redskins end Charley Malone (19) pulls down a 42-yard pass from "Slingin' Sammy" Baugh in the closing minutes of the first half of the 1940 championship game. (AP Photo)

8 | 1953: THE REMATCH: LIONS VS. BROWNS

Browns end Dante Lavelli (86), fullback Marion Motley (36), tackle Lou Groza (76), quarterback Otto Graham (14), Frank Gatski (52), and head coach Paul Brown in 1953. (AP Photo/NFL Photos/Pro Football Hall of Fame)

The 1953 World Champion Detroit Lions. (AP Photo/NFL Photos)

In 1950 the Cleveland Browns had won the NFL crown in their first season after joining the league from the folded AAFC. In the next two seasons they had made it back to the championship but lost both games, first in a rematch with the Los Angeles Rams and then to the Detroit Lions, who had also beaten them five straight times in regular-season games. So in 1953, when the 11-1 Browns made it to the NFL title game to face the Lions once more, they were looking for revenge.

But Cleveland's legendary quarterback Otto Graham—whose team had averaged 30 points per game—struggled on a muddy, slippery field in Detroit, producing the worst game of his career and perhaps the worst ever by a quarterback in an NFL title game. He would finish just 2-15 for four yards. His first-quarter fumble set up a Detroit touchdown, an interception set up a field goal, and he was even temporarily benched near the end of the first half.

"My hands were chapped terrible," he said. "I had no feel on my passes. I don't know what it was—I tried spitting on them, everything I could think of to moisten them. But they were chapped, and for some reason I just could not pass well at all that day."

Detroit took a 10–3 lead into halftime. But Cleveland kept hanging around, and a third-quarter interception set up a game-tying touchdown. When Graham's next two drives fell short, Lou Groza kicked field goals, and the Browns actually held a 16–10 lead with just 4:10 left.

Beginning at his own 20, Detroit quarterback Bobby Layne, a hard-partying maverick known for his leadership more than his passing, took control. Instead of going to his favorite targets, Layne turned to a defensive specialist named Jim Doran, who had caught just six passes all year but who

had come in after an injury to Leon Hart early in the game. Layne hit Doran for 17 and then 18 yards, moving the team to Cleveland's 33. All along, Doran kept saying he could beat his defender, the veteran Warren Lahr, deep. Not yet, Layne replied.

During a time-out, the coaches wanted a screen pass. Layne had other ideas. With Briggs Stadium nearly quiet in desperate anticipation, Layne turned to Doran. Now was the time. Doran wasn't fast, but he knew he could get behind Lahr, especially because Lahr was thinking more about making contact—Lahr had come at Doran hard all game. "He said he was gonna hit me in the mouth," Doran recalled. On the snap, when Doran extended his forearm as if he was going to block Lahr, the defender fell for it and rushed at Doran, looking for the hit. Doran slipped by and got 10 yards past him. Layne's pass was wobbly, but it didn't matter. Doran caught the ball and sauntered into the end zone.

Detroit had regained the lead, 17–16.

Graham had one final chance to make things right, but it was not going to happen on this day—he threw his second interception of the day, and the Browns once again were merely the runners-up. "Longest train ride I ever took," Groza said of the ride home. "That one stuck in the gut longer."

The following season, after enduring one more regular-season loss to Detroit, the Browns stomped the Lions, 56–10, in the championship to finally regain the crown. The Browns repeated in 1955, beating Los Angeles, but when these two teams met again in 1957, the Lions trashed the Browns, 59–14. With the emergence of the New York Giants, Baltimore Colts, and then Green Bay Packers, this rivalry was soon overshadowed, but when the NFL was building its popularity in the early 1950s, the Browns-Lions clashes were the centerpiece of the league.

DETROIT LIONS
1953 World Champions
NATIONAL FOOTBALL LEAGUE

Championship Game
BRIGGS STADIUM
December 27, 1953
Detroit Lions-17
Cleveland Browns-16

9 | 1945: THE GAME THAT LED TO THE "BAUGH/MARSHALL RULE"

It was the only game in NFL history where the goalpost should have been voted MVP.

In the first quarter of the 1945 NFL championship, the young and fast Cleveland Rams, playing in their first championship game, marched from their 21 to Washington's 5. But the Redskins, who had reached five of the previous nine title bouts (winning twice), slammed the door shut and took the ball over on downs.

In a game that was so cold—temperatures in Cleveland hovered near zero—that players on the bench wrapped their feet in straw in a desperate effort to keep warm, offense would be at a premium all day long. So the next set of downs proved crucial. The Redskins' famed quarterback Sammy Baugh dropped back to pass, fading into his own end zone. He fired downfield, only to have the pass blocked . . . by the goalpost (which in those days was in the front of the end zone). The rules stated that this was a safety, stunning the Redskins and giving the Rams an early 2–0 lead.

Then, late in the first half, with Washington leading 7–2, the Rams scored on a 38-yard touchdown pass by rookie quarterback Bob Waterfield. He was also the kicker, but his extra point lacked the zip of his pass—it wobbled and barely reached the goalpost, striking the horizontal bar before finally toppling over for a 9–7 Rams lead.

That point would prove vital because Waterfield missed his next extra-point attempt, giving the Rams 15 points. When Frank Filchock, replacing Baugh (who had bruised his ribs), threw his second touchdown pass in the third quarter, Washington had pulled to 15–14.

In the fourth quarter, the Redskins missed a 25-yard field goal and a 46-yarder, either of which would have won the game. Of course, without the safety, Washington would have had the lead—or without the fluke extra point, the game would have been tied. Instead, Cleveland held on, 15–14. Redskins owner George Preston Marshall was so furious that after the season he pushed through a rule change for the NFL: a pass off the goalpost would now be merely incomplete. But that play would never again happen in an NFL championship, and the Redskins would not capture an NFL title until the 1983 Super Bowl, nearly four decades later. This was the one that got away.

Rams back Don Greenwood (66) hangs on to the ball as he is tackled in the second quarter. (AP Photo)

Redskins end Joe Aguirre (19) attempts a field goal from the 25-yard line, but the ball sails inches short of the goalpost in the closing minutes of play in the 1945 championship game. (AP Photo)

10 | 1963: "THREE YARDS AND A CLOUD OF DUST" LEAD TO VICTORY

Giants quarterback Y. A. Tittle slams his helmet down, upset that his last-minute pass was intercepted by the Bears' Richie Petitbon. (AP Photo)

Giants halfback Phil King (24) attempts to gain yardage against the Chicago Bears. (AP Photo/NFL Photos)

Y. A. Tittle passes a snowball to halfback Frank Gifford (left) as they play around on a mound of snow at New York's Yankee Stadium a few days before the 1963 NFL championship game. (AP Photo)

When the New York Giants had won the NFL championship in 1956, it seemed like the start of a dynasty. But the team instead developed a terrible case of second-best-itis: they reached the championships in 1958, 1959, 1961, and 1962, but lost each time. The 1963 team had many of the same players—Sam Huff, Dick Modzelewski, Frank Gifford, Alex Webster—but they were aging and knew it might be their last great shot at glory. The offense that year had been unstoppable, scoring a whopping 448 points, 79 more than the next-best offense. The quarterback, Y. A. Tittle, was 37 years old, but he threw a record 36 touchdowns.

To win the championship, they would have to get by the Chicago Bears, whose defense, led by Doug Atkins, Joe Fortunato, and Richie Petitbon, had allowed just 144 points, 62 fewer than the next-best defense. In that sense it was a replay of the very first NFL championship game between these two franchises thirty years earlier. The results would be similar too.

Tittle ignored the kickoff temperature of 11 degrees and the frozen turf at Wrigley Field to lead the Giants on an 83-yard drive, topping it off with a 14-yard touchdown toss to Gifford. But Tittle

wouldn't last—his heroics would be undone by veteran Bears linebacker Larry Morris.

First, he administered a hit to Tittle's left knee that left the Giant quarterback wobbly. Then, after enduring his first season without a single interception since his sophomore campaign in 1956, he picked off a Tittle pass and ran it back 61 yards to set up a touchdown. Finally, he landed another hard but clean blow on Tittle, knocking him from the game.

At halftime, Tittle got Novocain and cortisone shots and had his leg taped up, then gamely declared himself ready to start firing again. Some Giants believed he should step aside or at least alter the game plan, but Tittle and coach Allie Sherman stubbornly refused. After Chicago grabbed a 14–10 lead, Tittle continually tried to rally his team but threw one interception after another, finishing with five on the day—his last came in the final minutes after he had driven 45 yards to the Chicago 39.

Once more, the Giants had come up just short. Morris walked away with the MVP Award, and for the first time since they beat New York in 1946, the Bears took home the NFL crown.

2 | THE 1962 AFL CHAMPIONSHIP

In the years before the NFL deigned to play a championship game against the winner of the upstart American Football League, most AFL championships were humdrum affairs. But the 1962 game between the Dallas Texans and the Houston Oilers provided more than just an intriguing Lone Star State showdown — there was a stirring comeback and dramatic finish too.

Houston had won the first two AFL crowns, but the first half of this game was a fiasco for the ageless quarter-back-kicker George Blanda, who had been plagued by interceptions—with a record 42—that season. First, he drove to the Dallas 5 only to be picked off and forced to watch as the Texans' Len Dawson steered his team into field goal range for a 3–0 lead. After Blanda missed a field goal, Dawson threw a 28 yard touchdown pass to running back Abner Haynes. After another Blanda interception, Haynes scored on a run for a 17–0 Dallas lead at halftime.

But with Dawson sticking to the ground in the second half to try to chew up the clock, Blanda, who had been AFL Player of the Year in 1961, returned to form in the second half. He went 3-4 on the team's first 51-yard drive, then led the team to another field goal and a touchdown in the fourth quarter to tie the game at 17. Unfortunately, however, he also missed a 42-yard kick to win it.

For the only time other than the 1958 NFL championship game, a season would be decided in over-time. After winning the toss, Haynes, the team cap-tain, made a huge mistake. Concentrating on the strong wind, he said, "We want to kick to the clock." But as soon as he said "kick," it meant that Houston got possession (a potential disaster in sudden-death play) and that the choice of direction would be theirs (making a field goal easier).

But Blanda's eagerness proved costly. He threw his fourth and fifth interceptions of the day. The last one, as time ran out in the first overtime, proved fatal. As the game moved into a second overtime, Dawson threw a 10-yard pass to Jack Spikes, and on the next play Spikes broke free for a 19-yard run. After nearly 78 minutes of play, Tommy Brooker kicked a 25-yard field goal, and Dallas had a 20–17 win in double over-time. Only one NFL game has gone longer, and no championship game has ever come close.

THE SUPER BOWL

The Super Bowl is world theater. — Marshall McLuhan, Canadian educator, philosopher, and scholar

1 | XLII: GIANTS 17, PATRIOTS 14
FEBRUARY 3, 2008

Patriots coach Bill Belichick. (AP Photo/ Paul Sancya)

Giants quarterback Eli Manning looks to pass. (AP Photo/ Ben Liebenberg)

With 2:39 to play in Super Bowl XLII, the New York Giants had one last shot at victory—not just any triumph, but an upset of epic proportions. The Giants, who hadn't won a Super Bowl in 17 years, had started the season 0-2 and only made the playoffs via the wild card. The New England Patriots, leading 14–10, had scorched the league in a relentless drive toward perfection, winning every game en route to what they expected to be their fourth crown of the decade.

Many fans and sportswriters had presumed that this game would be just another checkpoint on the Patriots' march into history. After all, the regular season—despite controversy when coaching mastermind Bill Belichick was accused of illegally videotaping opponents—was filled with big victories; the Pats won their first eight games by an average of 25 points, and only four times did

they win by less than 10. Yet their closest call was the season finale, a 38–35 win against these Giants, which actually felt like a psychological victory for New York.

Throughout most of this Super Bowl, the Giants had played crisp, physical football. Having held New England close, they suddenly had an opportunity to win. Yet nearly every play would bring another crisis, creating a sense of drama that only enhanced the stunning conclusion.

The Giants started at their own 17 but took nearly a minute to clear just 20 yards before facing a fourth-and-1 situation. Running back Brandon Jacobs shoved his way to a first down, setting the stage for quarterback Eli Manning.

On first down, Manning was nearly sacked but escaped to scramble for five yards. On second-and-5 from the 44, a safety blitz nearly got Manning. He rushed his pass toward receiver David Tyree, a special teams player who was often an afterthought on offense; he had nine tackles that year and only four catches (though he had caught a five-yard touchdown pass moments earlier). Giants fans gasped in horror as Manning's pass floated over Tyree and toward the waiting hands of Patriot cornerback Asante Samuel, who had 16 interceptions over the two previous seasons. If Samuel picked this pass, New England's dream season would be complete. But he mistimed his leap, and the ball glanced off his hands and fell harmlessly to the ground.

Giants receiver Plaxico Burress (17) jumps for the ball against Patriots Ellis Hobbs (27) and James Sanders during the first quarter. The pass fell incomplete. (AP Photo/David J. Phillip)

Giants receiver David Tyree (85) uses his head to snag Manning's 32-yard pass with this improbable catch, fending off the clutches of Patriots safety Rodney Harrison (37). (AP Photo/ Gene Puskar, File)

Manning had new life, but few believed that he had suddenly turned into his brother Peyton—the game's best quarterback who had won the previous Super Bowl with the Indianapolis Colts and now watched from a luxury suite. Eli may have lacked Peyton's skills, but he had shown calm and poise all season. Now, however, he was clearly frustrated, either with his blockers or with Tyree for running too short a route.

On third down, Manning set up in the shotgun. On the left were Plaxico Burress and Amani Toomer. Burress was hampered by leg injuries and the Patriots' extra coverage—he had seen just five passes, catching one—yet he remained Manning's favorite target, especially on big plays. The veteran Toomer had six catches already. Rookie tight end Kevin Boss had proved his mettle by setting up the Giants' sole touchdown with a 45-yard catch-and-run play. Lining up wide right was the talented rookie Steve Smith. Tyree, who had been dropping passes in practice all week, set up slot right, the least likely target of all.

Once again, however, the play broke down quickly, putting the Giants' hopes in jeopardy. The defensive line's attack was fierce and immediate. Adalius Thomas closed in on Manning, forcing him to step up, where he found Richard Seymour and Jarvis Green nearly on top of him.

Green grabbed Manning, but left guard Rich Seubert pulled him off. Green kept coming, and then Seymour clutched Manning's white number 10 jersey, trying to yank him to the ground. "I felt people grabbing me," Manning recalled. "You try to get small sometimes and keep the play alive." Referee Mike Carey was ready to blow the play dead, but Manning drove forward until he broke free. Then he ducked backward toward a patch of open space at his own 33. With three Patriots racing toward him, he whirled and fired downfield.

Manning had realized that with Patriot safety James Sanders moving toward Smith, Tyree should be free in the post; Tyree, seeing his quarterback in trouble, had come back in and toward the middle at the Patriot 24. Safety Rodney Harrison reached him just before Manning's bomb did.

The two men went up as one. Tyree got his hands on the football, but so did Harrison, and he knocked one of Tyree's hands away. As their descent began, it seemed certain that the ball would come loose. But Tyree cemented the ball to his helmet with his hand before landing on Harrison. Then he held on tight as Harrison tried to wrestle the ball away. "I thought it was falling out," said Harrison. "It was a wacky, crazy play."

But the Giants still had 24 more to go in 59 seconds, and the Patriots would fight for their lead with everything they had—especially since they had had to fight so hard to gain it. New England had scored only once in three quarters: the Giants offense had controlled the ball (their first drive netted only a field goal but consumed almost 10 minutes); the pass rush registered five hurries, two batted passes, eight knockdowns, and five sacks on Patriot superstar Tom Brady; and cornerback Corey Webster clamped down Brady's favorite target, Randy Moss.

Tyree's touchdown reception had put the Giants up 10–7 to start the fourth quarter. But with 7:54 left and the Giants defense finally showing fatigue, Brady guided an 80-yard drive and Moss broke out with three big catches, including one in the end zone that put New England in command.

Now, on first down after Tyree's miracle, the Patriots nailed Manning for a one-yard sack. Second down brought more pressure, forcing a wobbly pass that Tyree couldn't reel in. But on third-and-11,

Jacobs stayed back to block, giving Manning time to find Steve Smith, who got the first down, then got out of bounds at the 13 to stop the clock.

Finally, it was New England's turn to feel desperate. The defense loaded up with another blitz. Jacobs knocked off Harrison to give Manning the time he needed. Burress faked a slant inside and faded, unfettered, into the corner of the end zone, where he hauled in Manning's pass untouched. The Giants were just 35 seconds from an astonishing triumph.

New England began at its own 26, needing just to get into field goal range. They got nowhere instead. The Giants forced an incompletion on first down. Jay Alford sacked Brady on second down. Brady tried twice to go deep to Moss, but Corey Webster was there both times.

For the first time in Super Bowl history, the lead had changed three times in the final quarter. The slogan for Super Bowl XLII was "Who Wants It More?" Turns out, Manning and the Giants had the answer.

2 | III: JETS 16, COLTS 7
JANUARY 12, 1969

Joe Namath walks through the national media throng after being recognized as the MVP of Super Bowl III. (AP Photo/NFL Photos)

Colts tight end Tom Mitchell (84) attempts a catch as Jets defensive back Randy Beverly (42) intercepts the ball. (AP Photo/NFL Photos)

The first two showdowns between the best NFL and AFL teams were called the "World Championship Game." But by 1969 it had a new moniker: the "Super Bowl." Yet this new concept was almost over before it started. The NFL's Green Bay Packers had thoroughly dominated the first two games, and the 13-1 Baltimore Colts were favored by 17 to 19 points over the AFL's New York Jets in 1969, with Las Vegas oddsmaker Jimmy the Greek tacking on three extra points "for the NFL mystique and Don Shula's coaching" and *Sports Illustrated* projecting a 43–0 rout. Even though the two leagues were set to merge after the 1970 season, NFL commissioner Pete Rozelle held a press conference to declare he might change the setup to allow two superior (meaning NFL) teams to meet for the title. "Rozelle Indicates Tomorrow's Super Bowl Contest Could Be Next to Last," the *New York Times* announced.

Enter "Broadway Joe."

Coming from the University of Alabama, Joe Namath had spurned a $200,000 deal from the NFL's St. Louis Cardinals when the Jets doubled that offer.

This sparked a spending war between the establishment NFL and the radical newcomer AFL that led the NFL to offer a merger. Namath became a media sensation and a star, but NFL fans and players dismissed both the second-tier league and the long-haired loudmouth with a white mink coat, llama rug, and zebra pillows. Now they anticipated that Namath would get his comeuppance from the Colts, proudly conservative in their crewcuts.

Namath, however, grew more brazen than ever. When Jets coach Weeb Ewbank thanked his players' wives for their support, Namath thanked "all the broads in New York." Namath infuriated Shula by declaring Colt quarterback Earl Morrall—the NFL Player of the Year—inferior to all the "top young quarterbacks in the AFL." By implying that AFL quarterbacks were real men because they threw deep, Namath shrewdly hoped to provoke Morrall and lure the Colts defense to focus on his deep threat, Don Maynard, who was hiding an injured left hamstring.

Then came perhaps the most famous moment in NFL history to happen away from the playing field. At an AFL event in his honor days before the game, Namath was semi-drunkenly rambling through a speech when a Colts supporter heckled him. Tired of hearing how much better the Colts were, Namath responded with a bold declaration:

"The Jets will win Sunday. I guarantee it."

"The Guarantee," as it came to be known, drew minimal media attention, but the Colts noticed. "He's given our players more incentive," Shula sneered. Then at game time, announcer Curt Gowdy relayed Namath's boast to the entire nation.

It wasn't an empty boast. The Jets were outraged by the lack of respect they were being accorded and unimpressed by the Colts' traditional zones and static offense. Most older NFL quarter-

backs couldn't handle Baltimore's pass pressure, but Namath had fast feet, a deep backpedal, and an astonishingly rapid release. And while Namath's love of big plays had led to too many interceptions, he was savvy enough to suppress his style for the biggest game of his life. In Super Bowl III, he quarterbacked NFL-style, with restraint and precision.

The Colts, meanwhile, angered by Namath's taunts and feeling the pressure of being such heavy favorites—"If we blow it, we destroy the whole season," Shula said—played a riskier, thus sloppier, game. At New York's 19 in the first quarter, the Colts grew overeager, and a dropped pass, an overthrown one, and a broken play led to a missed field goal. Later, from the Jets' 6, Morrall forced a pass into traffic, where linebacker Al Atkinson deflected the ball into the hands of diving cornerback Randy Beverly, the first of Morrall's three interceptions. "We had the best defense in the American Football League, but nobody remembers that because our quarterback wore white shoes," defensive assistant and future head coach Buddy Ryan said later.

Namath, meanwhile, called audibles at the line, sidestepped Baltimore's blitzes, and patiently helmed a 12-play, 80-yard drive of short passes and handoffs to Matt Snell, who scored the touchdown. (Of the Jets' 74 plays, Snell rushed 30 times, gaining 121 yards.)

In the third quarter, the Jets chewed up the clock and added two field goals while stopping Morrall cold. With the score 13–0, Shula called on Johnny Unitas. Jet offensive lineman Dave Herman's "heart stopped for about 10 seconds," but the mystique no longer matched the reality—the injured veteran had little velocity. His first drive floundered, and after Namath guided another time-consuming drive for a field goal to start the fourth quarter, Beverly intercepted Unitas in the end zone.

Unitas finally got going with an 80-yard drive that pulled Baltimore within 16–7 with 3:19 left. When the Colts recovered their onside kick and Unitas clicked on three passes to reach New York's 19, the NFL superiority seemed to be reasserting itself. But the Jet defense—the game's real stars—stood firm. As Namath ran off, wagging his index finger high to symbolize that he and his

Namath (12) gives the ball to running back Matt Snell (32), who rushed for 121 yards. (AP Photo/NFL Photos)

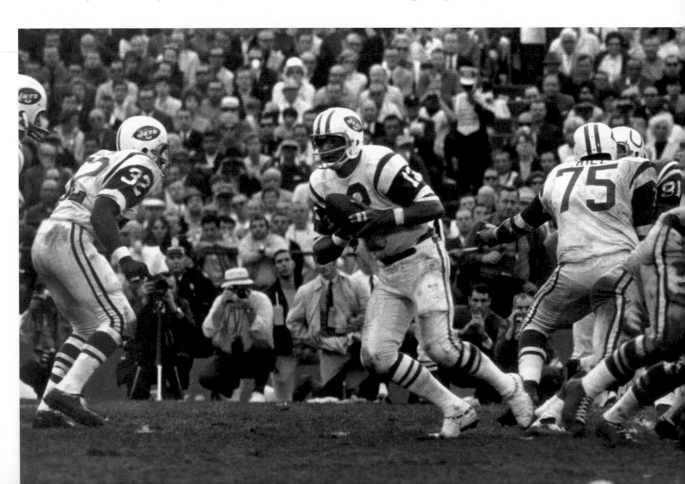

team were indeed number one, there was no doubt that despite his small-time numbers—17-28 for 206 yards, no fourth-quarter passes—his leadership had earned him the MVP Award . . . and a lasting place in football history.

Following the horrors of 1968—the murders of Martin Luther King Jr. and Robert Kennedy, the urban riots, the atrocities in Vietnam and protests over the war—this feel-good story captivated the nation. Namath was an anti-establishment star and the quintessential sign of the times.

Joe Namath legitimized the AFL-NFL merger, transformed the sport, and made the Super Bowl what it is today. This iconoclastic icon emboldened AFL owners to force the NFL to keep them together during the merger, while his swagger and style set the stage for the NFL in prime time on *Monday Night Football*. And the Super Bowl would grow rapidly—the audience quintupled in less than a decade, from 20 million viewers in 1969 to 102 million by 1978—as it set out on the path to becoming a national holiday that lives up to its name.

Jets fans are effusive in their support for Hall of Fame quarterback Joe Namath. (AP Photo/NFL Photos)

Hall of Fame Colts quarterback Johnny Unitas (19) plays in relief of starting quarterback Earl Morrall. (AP Photo/NFL Photos)

3 | XIII: STEELERS 35, COWBOYS 31
JANUARY 21, 1979

In 1972 the Dallas Cowboys won Super Bowl VI, shaking a reputation for just falling short. In 1978 coach Tom Landry's team won again. The next year the defending champion—which featured five Hall of Fame players, including Roger Staubach and Tony Dorsett, and was soon to earn the nickname "America's Team"—sought a third crown that would anoint it as the preeminent dynasty of the 1970s and perhaps all time.

In 1975 the Pittsburgh Steelers won Super Bowl IX, wiping clean decades of futility and frustration. The next year coach Chuck Noll's team repeated in a memorable comeback over the Cowboys. In January 1979, the Steelers—with nine Hall of Fame players, including Terry Bradshaw, Lynn Swann, Joe Greene, and Jack Lambert—sought a third crown that would anoint them as the NFL's preeminent dynasty of the 1970s and perhaps all time.

Super Bowl XIII was the ultimate clash of the titans.

In their first confrontation, the defenses had dominated—though Swann made four stunning catches, including a 64-yard touchdown—and the famous Steel Curtain keyed Pittsburgh's victory with seven sacks of Roger Staubach and three interceptions, including one in the end zone to preserve the 21–17 win. By contrast, Super Bowl XIII, reflecting new rules designed to open up offenses, would produce 66 points, a record that stood until 1993 and that has been surpassed only in routs decided by at least three touchdowns. The quarterback shootout in this Super Bowl between Staubach and Bradshaw, the NFL MVP, went down to the final clicks of the clock.

Bradshaw struck first, hitting John Stallworth for a 28-yard touchdown. But as the first quarter ended, Staubach withstood an eight-man blitz to fire a 39-yard touchdown pass to Tony Hill.

When the Cowboys scored on a fumble recovery, Pittsburgh struck back immediately. To blitz Bradshaw, the Cowboys often covered Swann and Stallworth man to man. So when Stallworth pulled in a 10-yard pass on his own 35 and broke Aaron Kyle's tackle, he suddenly had the field to himself. Stallworth outraced everyone for a 75-yard touchdown, tying the record for the longest pass in Super Bowl history. And when Mel Blount intercepted Staubach at the Pittsburgh 15 and Bradshaw led a five-play drive, highlighted by passes to Swann of 29 and 21 yards, Pittsburgh finished the first half with a 21–14 edge.

In the third quarter, it was a dropped pass, not a great catch, that made the difference. On third-and-3 from Pittsburgh's 10, running back Scott Laidlaw staved off a blitzing Jack Lambert, giving Staubach time to find tight end Jackie Smith in the end zone. Smith, a longtime Cardinal and future Hall of Famer, had suffered a neck injury in 1977 and retired, but the Cowboys had persuaded him to come back. Staubach's pass came in low, and Smith then slipped on the soggy turf; after the ball caromed off his hip, the Cowboys had to settle for a field goal instead of a game-tying touchdown. "I think it surprised him that the ball got to him that fast, and I threw it a little bit low and he kind of slipped," Staubach later said.

Forgiving a teammate's mistake is easy, but enduring a bad call while trailing 21–17 in the fourth quarter is another matter. With Stallworth sidelined by a muscle cramp, Bradshaw kept going back to Swann. On this bomb, the receiver and cornerback Benny Barnes ended up on the ground, and field judge Fred Swearingen threw the flag for tripping. "The worst call in the history of football," Staubach called it years later. Commissioner Pete Rozelle later said it was a bad call, but there was no instant

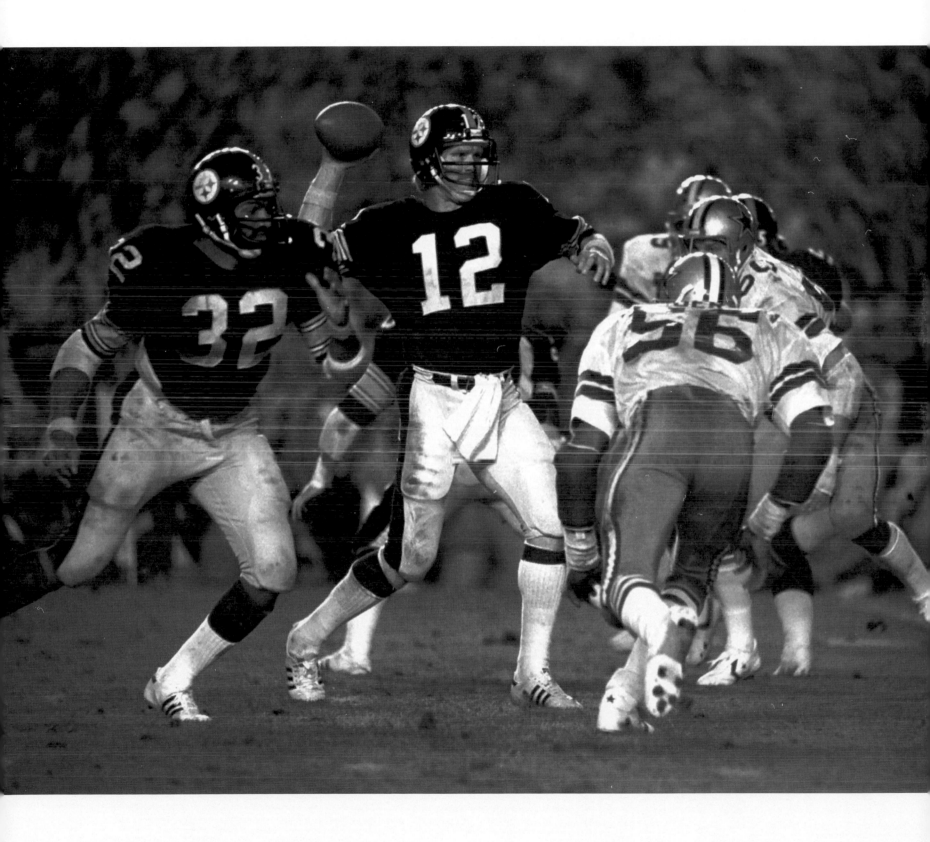

Steelers wide receiver John Stallworth (82) goes high to haul in a pass from Bradshaw and score the first Steeler touchdown of Super Bowl XIII. (AP Photo)

replay then, and the Steelers got new life on the Cowboy 23.

Two plays later, the Steelers should have called a pass play on third-and-9, but running back Franco Harris, furious at Dallas linebacker Thomas "Hollywood" Henderson for taunting him, demanded that Bradshaw hand off to him. Bradshaw understood. He had been outraged before the game when Henderson stoked the rivalry's flames by reviving an old knock on his own intelligence with a new quip: "Bradshaw couldn't spell 'cat' if you spotted him the C and the T."

So, with the Cowboys expecting a pass, Bradshaw called a draw play, and Harris burst through a huge hole in the middle and chugged in for a 22-yard touchdown.

The dramatics never let up. Kicker Roy Gerela lost his footing on the kickoff, sending a bouncer down the middle of the field, where it found Pro Bowl defender Randy White, who was playing with a fractured thumb. White lost the ball, and Pittsburgh recovered on the Cowboys' 18. Bradshaw instantly went for the kill: even though Swann was double-teamed by Kyle and Cliff Harris, Bradshaw threw the pass so high that only the unstoppable Swann could soar to it. Touchdown Pittsburgh.

Had Dallas folded and Pittsburgh won 35–21, we would remember Super Bowl X as the best of those 1970s Super Bowls. "A lot of our guys were celebrating as though the game was over," Franco Harris recalled, but he was worried about Dallas "[having] a history of coming back."

Against the judgment of some Steelers players, like L. C. Greenwood, the Pittsburgh coaches ordered a prevent defense . . . which Staubach quickly picked apart. First came an 89-yard touchdown drive. Then Dallas recovered an onside kick and Staubach engineered another touchdown, making it 35–31 with 22 seconds to play. This time, however, veteran Steeler running back Rocky Bleier successfully snatched the onside kick and the game was over.

Swann finished with seven catches for 124 yards; Bradshaw, who certainly knew how to spell MVP, was 17-30 for 318 yards and four touchdowns. "It was the most disappointing game I ever played in," Staubach later said, while Pro Bowl safety Cliff Harris has argued that a Cowboys win, cement-

ing his team's winning reputation, would have led to his induction in the Hall of Fame. The Steelers, meanwhile, would repeat the next year for their fourth title, leaving little doubt about their place in history.

"We resented—and still resent—that anyone referred to the Cowboys as 'America's Team,'" Lynn Swann said later. "You know what America's Team is? A team that wins the Super Bowl. . . . That was us, four times."

Steelers running back Franco Harris (32) carries the ball into the end zone for a touchdown in the fourth quarter. (AP Photo)

4 | XLIII: STEELERS 27, CARDINALS 23
FEBRUARY 1, 2009

Some Super Bowls are defined by a signature play or a dramatic drive. Super Bowl XLIII had an abundance of both.

The first drive featured Pittsburgh's quarterback, Ben Roethlisberger, scrambling for a touchdown only to have it overturned by the referees when they decided he didn't get in. The Steelers settled for a field goal but scored a touchdown on their next drive.

Then it was the Arizona Cardinals' turn. While the Steelers were used to the big game—they were going for their record sixth trophy and had won one just three years earlier—the presence of the Cardinals, who had finished just 9-7, was a total surprise.

The Cardinals had never reached the Super Bowl—in Arizona or St. Louis—and in fact had not won an NFL championship since 1947, when they were in Chicago. In fact, they had finished above .500 and made the playoffs only once in the previous quarter-century, both in 1998. In 2007 the Cardinals had hired a new head coach, Steelers' offensive coordinator Ken Whisenhunt, who had guided Roethlisberger and company during their Super Bowl XL win. The team finished 8-8 his first season, but still suffered from an unresolved situation at quarterback, where youngster Matt Leinart and aging veteran Kurt Warner split time. In 2008 Whisenhunt handed the reins to Warner, who, looking rejuvenated, passed for 4,583 yards and clinched the NFC West in a win against his former team, the St. Louis Rams.

Now, with his team trailing 10–0, Warner looked to make the big plays that had earned him the Super Bowl MVP in 2000. He fired a 45-yard pass to Anquan Boldin on an inside-out route to set up a score. Then, in the first half's closing moments, he completed passes to running back Tim Hightower

Arizona receiver Larry Fitzgerald races past the Steelers defense to score after an eight-play touchdown drive. (AP Photo/ Ben Liebenberg)

and receivers Larry Fitzgerald and Boldin, bringing his team to the 1 with just 18 seconds left. The Cardinals were on the verge of a 14–10 halftime lead.

But history can change in an instant, and often in the least expected ways. Boldin set up in the wrong spot, and Warner didn't notice. On the other side of the ball, Pittsburgh linebacker James Harrison blew his assignment, forgetting to blitz. The combination of those two mistakes proved fatal for Arizona.

When Boldin ran his slant, he ended up cutting behind Harrison. "I couldn't see [Harrison] around our lineman and the pressure," Warner said. "I thought I had Anquan for a second."

The pass was caught instead at the goal line by Harrison, and the 240-pound linebacker, who had been cut four times earlier in his career, began the longest run of his life. As blockers cleared a path, he broke several tackles (including Warner near midfield) and even leaped over a falling teammate. He just kept on rumbling. Near the end, Arizona receivers Larry Fitzgerald and Steve Breaston were gaining on him. He and Fitzgerald went down for good, right on the goal line, 100 yards from where the play started. While the officials reviewed whether he had actually scored, Harrison was wearing an oxygen mask. "Those last couple of yards was probably tougher than anything I've gone through in my life," Harrison said. (The following weekend *Saturday Night Live* did a skit in which cast member Kenan Thompson portrayed Harrison as still out of breath.)

Harrison was in the record books with the longest Super Bowl touchdown, and that 14–10 Cardinals lead had become a 17–7 Steelers advantage.

Arizona didn't begin to recover until it was trailing 20–7 in the third. Warner went to a no-

Steelers quarterback Ben Roethlisberger (7) rolls into the end zone against Cardinals defensive tackle Darnell Dockett (90). (AP Photo/Julie Jacobson)

huddle offense with four wide receivers. Fitzgerald, who had been smothered with extra coverage all game, caught four passes in an eight-play touchdown drive. Then Pittsburgh center Justin Hartwig, playing hurt, was called for holding in his own end zone, which is a safety. That meant a 20–16 score with Arizona getting the ball back.

Suddenly momentum turned into results. On Arizona's second play, Fitzgerald transformed a seven-yard pass over the middle into a 64-yard touchdown with a burst of dazzling speed that left the NFL's best defense behind. All season, the Steelers had yielded just two passes of more than 40 yards. Now Boldin and Fitzgerald had equaled that total in one game.

Pittsburgh was behind for the first time all day and had just 2:37 to rectify the situation. A holding penalty pushed them back to their own 12.

But Roethlisberger—who had seen his reputation tarnished after that first Super Bowl win when he crashed his motorcycle while riding without a helmet—and receiver Santonio Holmes—who had been arrested for marijuana possession and subsequently benched twice during the regular season—proved as dynamic a duo as Warner and Fitzgerald. On first-and-20, Roethlisberger escaped pressure and found Holmes for 14 yards. On third down, they connected for a 13-yarder. After the drive reached Cardinal territory, the Steelers produced another big play. A pump-fake by Roethlisberger froze the defense long enough for Holmes to break free, catch the pass at the 39, and race all the way to the 6.

On the very next play, Holmes got open in the end zone, but Roethlisberger's perfect pass went right through his hands. Redemption came on

Steelers linebacker James Harrison takes in some oxygen after scoring a 100-yard touchdown. (AP Photo/ Gene J. Puskar)

the very next play: Holmes got open in the corner of the end zone, and Roethlisberger went to him one more time, rifling a pass just beyond an outstretched defender. Holmes had absolutely zero margin for error, needing to stretch his body up to the ball, then land with perfect precision to get his toes down in the end zone. Afterward, legendary Steeler receiver Lynn Swann compared this catch favorably to some of his own greatest plays and to David Tyree's miracle catch from the previous year. "It won't seem to be as spectacular to a lot of folks because they don't understand how difficult, how hard a catch like that is to make, but it was terrific," Swann said.

Pittsburgh had a 27–23 lead with 29 seconds left, and Arizona, despite a few more desperate passes by Warner, had run out of time. Holmes had reeled in not just a pass but a Super Bowl title.

5 | XXXIV: RAMS 23, TITANS 16
JANUARY 30, 2000

Titans quarterback Steve McNair (9) flings a pass. (AP Photo/NFL Photos)

One foot. The difference between champion and runner-up in Super Bowl XXXIV was as small as it gets.

Few people expected either the Tennessee Titans or the St. Louis Rams to even be in the Super Bowl in 2000. The Titans' last winning season was 1993 as the Houston Oilers, who had never reached the big game. The Rams' last winning season was 1989 in Los Angeles. They had owned the NFC's worst record for the 1990s and had seen only one Super Bowl, a 1979 loss.

But the Titans had earned a wild-card spot with a 13-3 record and won their wild-card game on a 75-yard kickoff return with a cross-field lateral in the final seconds of the game that became known as "the Music City Miracle." Meanwhile, the Rams were transformed when their starting quarterback, Trent Green, was injured in the preseason. Their second-stringer—who had been rejected by NFL teams and had bounced from Arena Football to NFL Europe—was Kurt Warner. He stepped on-stage, threw for 4,353 yards, and led the team to an astonishing 526 points, a 13-3 record, and the Super Bowl.

The first half of the big game showed off Warner's high-flying offense and the Titans' resilient defense—the Rams posted 294 yards (to the Titans' 89), getting inside the Titans' 20 on five straight drives, yet at halftime they held just a 9–0 lead on three field goals. In the second half, the Rams finally finished one of those drives, gaining a 16–0 lead.

It looked like the only reason to keep watching would be to check out the newest commercials—after all, no Super Bowl team had ever overcome a deficit of more than 10 points. Tennessee could not seem to stop Warner and had not managed to get on the board.

But Tennessee quarterback Steve McNair rallied his team on the next drive, with his passing and a 23-yard scramble. The Titans defense stiffened, and McNair followed up with another long drive and a touchdown. With just 2:12 left in the game, McNair had moved his team into field goal position and suddenly the score was tied at 16.

It was an impressive comeback, and with St. Louis wearing down—not only was the defense faltering, but the Rams offense had gone three-and-out twice in a row—Tennessee seemed poised to take control. But the Rams erased the Titans' accomplishments in an instant. On their first play, with the Titans expecting a conservative push toward field goal range, the Rams sent receiver Isaac Bruce on a deep route. The Titans blitzed, and Warner was hit as he released, leaving the ball slightly short. "Bruce saw the ball underthrown," coach Mike Martz recalled. "It wasn't like he beat the coverage or anything, but the corner didn't see the ball." Bruce slowed down, made the catch, then faked out safety Anthony Dorsett. He then cut inside toward the middle and ran the ball for a 73-yard touchdown.

Tennessee was almost relieved—had Bruce been tackled, the Rams might well have run a few plays, run down the clock, and kicked a game-winning field goal. Now there was at least time on the clock.

After a penalty on the kickoff, Tennessee had only 1:48 to travel 88 yards for a tie. Two short passes and two penalties brought the Titans to the Rams' 40 with 59 seconds left. The Rams defense was "gassed," coach Mike Martz confessed later. Suddenly, a fourth straight scoring drive seemed very possible. Yet the clock kept ticking, and soon just 22 seconds remained, with the Titans on the 26 and Rams linemen Kevin Carter and Jay Williams hunting McNair in the backfield. Somehow he slipped their grasp and found receiver Kevin Dyson at the 10. The Titans used their final time-out with six seconds left.

The Titans had one more shot at the end zone. Tight end Frank Wycheck ran straight up the right side, pulling linebacker Mike Jones away from Dyson, who slanted over the middle. But Dyson had made too shallow a cut. When Dyson caught McNair's pass, he was still more than four yards out. "If Dyson would have taken it up two more yards vertically, he would have caught the ball and walked in," McNair said later.

That foreshortening allowed Jones to cut back, wrap up Dyson at the waist and knee, and bring him down at the 2. "When he first hit me, I thought I could run through his arm," Dyson recalled. "Then all of a sudden my feet stopped. All I needed was one more step, but I couldn't get my left leg moving."

Dyson, at 6'1", was more than two yards long himself. As the two men fell toward the turf Dyson desperately lunged forward, his arm outstretched, hoping to break the plane of the end zone. "Even when I was going down, it seemed like that end zone was so close," Dyson said.

He was less than a yard away, maybe less than a foot, when his shoulder hit the ground. Dyson later called it the perfect tackle. "The smartest thing I did on that play was not overtry," Jones said. "If I had tried to put a kill shot on Dyson, he might have bounced off and gone in. I just wrapped him up and took him down, the old textbook tackle."

The drive was short. The game was over. An entire stadium exhaled. The Rams were champions.

Titans wide receiver Kevin Dyson (87) fails to get the ball into the end zone as he is tackled by the Rams' Mike Jones on the final play of the game. (AP Photo/ John Gaps III)

Rams quarterback Kurt Warner (13) is sacked in the second quarter of Super Bowl XXXIV. (AP Photo/Dave Martin)

6 | XXXVI: PATRIOTS 20, RAMS 17
FEBRUARY 3, 2002

Patriots kicker Adam Vinatieri (4) kicks a game-winning 48-yard field goal as the Rams' André Bly (32) approaches. (AP Photo/NFL Photos)

For three straight seasons, the St. Louis Rams had scored at least 500 points, an NFL record. "The Greatest Show on Turf" offense headed by Kurt Warner was also backed by a strong defense, and it was that combo that made the Rams, with the 2000 crown to their credit, 14-point favorites in Super Bowl XXXVI—the third-highest spread ever. Their foe, the New England Patriots, had installed a young, unknown Tom Brady at quarterback early in the season only after veteran Drew Bledsoe got hurt. The team was 11-3 under Brady's guidance, and coach Bill Belichick knew about defense and Super Bowls—as defensive coordinator for the New York Giants, he had designed the plan that

shut down Jim Kelly's Buffalo offense in Super Bowl XXV. To disrupt the Rams' game plan, Belichick keyed on all-purpose running back Marshall Faulk, who had not only rushed for 1,382 yards but caught 83 passes.

Although the Rams were heavy favorites, this was the first Super Bowl after the terrorist attacks of September 11, 2001 (the game had been pushed back a week), and the Patriots picked up fans simply because of their name and their red-white-and-blue approach. The Patriots also impressed everyone—and started a new tradition—by coming out as a team instead of individually, to emphasize their cohesion in the face of adversity. (The halftime show featuring U2 was also considered one of the most memorable: during the band's classic "Where the Streets Have No Name," two backdrops were revealed, listing the names of those who died on September 11, and Bono opened his jacket to reveal an American flag stitched on the inside.)

Shocking everyone but the Patriots, Belichick's defensive plan worked brilliantly.

Quarterback Kurt Warner couldn't find a rhythm, scoring just one field goal across three quarters. Thanks in part to a 47-yard interception return for a touchdown, the Patriots held a 17–3 lead with 10 minutes to play. The Patriots defense was worn down, however, and Warner finally got going. Two touchdowns later, the score was tied.

With 1:21 left, the Patriots got the ball at their 17. They had no time-outs left. They had been forced to punt eight out of the 10 times they had the ball and had only 214 yards total offense. Given those results, Belichick wanted Brady to remain conservative, to avoid mistakes. But if the game went to overtime, the Rams seemed certain to win. According to legend, as Brady was heading out, Bledsoe told him, "Just go out there and win it. Don't worry about being careful."

The Rams didn't give Brady a chance for a big pass, but Brady's teammates made big plays that turned the quarterback into a hero. Under pressure, he barely got off two short passes and then spiked the ball at the 30 with 41 seconds left. Running back J. R. Redmond caught a pass behind the line of scrimmage but took a hit from linebacker Tommy Polley when cornerback Dré Bly missed a tackle. However, Redmond kept going until he had picked up 11 yards and—of equal importance—got out of bounds to stop the clock.

Facing a blitz, Brady dumped a pass to Troy Brown just two yards past the line, and Brown

slipped past two Rams and raced for 23 yards before getting out of bounds. The Patriots were closing in. Brady beat the Rams blitz again with what by then seemed like a relatively deep play— a six-yard pass to tight end Jermaine Wiggins. He then spiked the ball with seven seconds left.

It was time for Adam Vinatieri. The Patriots' kicker was "Mr. Clutch"—12-13 on game-winning attempts, including four straight that season. He had single-footedly beaten Oakland in the playoffs, ignoring four inches of snow to nail a 45-yarder as time ran down and then a 23-yarder in overtime.

As the clock wound down to zero, Vinatieri stepped up for the biggest kick of his career and drove it through the uprights. The scoreboard read PATRIOTS 20, RAMS 17, "the Greatest Show" was over, and a new dynasty was born.

A mural honors the fallen of the 9/11 tragedy during U2's performance of "Where the Streets Have No Name" at halftime of Super Bowl XXXVI. (AP Photo/NFL Photos

Patriots quarterback Tom Brady (12) looks for a receiver. (AP Photo/Steven Senne)

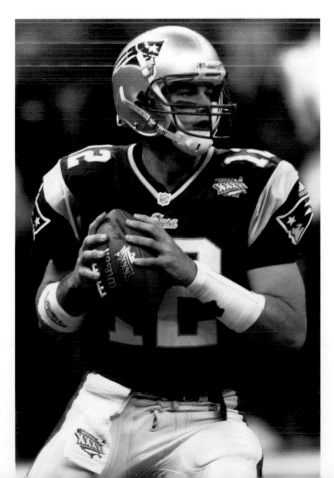

7 | XXIII: 49ERS 20, BENGALS 16
JANUARY 22, 1989

Coaching legend Bill Walsh counsels 49ers quarterback Steve Young. (AP Photo/NFL Photos)

Joe Montana (16), John Taylor (82), and Roger Craig (33) celebrate Taylor's game-winning 10-yard touchdown reception. (AP Photo/NFL Photos)

Bill Walsh had created the high-scoring "West Coast Offense," helped mold Joe Montana into the game's top quarterback, and coached the San Francisco 49ers to two Super Bowl titles. The legendary coach planned to retire after Super Bowl XXIII—although he hadn't told his team because he did not want to put pressure on them or shift the spotlight to himself—and he wanted to go out a winner. It would not be easy.

The team struggled to a 6-5 start. With the playoffs slipping from view, Walsh looked to Montana, who had been at the helm for four straight wild-card wins. He threw for two touchdowns, including an 80-yarder, the next week, and three more, including a 96-yarder, the week after. He continued his stellar play in the postseason, throwing six touchdown passes (and just one interception) in two NFC playoff games.

In the Super Bowl, they faced off against the Cincinnati Bengals, the team they had beaten in 1982 for their first title. The Bengals were coached by Walsh protégé Sam Wyche, who had NFL MVP Boomer Esiason at quarterback, so expectations ran high for an offensive game. Instead, the score was just 6–6 with a minute left in the third. The 49ers had generated plenty of yardage (453 by game's end) but couldn't finish, while the Bengals sputtered—perhaps in part because fullback Stanley Wilson had gone AWOL on a cocaine bender.

When Cincinnati's Stanford Jennings notched the game's first touchdown on a stunning 93-yard kickoff return, it gave the Bengals momentum. But Montana struck back coolly and quickly. He connected with receiver Jerry Rice for 31 yards, running back Roger Craig for 40 on the first play of the final quarter, and then, one play later, Rice for

a 14-yard touchdown. The 49ers then stopped the Bengals but missed a 49-yard field goal attempt, and when Esiason's 10-play drive produced a Cincinnati three-pointer and a 16–13 lead, Walsh's hopes for a final crown looked grim.

After a blocking penalty, the 49ers were pinned at their own 8, with just 3:10 left. But there was a reason people called Montana the game's greatest quarterback. It wasn't his size, speed, or powerful arm. It was his persona.

Montana looked around the huddle, and instead of barking out a play, he pointed to the stands, where he had done some celebrity-spotting, and asked, "Isn't that John Candy?" The team relaxed. Joe Cool was in charge. (The persona was in part a facade—at one point during the drive Walsh had to call time-out because Montana was so revved up that he was hyperventilating and dizzy.)

Using a twist on Walsh's strategy of short, controlled passes, Montana surprised the Bengals by throwing over the middle to start the march downfield, letting the clock run. After escaping the shadow of his goalpost, Montana opened up a bit, connecting with Rice for 17 and Craig for 13. Then a penalty left the 49ers facing second-and-20. Walsh called another play for Rice;

Montana delivered a 12-yard pass while getting hit, and Rice then ran for another 15. On the next play, Montana absorbed another hit while finding Craig for eight yards.

Now the 49ers held the cards on the Bengals' 10 with 39 seconds, Walsh told Montana he could have two end zone passes before they went for a field goal. Montana only needed one. Rice, with 11 catches for 215 yards, would be double-teamed, so Craig would repeat his last route as the primary target. But the Bengals' linebackers picked him up. So Montana threaded a perfect pass to John Taylor, who hadn't caught a pass all day. Vintage Montana. And a 20–16 win for Walsh.

49ers wide receiver Jerry Rice (80) after making a catch during the game-winning drive in the final moments of the 49ers' 20–16 victory over Cincinnati. (AP Photo/NFL Photos)

Bengals quarterback sensation Boomer Esiason (7) rolls out of the pocket and looks for an open receiver. (AP Photo/NFL Photos)

8 | XXXVIII: PATRIOTS 32, PANTHERS 29
FEBRUARY 1, 2004

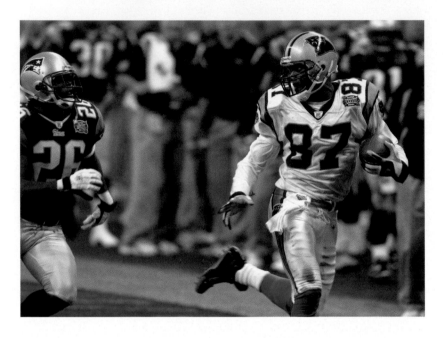

Panthers wide receiver Muhsin Muhammad (87) beats Patriots cornerback Eugene Wilson (26) on an 85-yard touchdown in the fourth quarter. (AP Photo/ Morry Gash)

Super Bowl XXXVIII gave fans two games for the price of one, or maybe it was four games.

For most of the first half, the league's stingiest defense (New England's) and the NFC's fourth-best defense (Carolina's) battled each other to a scoreless draw—for their first 20 plays, the Panthers "produced" a total of negative nine yards. New England's two scoring opportunities fell short when Adam Vinatieri, usually so reliable in big games, missed a 31-yard field goal and had a 36-yarder blocked.

In fact, the first score, with just 3:05 left in the half, was set up by New England's defense, which caused a fumble and recovered at Carolina's 20.

It was the longest scoreless start for a Super Bowl, but once the floodgates opened, the offensives burst through. Panthers quarterback Jake Delhomme responded with a 95-yard drive, capped by a 39-yard touchdown pass to Steve Smith. Then New England's Tom Brady and receiver Deion Branch offered up their own highlight footage

on a 52-yard play that led to another touchdown. With just 18 seconds remaining in the half, the Panthers took advantage of a squib kick by New England—when the Patriots guessed pass play, Stephen Davis ran for 21 yards to set up a 50-yard field goal and a 14–10 halftime score.

After Janet Jackson's instantly infamous "wardrobe malfunction" during intermission, the defenses returned to form in the third quarter with no points going up on the board, though New England started a drive that yielded a touchdown at the start of the final quarter, inciting another offensive outburst—the 37 points put up by the two teams in the fourth quarter remain a single-quarter Super Bowl record.

Some of the scoring was the result of the heat inside Houston's Reliant Stadium combined with a tiring New England defense (the Patriots were the league's oldest team). But credit the Panthers for their accomplishment.

Delhomme led the charge, connecting with receivers Muhsin Muhammad and then Steve Smith twice to set up DeShaun Foster's 33-yard TD run. After the Panthers shocked Patriots fans by intercepting Brady in the end zone, Delhomme took advantage of the Patriots' fatigue—which gave him more than six seconds in the pocket—to launch a historic bomb, an 85-yard touchdown pass to Muhammad that went the first 51 yards in the air in a perfect spiral. Muhammad reeled it in, pushed away cornerback Eugene Wilson, and ran the rest of the way unopposed. The Panthers finally had a lead. But on both touchdowns, Carolina went for the two-point conversion and failed—instead of having a 24–21 edge, they were up by just 22–21. That decision would haunt them.

Meanwhile, on the Patriots' sideline, safety

Rodney Harrison turned to a teammate and said, "Hey, man, there's no reason for us to worry. We've got Tom Brady."

Brady proved Harrison's point with a 68-yard drive, and when New England converted its two-point attempt, the Pats held a 29–22 lead. Still, Delhomme kept coming, slicing and dicing the exhausted New England defense — 19 yards to Muhammad, 31 to Ricky Proehl, and then a 12-yarder to Proehl to tie the game at 29.

With just 1:08 left, the Super Bowl seemed destined for its first overtime. But John Kasay somehow sent the kickoff out of bounds, automatically putting New England at the 40-yard line. "We saw the kickoff go out of bounds, and everybody was jacked up," receiver Troy Brown said.

"Tom is at his best in those two-minute situations," Belichick said. "Or one, as the case may be."

Now the Panthers defense was panting. Brady, working from the shotgun, threw four clutch passes for 47 yards, including a 17-yarder to Deion Branch on third down. That got the Patriots into field goal range and gave Vinatieri one last shot, from 43 yards out. Despite his poor first half, he had kicked 15 game-winners and proven himself on the Super Bowl stage, when he finished off the St. Louis Rams in 2002.

And just like Brady, Vinatieri proved he was every bit as good in 2004 as he had been two years earlier, splitting the middle of the uprights. The thrill ride was over, and the Patriots could start talking dynasty.

Patriots wide receiver Deion Branch (83) eludes a tackle by Carolina Panthers cornerback Terry Cousin (21) in the first quarter. (AP Photo/Elise Amendola)

Patriots kicker Adam Vinatieri (4) kicks his game-winning field goal. (AP Photo/Brett Coomer)

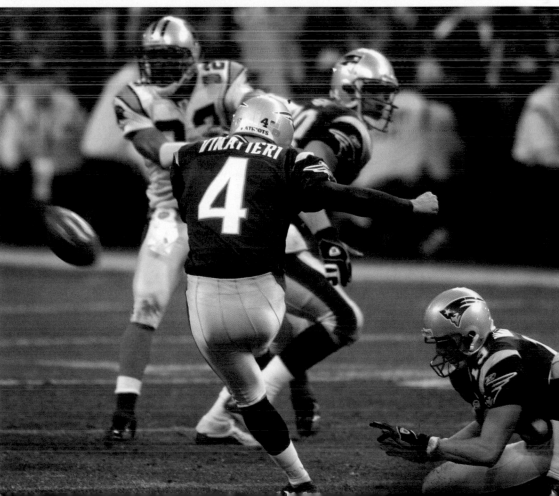

9 | XXV: GIANTS 20, BILLS 19
JANUARY 27, 1991

Buffalo Bills running back Thurman Thomas (34) carries the football for an 11-yard gain before being stopped by Giants cornerback Mark Collins (25). (AP Photo/NFL Photos)

Giants quarterback Jeff Hostetler (15) runs from the field carrying the game-winning ball in New York's 20–19 victory over the Buffalo Bills. (AP Photo/Ron Heflin)

Buffalo Bills wide receiver James Lofton (80) focuses to catch a tipped pass, then advances for a 61-yard gain. (AP Photo/NFL Photos)

In Super Bowl XXV, the solid favorites were the Buffalo Bills, who had the league's most potent offense thanks to quarterback Jim Kelly, running back Thurman Thomas, and receivers Andre Reed and James Lofton. The New York Giants, by contrast, had finished just 15th in points scored, and they had been forced to rely on backup quarterback Jeff Hostetler after starter Phil Simms was injured.

But Giants coach Bill Parcells preached ball control, and his defensive coordinator, Bill Belichick, was a superb tactician; as a result, the Giants had yielded the fewest points in the NFL. They brought that same game plan to the Super Bowl. Sure, Lofton caught a 61-yard pass from Kelly, Reed set a record with five first-quarter catches, and Thomas rushed for 135 yards, including a 31-yard touchdown. But you can't put up points if you don't touch the ball, and the Giants set a "time of possession" record by keeping the ball for 40 minutes, 33 seconds.

The critical drive came when the Giants turned a 12–10 halftime deficit into a 17–12 lead. The 14-play march featured four third-down conversions, including a 14-yard catch by Mark Ingram

on third-and-13; more significantly, it chewed up nine minutes and 29 seconds, a Super Bowl record (since broken by the Giants in Super Bowl XLII).

Yet skills nearly overcame tactics when Thomas's touchdown run gave Buffalo back the lead. But the Giants grinded out another 14-play drive, this one eating 7:32 off the clock before producing a field goal for a 20–19 lead. The Bills had time for two more tries. Their first failed, and the second began with just 2:16 left at their own 10. Thomas gained 22 on one draw play, and 11 on another, but Kelly struggled, completing just two passes and scrambling three times, which used up precious time needed to get into field goal range.

With eight seconds left, the Bills were at the Giants' 29—a 47-yard kick for Scott Norwood, a former Pro Bowler, whose numbers had been in sharp decline.

The Giants called time to let the pressure build. Norwood was concerned about the distance, but he drilled the ball high and far. It was up and it was . . . no good.

Wide right.

Game over.

10 | XIV: STEELERS 31, RAMS 19
JANUARY 20, 1980

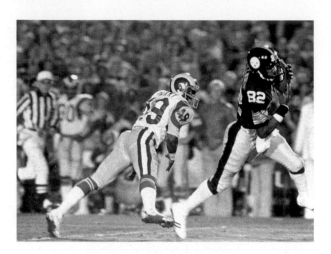

Steelers receiver John Stallworth (82) makes a touchdown ahead of Rams defender Rod Perry (49) during the fourth quarter. (AP Photo)

Steelers quarterback Terry Bradshaw (12) embraces coach Chuck Noll on the sidelines shortly after Bradshaw threw a touchdown pass in the second half. (AP Photo)

The outlook wasn't bright for the mighty Steelers that day. Winners of three Super Bowls in the 1970s, the Steelers' dynamic offense and Steel Curtain defense had dominated all season long and expected to do so in Super Bowl XIV. The Los Angeles Rams had lost their owner, Carroll Rosenbloom, in a drowning accident (which was later alleged to have been a mob-related murder) and numerous players, including quarterback Pat Haden, to injury, and they had barely made the playoffs with a 9-7 record.

But the aging Steelers stars suddenly looked vulnerable. They trailed 13–10 at the half, and despite one of Terry Bradshaw and Lynn Swann's patented touchdown passes—for 47 yards—they were losing 19–17 to start the fourth quarter. With Swann subsequently sidelined with a concussion and blurred vision and Bradshaw having thrown three interceptions, the dynasty was in peril.

Facing third-and-8 early in the final quarter, Steeler coach Chuck Noll sent in a special play called "60 Prevent Slot Hook and Go." The play had never worked in practice, and Bradshaw had refused to call it when Noll wanted to use it earlier. Even this time he almost changed the call, knowing John Stallworth, the lone deep threat, would be double-teamed. But Bradshaw also realized that the coach knew best. "I should've been bombing away earlier," he said later. "Their secondary wasn't that good. We played into their hands by throwing underneath."

Stallworth was in the slot; he ran 15 yards, faked the hook, and took off. "The safety [Eddie Brown] bit on it, and Stall was one on one with the corner [Rod Perry]," Bradshaw recalled. "I just let it fly."

Bradshaw's beauty sailed over Perry's fingertips 39 yards downfield, and Stallworth made an over-the-shoulder catch before galloping 34 more yards for a 73-yard touchdown. It was the seventh lead change—a Super Bowl record—but this time it would stick. The Rams threatened once more, reaching Pittsburgh's 32, but linebacking great Jack Lambert intercepted a pass, and moments later Stallworth took off from the slot again and hauled in a 45-yard bomb. This set up one final touchdown to cap off the last stand by the game's greatest dynasty.

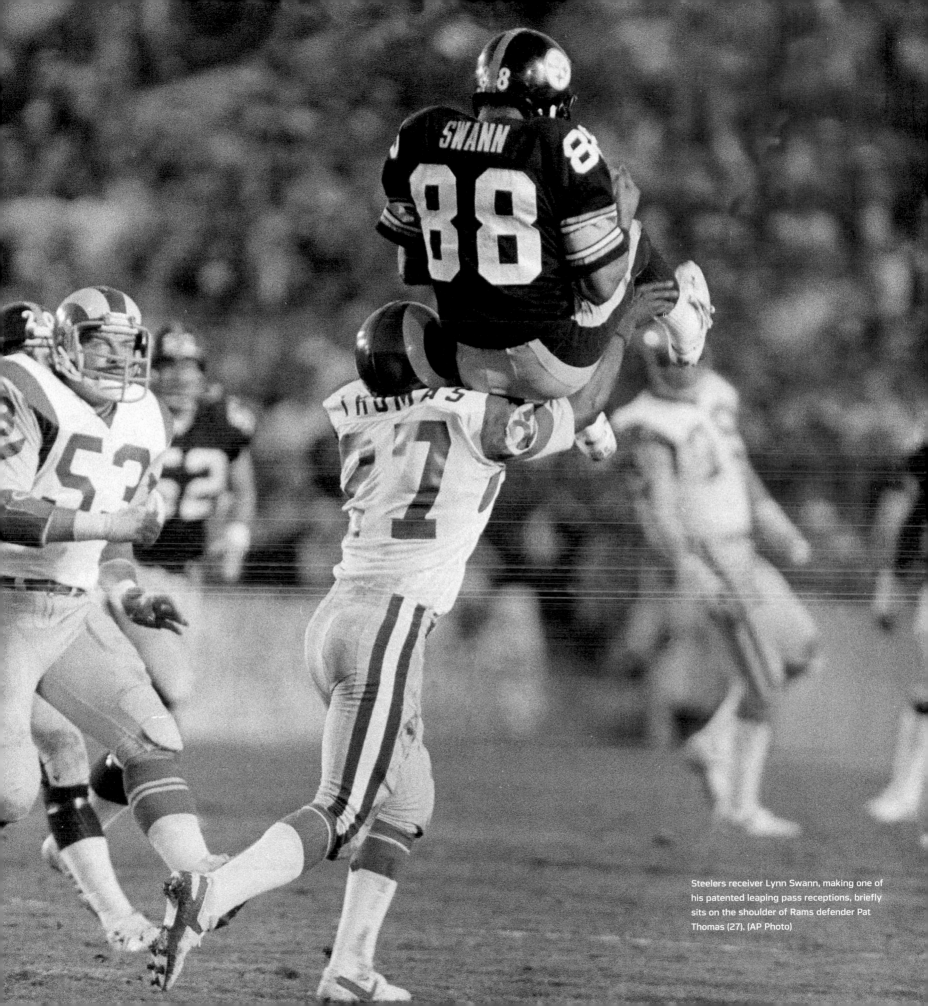

Steelers receiver Lynn Swann, making one of his patented leaping pass receptions, briefly sits on the shoulder of Rams defender Pat Thomas (27). (AP Photo)

BEST SUPER BOWL STORY LINES

XLIV: Drew Brees and New Orleans Finally Get a Big Win

The New Orleans Saints were long associated with NFL futility—their woeful 0-14 start in 1980 had fans wearing bags over their heads and calling their team the "Aints." So it might have made sense for the team, like so many of the residents of New Orleans, to flee after Hurricane Katrina hit the city in 2005 and start over with a new identity. Owner Tom Benson flirted with San Antonio and other cities, but pressure from the fans and commissioner Paul Tagliabue brought the team back to the Big Easy in 2006.

The team had a new coach, Sean Payton, and a new quarterback, former San Diego Charger Drew Brees. Payton had persuaded Brees that signing with New Orleans would be about more than just football. This was a team that could help rebuild a city's spirits.

In his first huddle, Brees told the offense, "I'm here to lead you to a Super Bowl, and anything else is despicable."

The home opener at the Superdome became a major event, with Green Day and U2 performing "The Saints Are Coming" beforehand; ESPN's ratings were the second-highest for any cable show ever. The team experienced an on-field rebirth as well: the Saints reached the playoffs for the first time since 2000. After losing the NFC championship, the team struggled for two straight years, but 2009 proved special beyond their wildest dreams.

The team won its first 13 games, then marched through the playoffs to face Peyton Manning and the Indianapolis Colts in the Super Bowl. Before the game, the Saints watched a video that interspersed highlights from the 2009 season with clips of the devastation wrought by Katrina, including the overcrowded Superdome. The city had slowly been reviving.

A win that day would give more hope for a brighter future. "It placed us in history," said cornerback Greg Fassitt. "It gave this game a context. The room was dead quiet. You could hear people breathing hard. You could hear sniffling."

But beating the Colts required more than inspiration—they were considered the NFL's premier team and played like it for most of the game. Indianapolis built a 10–0 lead and held a 17–16 advantage when the final quarter started. But then the Colts missed a field goal. Brees, who had become extremely involved in the New Orleans community, told his team, "Let's be special." Then he began a 59-yard drive that featured seven completions to seven different receivers. (He would complete 29 of his final 32 passes.) The touchdown made it 22–17, so Payton went for a two-point conversion, with Brees passing to an eighth receiver, Lance Moore. When the pass was initially ruled incomplete, Payton challenged the call, which was overturned when it was shown that Moore had maintained possession and stretched the ball over the goal line as he fell.

When it was over, the Saints had won, 31–17. On the field in Miami afterward, Brees held his one-year-old son, Baylen. His wife Brittany later said, "My only wish is that everybody from New Orleans was here with us right now." In a way, everyone—not just New Orleans—was in fact there. As if proving this was more than just a game, America had made Super Bowl XLIV not only the most-watched Super Bowl ever but, with 106.5 million viewers, the most-watched television program of all time, breaking the record set by the last episode of *M*A*S*H*.

Saints quarterback Drew Brees shares the Vince Lombardi Trophy with head coach Sean Payton. (AP Photo/David J. Phillip)

XXXII: John Elway Leads the Broncos to the Title — Finally

Broncos quarterback John Elway scrambles during the first half of Super Bowl XXXII. (AP Photo/Elise Amendola)

The scarlet letter in the NFL is "L," as in Loser. Fran Tarkenton may be in the Hall of Fame, but he is remembered for falling short in three Super Bowls. Jim Kelly is a Hall of Famer with four Super Bowl defeats forever attached to his name.

Denver Broncos quarterback John Elway looked like he was heading in the same direction. Elway lost three Super Bowls in four years, beginning in 1987, and all were blowouts (39–20, 42–10, 55–10) in which Elway threw just two touchdowns but six interceptions.

"They'll never, ever forgive me for this," he said of Bronco fans after the last loss.

As the Broncos faltered in the 1990s, it looked like those games—more than his toughness, his talent, his monumental regular-season statistics, or his great playoff comebacks—might be Elway's legacy.

Then, in 1998, Elway, at age 37, guided the wild-card Broncos back to the Super Bowl one last time. The defending champion Green Bay Packers, with the reigning MVP, Brett Favre, were 11½ -point favorites.

"We've heard all about poor John Elway," Packer defensive tackle Santana Dotson said before the game. "We're all very touched. . . . As long as we're the focus of the postgame story, that's cool."

Elway, once the game's premier gunslinger, no longer could match Favre's arm—he would pass for just 123 yards all day and failed to hit a wide receiver until the third quarter—but his leadership and drive remained intact. One play, with the game at 17–17 in the third quarter, defined Elway. Beginning at Denver's 8, Elway took the team to Green Bay's 12, a drive highlighted by a 36-yard pass to Ed McCaffrey. On

third-and-6, Elway saw no open receivers, so he burst through the line of scrimmage himself. Most quarterbacks would have headed for the sidelines or slid to safety. Not Elway.

He cut to the right, but as he neared the first down, Packer strong safety LeRoy Butler threw himself toward Elway. The quarterback didn't shy away but instead launched himself into the air. The hit spun him around, and he took another blow from defensive back Mike Prior. Elway landed at the 4, a first down. Better still, he jumped up and got right back to the business of leading his team to the promised land of the end zone.

"The Helicopter," as his flying first down became known, gained more than yardage. "When I saw him do that and then get up pumping his fist, I said, 'It's on.' That's when I was sure we were going to win," said Shannon Sharpe, the Broncos' All-Pro tight end.

Elway later threw an interception, but after Green Bay tied the game, he came up with a huge 23-yard pass to fullback Howard Griffith to set up the final score in a memorable 31–24 victory.

"That was the ultimate win, there's no question," Elway said. "There have been a lot of things that go along with losing three Super Bowls and playing for 14 years and being labeled as a guy who has never been on a winning Super Bowl team."

XXII: Doug Williams Becomes the First African-American Quarterback in the Super Bowl . . . and the MVP

Doug Williams wasn't the first African-American quarterback. But in 1988 he became the first to start and win a Super Bowl. And he did it with élan, after overcoming more than his share of adversity.

A first-round draft pick in 1978, Williams led Tampa Bay, a team that had never reached the playoffs. He took them there three times in four years, but was still paid far less than every white starting quarterback and many backups. So in 1983 he jumped to the upstart United States Football League (and the Buccaneers fell to 2-14). Williams, who had lost his wife to a brain tumor, never found happiness in the USFL. When he returned to the NFL upon its demise, he was relegated to a backup role in Washington.

He played sporadically during the season and outperformed starter Jay Schroeder, so coach Joe Gibbs chose Williams to lead the team during the playoffs. Before the Super Bowl, Williams faced both a root canal and an endless blitz of questions about his race.

He said he was glad if he had "opened doors" for other African-American quarterbacks, but emphasized that "Joe Gibbs and [general manager] Bobby Beathard didn't bring me in to be the first African-American quarterback in the Super Bowl. They brought me in to be the quarterback of the Washington Redskins."

Williams almost didn't get the chance to do that —he wrenched his knee in the first quarter and was briefly sidelined as Denver's John Elway ran up a 10–0 lead. No team had overcome a 10–0 Super Bowl disadvantage before. But no team had seen a second quarter like the spectacle unleashed by the 32-year-old Williams.

The Redskins had the ball five times in the second quarter. They ran just 19 plays, yet scored 35 points. Williams went 9-11 for 228 yards with four touchdowns, including one of 50 yards and one of 80. No team and no quarterback—black or white—had ever pulled off such a feat. The game ended 42–10, and Williams was the clear choice for Super Bowl MVP.

Washington Redskins quarterback Doug Williams warms up before Super Bowl XXII. (AP Photo/NFL Photos)

FANTASTIC FINISHES

Football is an incredible game. Sometimes it's so incredible, it's unbelievable. — Tom Landry, NFL coach

1 | THE IMMACULATE RECEPTION, 1972

Franco Harris races down the sideline with the controversial 60-yard pass from Terry Bradshaw. (AP Photo/ NFL Photos)

When Pittsburgh Steelers quarterback Terry Bradshaw faded back to pass with his team trailing 7–6 and just 20 seconds left in the 1972 AFC divisional playoff game against the Oakland Raiders, expectations ranged from low to negligible. The Raiders had a winning tradition, having compiled a 63-15-6 record since 1967 and reaching the postseason every year but one. The Steelers, by contrast, were losers.

The hapless Steelers had reached the playoffs just once, back in 1947. They had won nine games only once since then; the nadir arrived in 1965, when the team hit a 14-53-3 skid. But 1969's 1-13 season actually marked a rebirth under their rookie coach Chuck Noll, who was piecing together a talented roster that broke through with an 11-3 record in 1972.

With 20 seconds remaining in this game, however, the new beginning seemed headed for an abrupt conclusion. It was a defensive battle in which the Steelers had kicked a field goal to open the scoring . . . in the third quarter. Pittsburgh added a field goal in the fourth quarter. But when Oakland's Ken Stabler, who had replaced the injured Daryle Lamonica, evaded a Steeler blitz and ran 30 yards for a touchdown and a 7–6 Oakland lead with about 1:17 left, the locals resignedly sighed "SOS"—Same Old Steelers.

The Steelers just needed a field goal, but they made little progress. With 22 seconds left, they faced fourth-and-10 from their own 40.

Then came the most famous—and most controversial—play in NFL history.

It fueled the classic Steelers-Raiders rivalry of the 1970s and transformed Pittsburgh's mind-set, providing a crucial stepping-stone on the path to the game's greatest dynasty. "We had a lot of important wins after that, but I think that one was the game that set the pattern," said cornerback Mel Blount.

Bradshaw's initial target was Barry Pearson, who was running a quick route over the middle. But Pearson was covered, and Bradshaw ducked out of the pocket to escape Oakland's 255-pound Horace Jones, who briefly got a hand on him. With three Raiders closing in on the scrambling quarterback, he was lucky to see halfback John "Frenchy" Fuqua hooking into the middle of the field, wide open.

"I was about to get hit. I unloaded it," Bradshaw said.

Bradshaw fired a pass about 37 yards. It was right on the money, but it arrived at the same time as Oakland's Jack Tatum, who had left his man after seeing the pass released. Tatum, who would gain the nickname "Assassin," was a hard hitter (he would paralyze New England receiver Darryl Stingley in 1978), but here his aggression proved fatal to Oakland.

"I said in my mind, 'He's coming, no doubt about it,'" Fuqua recalled later. "I hear footsteps. . . . I hear [Tatum] breathing. . . . I'm hauling ass to get to a point, and he's coming at the same speed to

Harris gathers the controversial pass from Bradshaw in the 1972 AFC divisional playoff game. (AP Photo/ NFL Photos)

destroy whatever's coming to that same point."

Tatum should have focused on knocking down the pass or, if Fuqua caught it, just wrapping him up. But thinking the ball would beat him there, Tatum was intent on jarring the ball loose by hitting Fuqua full force, which he did with a forearm to the head, sending the Steeler to the ground. As he did, the ball ricocheted hard—either off Tatum, Fuqua, or both men—back toward the line of scrimmage.

"I hit him, and I thought the game was ours," Tatum said. Behind the play, defensive back Jimmy Warren lifted his arms in celebration, which soon proved to be another costly mistake. The Raiders presumed that the ball would land on the turf carpet for an incompletion. The game appeared to be over, a victory for Oakland.

But Pittsburgh's 230-pound rookie fullback Franco Harris presumed nothing. He was supposed to have blocked the outside linebacker, then slipped out if all the receivers were covered. At Penn State, he had learned to follow the ball, so he decided to run toward Fuqua in the hopes of blocking for him. With Bradshaw in trouble, Harris headed downfield, somewhat aimlessly at first.

As NBC announcer Curt Gowdy was saying, " . . . broken up by Tatum," Harris, a burly black-and-gold superhero, swooped in to grab the ball, eight yards from the collision, just before it hit the ground. Then he rumbled the remaining 40 yards toward the end zone.

"I didn't see Franco catch the ball," Tatum said later. "I thought, 'He's sure in a hurry to get to the locker room.'"

Stunned, the Raiders gave a desperate but belated pursuit. Tight end John McMakin took out linebacker Phil Villapiano, who had been covering Harris, and just before the end zone Harris stiff-armed Warren—who had lost that crucial split second with his misguided reaction—and ran in for the score.

Or did he? Oakland immediately besieged the referees, arguing that the ball bounced off Fuqua, not Tatum, and that since a player can't catch a teammate's deflection, the pass was incomplete. (The league changed the rule in 1978.)

The refs quickly gathered. If only Fuqua touched the ball, it would be Oakland's ball with their 7–6 lead intact. If the ball touched either just Tatum or both players, then the touchdown stood and Pittsburgh would have a 12–7 lead with an extra point to come.

The teams, the fans, and the viewers on television could do nothing but wait.

Referee Fred Swearingen finally went to the Pittsburgh Pirates dugout and used the phone there to call the NFL supervisor of officials, Art McNally, who was up in a booth.

Swearingen just told McNally that two officials believed the ball had been touched by opposing players; McNally, who had confirmed that view with a brief glance at the replay on TV, responded, "Everything is fine. Go ahead and go."

When Swearingen signaled a touchdown, some Pittsburgh fans raced onto the field to celebrate the team's first playoff win ever. Oops, there were still five seconds left on the clock, and Pittsburgh had to kick the extra point. Then the game was over. But the play's legacy was just getting started.

That night, journalist Myron Cope was preparing to deliver his commentary on WTAE's 11:00 p.m. news when he got a call from a fan named Sharon Levosky. She was celebrating with a friend named Michael Ord, who had toasted the victory by declaring, "May this day forever be known as the Feast of the Immaculate Reception."

Bradshaw claimed that the ball could only have bounced that far back if it hit Tatum, who was running upfield, not Fuqua, who was running across and down. "Tatum's momentum carries the ball backward," Bradshaw said years later. Several physicists who studied the footage and ran tests on momentum and velocity agreed with that assessment, with one emphasizing that the ball bounced back before Tatum and Fuqua made contact.

In 1998, NBC finally rebroadcast its footage, which Bob Raissman of the *New York Daily News*

called "football's version of the Zapruder film." It seemed to confirm that Tatum had hit the ball.

With all the debate, what is often forgotten is that Pittsburgh lost the next week to Miami, which was en route to its perfect 17-0 season, and to Oakland in the divisional playoffs the following year. Still, Fuqua and others argued that this play marked the team's turnaround, blazing the path for the dynasty that followed.

Harris said that "1972 was a magic year for us. Part of that magic was capped off in the playoff game with the Immaculate Reception. That was just the start of a great decade."

Bradshaw (left) gets a hug from reserve quarterback Terry Hanratty in the dressing room after the Steelers defeated the Raiders. (AP Photo)

2 | THE ICE BOWL, 1967

Cowboys quarterback Don Meredith (17) falls back as players chase a fumble. (AP Photo/File)

Quarterback Bart Starr (15) digs his face across the goal line to score the winning touchdown against the Dallas Cowboys to bring the Packers their third consecutive NFL championship. (AP Photo)

On New Year's Eve 1967, it was 13 degrees below zero in Green Bay, Wisconsin. That was the city's coldest December 31 ever, and the temperature reading didn't even account for the winds pushing through at up to 30 miles per hour.

The NFL considered postponing the championship game between the Green Bay Packers and the Dallas Cowboys, which would become the coldest NFL game on record. The special heating system that Green Bay coach Vince Lombardi had installed beneath the grass at Lambeau Field worked fine during Saturday practice, when the temperature reached the 20s, but the system broke down in the arctic conditions on Sunday. In the end, at least five members of the Cowboys and several Packers, including quarterback Bart Starr, would either suffer serious frostbite or require medical treatment for exposure.

"The field was exactly like playing on an ice rink," said Cowboy Walt Garrison.

In the broadcast booth, former Giants great Frank Gifford quipped, "I think I'll take another bite of my coffee."

But it wasn't just the bitter weather that made the Ice Bowl an instant classic. It was the football itself, especially the final drive.

The Packers were the defending champion, but they were nearing the end of their dynasty. Coach Vince Lombardi had decided to retire, though he hadn't told anyone yet. The Cowboys, coached by Tom Landry, who had made his name running the New York Giants defense when Lombardi was running the Giants offense, were just beginning their run as a premier team.

"Coach Lombardi was quick to point out all week long how good the Cowboys were and what respect he had for them," Starr said. But on game day Lombardi told his players that they were better prepared for the weather than the team from Dallas. "It's our kind of day, boys," he said, adding that his players wouldn't wear gloves because it would interfere with their hands. Some Packers thought otherwise: "The question ultimately is whether anyone can survive playing in these conditions," said defensive end Willie Davis later, after suffering frostbite on his fingertips.

The Packers took a 14–0 lead, but two Green Bay fumbles let Dallas back into the game. "Maybe we started to think about the cold and the conditions more than we thought about our own execution," Starr admitted later.

The halftime marching band was canceled. The line judge's whistle froze to his lips. But perhaps nothing was more chilling to Green Bay fans than watching Dallas take a 17–14 lead in the fourth quarter.

With 4:54 left, the Packers began one final push from their own 32. Starr thought about giving his men a pep talk in the huddle but saw in their faces that they didn't need one. "Everyone in the huddle was calm," said fullback Chuck Mercein. "I didn't sense any anxiety or desperation."

Starr mixed handoffs and short passes to bring the team to the Cowboy 3 with 1:11 left. But it took three plays and most of that time to get to the 1. There was time left for just one more play.

With 16 seconds left in the Ice Bowl, the Packers used their last time-out. On the sidelines, Starr and Lombardi never really considered going for the tie. It was all or nothing. Lombardi wanted to go out a winner.

The play they settled on was "31 Wedge," which Lombardi had just added that week because guard Jerry Kramer thought he had found a weakness in

the Cowboys' short yardage defense. On the play, Starr would hand the ball to Mercein, who would plunge ahead. "Run it and let's get the hell out of here," Lombardi said.

But the footing was treacherous, and Starr worried about Mercein slipping or fumbling—he would have only a split second to hit the hole. The year before, Starr had improvised a quarterback sneak in icy conditions, so even though he called "31 Wedge" in the huddle, he decided—without telling the linemen or Mercein—to keep the ball himself. On the play, Kramer and center Ken Bowman cleared Cowboys defensive tackle Jethro Pugh. Starr found the opening and shot through. The sneak had worked.

The Packers were NFL champions for the third straight year and were heading back to the Super Bowl. The play gained even greater stature because one CBS camera, which was supposed to shift to follow a wide receiver, had frozen in position and was trained right on Kramer. The play showing Kramer's block and Starr's score was shown again and again, becoming part of NFL lore.

"To have it come down to such brutal conditions and to win it in that fashion, from our perspective, we think it was the greatest game of all time," Starr said.

3 | THE CATCH, 1982

The 49ers' Dwight Clark leaps high in the end zone to catch a Montana pass to tie the game. (AP Photo/ *Dallas Morning News*, Phil Huber)

onships and advanced to five Super Bowls, while the San Francisco 49ers had never reached the Super Bowl and were in their first postseason since 1973.

The Cowboys had two time-outs and needed only a field goal to win. But after Pearson—who, in the twilight of his career, hadn't caught a ball all day—grabbed Danny White's bullet of a pass and San Francisco's rookie defensive backs Ronnie Lott and Carlton Williamson collided, Pearson tore down the sideline thinking he had a 75-yard game-winning touchdown. But it was not to be.

Moments earlier, Dwight Clark had run a route for San Francisco as the secondary target on the "Sprint Right Option," a play that had produced a touchdown catch early in the game. But Freddie Solomon, the primary receiver, made that score; in three years of running this play in games, quarterback Joe Montana had never thrown to Clark. They had tried it in practice, but Clark had never made a catch, much less *the* catch, on the play.

The 49ers trailed the Dallas Cowboys, 27–21, with less than a minute to go, but they remained determined. Montana was in his first full season as a starter and had led the league in pass completion percentage, but he had had a rough game, throwing three interceptions and fumbling once. (Turnovers and penalties had set up 24 of the Cowboys' 27 points, 10 of which had come in the fourth quarter.) San Francisco owner Eddie DeBartolo had headed to the locker room to see his team. "It looked hopeless. I wanted to get in the locker room to commiserate with them."

Then Montana, along with head coach Bill Walsh and assistant coach Sam Wyche, engineered an 83-yard march to the 6-yard line. Walsh's innovative West Coast Offense replaced runs with short passes, but after an incompletion he and Wyche

Drew Pearson saw nothing but open field. As the veteran Dallas Cowboy receiver accelerated toward the end zone with time ticking down on the 1982 NFC championship game, it seemed for a moment that he had made "the Catch"—the biggest play of his career in the most fantastic finish ever to an NFL game, giving the Cowboys one more shot at being king of the mountain.

With a minute left and behind by a single point, 28–27, the Cowboys were undeterred. After all, they had reached eight of the previous 11 NFC champi-

suddenly switched gears and began running to set up the pass. It was especially effective because Dallas defensive coordinator Ernie Stautner was so worried about deeper passes that he had gone to a nickel defense—four linemen, one small, quick linebacker, and six backs—over the heated protests of veteran safety Charlie Waters, who wanted to play more aggressively. The 49ers exploited Stautner's scheme effectively, and by the time they were inside the Cowboys' red zone, right guard Randy Cross saw a defense on the defensive.

"I saw on [the Cowboys'] faces the same look Thomas Hearns had when Sugar Ray hit him a few times," Cross said. "They had had us backed up, but now they were no longer the aggressors. They were fighting for their lives."

Walsh went for broke, sending Solomon into the left corner of the end zone—he was open, but Montana's pass was off target. "I thought that was the championship right there," Walsh said afterward. "We were never going to get that open again."

San Francisco got to the Dallas 6 on a run, for third-and-3; two chances for a touchdown, or even a first down.

Solomon slotted inside, and Clark was supposed to set a pick, then cut across the back of the end zone, first one way and then the other. But the Cowboys finally abandoned the nickel defense, returned to the 4-3, and sent D. D. Lewis in to blitz. Lewis, "Too Tall" Jones, and Larry Bethea all chased Montana as he rolled right toward the sideline. Solomon lost his footing, then couldn't get open.

Montana saw Clark briefly, pump-faked to throw off Jones, and then went up on the wrong foot for an off-balance throw to where he thought Clark would be. The quarterback got hit and went down. The pass sailed toward the back of the end zone but was clearly going to be out of anyone's reach. It went beyond an outstretched Dallas defender, Everson Walls.

"It was over my head," Clark said. "I thought, 'Oh oh, I can't go that high.'"

Most of Clark couldn't, but his fingertips could—and did. They brought the ball down. Suddenly, the Cowboys' 27–21 lead was gone, and San Francisco held a one-point edge with time running out.

But then Pearson made his catch and took off downfield. Another rookie defensive back, Eric Wright, somehow caught up enough to get his left hand on Pearson's shoulder pad. Wright couldn't tackle Pearson like that, but he slowed him down enough so that he could yank the Cowboys receiver down with his other hand by the back of the shoulder pads. (This "horse collar" tackle was banned in 2005.)

Wright had, for the moment, saved the day. But Pearson had gained 31 to the 49er 44. Danny White faded back again, needing one more pass to get into field goal range. But defensive end Lawrence Pillers nailed him, causing a fumble (White argued that his arm was moving forward, making it an incomplete pass), and Jim Stuckey recovered. It was only then—with a 28–27 victory and a trip to the Super Bowl sealed—that Clark's catch became "the Catch."

The play took on even larger implications when San Francisco won the Super Bowl, beginning a dynasty that would capture four crowns in the decade while Dallas stumbled toward mediocrity. With the 49ers at the top of the football world, footage of Clark's touchdown gained new life in a Kodak commercial. Montana to Clark for "the Catch" had indeed created an indelible image . . . even if it took Wright's tackle and Pillers's hit to make it last.

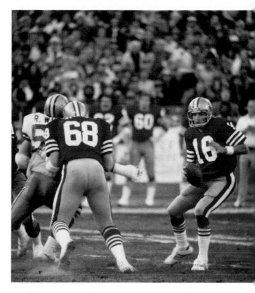

San Francisco quarterback Joe Montana (16) pump-fakes in the 1982 NFC championship game. (AP Photo)

4 | EPIC IN MIAMI, 1982

Dan Fouts (14) carries the ball in the AFC divisional playoff game. (AP Photo)

Wes Chandler (89) pulls in a pass in early action. Chandler returned an early punt for a 56-yard Chargers touchdown in the first quarter. (AP Photo)

The 1982 AFC divisional playoff game was a non-stop thriller for the fans. For the players, slugging it out in the horrific heat and humidity, it felt more like a war of attrition.

The San Diego Chargers, led by their head coach, the master offensive tactician Don Coryell, and their quarterback, Dan Fouts, had led the NFL in scoring and yardage in 1981, with Fouts setting a record by passing for 4,802 yards. They were stacked up against the Miami Dolphins, whose defense had allowed the fifth-fewest points in the league. That should have been the story line, but the script was tossed out almost immediately.

The Chargers shot out to a 24–0 lead with barely any magic required from Fouts—they scored on a punt return, recovered a kickoff to set up one touchdown, and then intercepted a pass to set up another.

But Miami had a savvy coach too—the legendary Don Shula. Knowing he needed a dramatic change, he turned to backup quarterback Don Strock, who led the team back to tie the game by early in the third quarter.

But it was untied when Fouts threw a touchdown pass to tight end Kellen Winslow. The play was especially rewarding for Winslow, who had led the league in receptions for the second straight year but who had a rep for being soft by tight end standards. Miami had hit him hard as often as possible; they cut his lip, gave him a swollen eye, and left him with a pinched nerve in his left shoulder that flared with each hit he took. But Winslow created a new reputation in this game—he just kept on coming. After catching this pass, he hobbled to the bench as his legs cramped up.

Strock responded with a 50-yard touchdown pass to his tight end Bruce Hardy, and Miami's

defense produced an interception to set up a touchdown. Shockingly, Miami led, 38–31, as the fourth quarter began. Now they just had to stop San Diego. It looked good. Coryell's year had started miserably when stars John Jefferson and Fred Dean left over contract arguments. He and his team had been accused of lacking character during the season. Now he was bent down, hands on knees, looking as if the world were ending soon. But San Diego forced a fumble, putting the game back in Fouts's hands.

The ball was soon flying out of Fouts's hands—eight passes, seven completions, and a 38–38 tie with just 52 seconds left. Miami used that limited time perfectly, getting down to the Chargers' 26. Uwe von Schamann, who had kicked three game-winners that year, came on the field. But so did Winslow. Battered and exhausted, Winslow knew that, at 6'5", he had the best chance to block the kick, even though he wasn't part of the field goal blocking unit and had never blocked a kick before.

That extra height was the difference between victory and defeat. Von Schamann's kick was interrupted on its journey to the uprights by nothing more than a right pinkie. But Winslow's littlest finger caused enough of a disruption to save the day. "It was the biggest thrill of my life," Winslow said. "I felt like I scored three touchdowns."

Still, his spasms had now spread to his back and were so bad that he had to be carried off the field. Both teams were feeling the heat, the humidity, and the hits.

In overtime, San Diego had a chance to win from the Miami 8, but kicker Rolf Benirschke, who hadn't missed inside the 30 all season, hooked the ball to the left. Sickened, he trudged off the field, knowing how von Schamann had felt.

Everyone else felt even worse. The game wouldn't end. Most of the players could barely stand. But the more exhausted they got the more impossible it seemed to sustain a drive. Back and forth. Back and forth.

Von Schamann got a shot at redemption, but haunted by Winslow's block, he rushed the kick—his foot hit the ground first, the kick never got high enough, and Charger Leroy Jones blocked it.

This sparked the San Diego offense back to life (or maybe knocked the life out of Miami's defense). "When you get a little desperate, you find something extra," Fouts said. After 13:52 of overtime, Benirschke got a shot at redemption as well. Unlike von Schamann, he made the most of his—the kick was good, 41–38. Game over. Finally.

A Dolphin player helped Winslow up, but after the tight end—who had caught 13 passes for 166 yards, both playoff records—took a few steps,

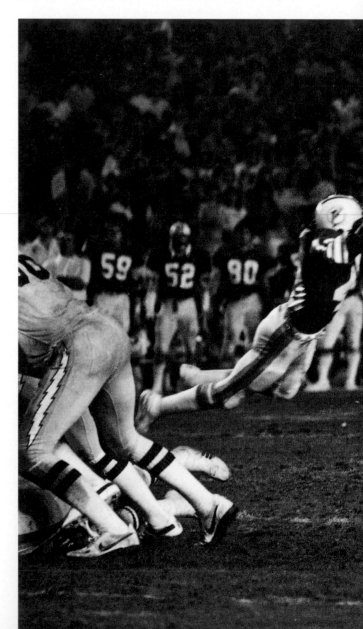

he fell again, cramping all over. His teammates carried him off, while lineman Louie Kelcher and 270-pound guard Ed White lay at the line of scrimmage. After everyone had left, White said, "Louie, you know we're gonna have to get up and walk. They don't carry fat guys off the field."

In the locker room, White needed an IV drip, Kelcher had to have his socks cut off his feet, and Winslow's temperature hit 105 degrees. (He lost 13 pounds during the game.)

In a bitter irony, the Chargers lost the next week to Cincinnati in a game played in freezing temperatures with a −59° windchill. And Miami would beat San Diego in the playoffs the next year en route to the Super Bowl.

But nothing could top the 1982 epic in Miami, one that stands out more than most Super Bowls, and not just for the final score. "People remember all kinds of details from that game," Winslow said nearly two decades later, "but they can't remember who won, because it wasn't about who won or who lost."

The Chargers' Rolf Benirschke (6) kicks the winning field goal in overtime. (AP Photo)

5 | MUSIC CITY MIRACLE, 2000

Do you believe in miracles? For one shining moment in Nashville in January 2000, all of Music City did.

When the Tennessee Titans kicked a field goal to grab a 15–13 lead with 1:48 left, they believed they had won the AFC wild-card game. But when Buffalo came back and snatched a 16–15 lead with a mere 16 seconds left, the Bills were sure they had it won.

Then came the kickoff and a 75-yard touchdown return on a lateral that many in the NFL called the greatest (and most disputed) play since "the Immaculate Reception."

The nickname "Music City Miracle" was a bit misleading, since the dizzying spectacle that produced it was born out of Titans coach Jeff Fisher's dedication to preaching preparation and poise. The preparation: the Titans' special teams unit had practiced a play called "Home Run Throwback" all season long, just waiting for a chance to use it. The poise: when the play's time finally came, nearly every element had to be improvised.

Home Run Throwback was designed by special teams coach Alan Lowry, who had been fired by the owner as receivers coach, but rehired when Fisher persuaded the bosses to keep him on in a new job. The idea was that tight end Frank Wycheck would field a squib kick and make a short lateral to receiver Isaac Byrd, who would run upfield and then toss it back one more time to returner Derrick Mason, who could get the team into field goal range.

But Mason and the second returner, Anthony Dorsett, had been sidelined by injuries, so wide receiver Kevin Dyson—who had never practiced the play and had never even returned a kick—was given last-second instructions by Fisher and thrust into the spotlight.

For some reason, the Bills' Steve Christie didn't kick a squib but rather a short, high ball to Tennessee's 25. Running back Lorenzo Neal caught it and started the improvising by meeting Wycheck on the run for a handoff. But Byrd was now way out of position. So Wycheck kept running right to dis-

Bills kicker Steve Christie (2) is lifted up by holder Chris Mohr after Christie kicked a field goal with 20 seconds remaining in the fourth quarter to put the Bills ahead of the Tennessee Titans, 16–15, in the AFC wild-card game. (AP Photo/Mark Humphrey)

guise the play as a reverse. Then he stopped short, pivoted, and lateraled the ball back to Dyson on the left side. The toss was low, but Dyson scooped it up and took off. "I was real excited," he said. "There was nobody there."

The only players in front of him were blocking Titans and Christie, who was wiped out by Tennessee linebacker Terry Killens. "At first I was, like, 'Get out of bounds so we can kick a field goal,'" Wycheck said. "But he was, like, flying."

And he didn't come in for a landing until the end zone. Buffalo's players immediately howled that Wycheck's pass had gone forward, not laterally, and was thus illegal. "Everybody knew that was illegal—it was a forward pass," said cornerback Thomas Smith.

Referee Phil Luckett went to examine the replay. For several moments, the 66,000 fans packed into Adelphia Coliseum held their collective breath. If in fact the pass was forward by a few inches, it wasn't clear enough on camera to overturn the call. And while the Bills moaned about being robbed, the Titans and their fans exploded in celebration. "There's something to be said about destiny and belief and expectation," said Fisher.

Titans wide receiver Kevin Dyson (87) returns a kickoff with seconds remaining in the fourth quarter. The ball was lateralled twice on the return, and Dyson took it to the end zone. Looking on from the sideline is Titans quarterback Steve McNair (9). (AP Photo/Wade Payne)

6 | THE "TUCK RULE" GAME, 2002

Patriots head coach Bill Belichick watches his team in action against the Oakland Raiders in the AFC divisional playoff game on January 19, 2002. (AP Photo/ Steven Senne)

Raiders head coach Jon Gruden shouts instructions from the sidelines. (AP Photo/ Winslow Townson)

The Pittsburgh Steelers' 1970s dynasty was born out of the astonishing "Immaculate Reception." The San Francisco 49ers' reign of the following decade started with the Catch. In 2002 a referee's call and a field goal kicked off the New England Patriots' dynasty with less glitz and more grit—but just as much drama.

Snow covered the field for the final game at Foxboro Stadium, the AFC divisional playoff between the Patriots and the Oakland Raiders. With swirling winds and the footing growing ever more treacherous, Oakland's 13–3 lead looked much bigger as the fourth quarter started.

New England quarterback Tom Brady was not yet an icon—he had gone from fourth-stringer his rookie year to backup in this, his second season.

Brady had taken over when Drew Bledsoe got hurt and led the team to an 11-3 record, but he had scuffled in his last five games, with only two touchdowns and five interceptions. And now, through these quarters, he had gone just 12-24.

With the season on the line, however, Brady would prove his mettle. After throwing nine consecutive completions, he scored on a six-yard scramble. And then, in the waning moments, Brady began another march down the field. But this one was rudely interrupted at Oakland's 42 with 1:50 left. After Brady coolly scrambled for a first down, Oakland star cornerback Charles Woodson blitzed and nailed the quarterback just as he finished a pump-fake. The ball was jarred loose, and linebacker Greg Biekert recovered. As Brady shuffled

Quarterback Tom Brady prepares to pass during the snowy game. (AP Photo/Elise Amendola)

off the field with his head down, the season seemed over—he knew it, the fans knew it, and the announcers on TV knew it.

Only the referees didn't know it—because it was the final two minutes, they could automatically review the play without a challenge. On the replay it could be clearly seen that Brady started to pass—which would make it an incompletion, not a fumble. But then he changed his mind and seemed to start tucking the ball in for protection. At the press conference after the game, he said slyly, "Yeah, I was throwing the ball. He hit me as I was throwing. How do you like that?"

But he didn't actually have to be throwing. Rule 3, section 21, article 2, declares that, "any

intentional forward movement of [the thrower's] arm starts a forward pass, even if the player loses possession of the ball as he is attempting to tuck it back toward his body." Only if he completed the tuck to become a runner would it have been a fumble. Because Brady hadn't finished the tuck, the referees correctly called the play an incompletion.

The Raiders were furious, believing they had been robbed (although replays also showed Woodson hitting Brady in the head, which could have been called roughing the passer). But they still could have stopped the Patriots.

Or maybe not. It wasn't just Brady—his receivers did yeoman's work, finding footing, catching and holding the ball, and fighting for extra yardage.

Brady (12) loses the ball after being brought down by the Raiders' Charles Woodson (right), while Greg Biekert (54) moves to recover the ball. (AP Photo/ Elise Amendola)

On the very next play, Brady found David Patten, who caught a low pass and then scratched and clawed for 13 yards and the first down.

The drive then stalled at the 28. So Adam Vinatieri came out to try for a 45-yard field goal. Giving hope was the wind at his back, but he had missed four of his last five from 40 to 49 yards, and none of those had been in a snowstorm. With no time-outs, the Patriots didn't even have a chance to clear a spot.

But Vinatieri would prove as clutch—and as critical to the Patriot dynasty—as Brady. With 27 seconds left, he barely cleared the goalpost, tying the game at 13–13. "I kind of line-drived it," Vinatieri said. "I knew it was straight enough. I had to wait a while to see if it was long enough."

Even with this inspiring drive, the game still wasn't won. Brady, however, had found his rhythm, and in overtime he threw nothing but completions, thanks again to his receivers. At the Raiders' 28, when the Patriots faced fourth-and-4—and felt it was too much to expect Vinatieri to boot another long field goal—Patten made a diving catch on a low pass for a six-yard gain.

Moments later, after a time-out that allowed New England's players to clear a patch of grass, Vinatieri came out for a 23-yard field goal. When it soared through the uprights, New England safety Lonie Paxton lay on the ground and made snow angels. The rest of the team hoisted their kicker high in the air.

Much later, after kicking two game-winners in Super Bowls, Vinatieri looked back with appreciation, not at the game-winner, but at the kick that tied it up. "There were five inches of snow on the ground, and I don't have much experience—hell, nobody does—kicking in those kinds of conditions. Then, when you consider what was on the line, that if I missed that kick our season was over, I'd have to say that was the one."

The Patriots' Adam Vinatieri (4) kicks a 45-yard game-tying field goal with 27 seconds left in the fourth quarter. (AP Photo/Elise Amendola)

7 | THE DRIVE, 1987

Broncos quarterback John Elway (7) eludes Cleveland defender Reggie Camp as he scrambles out of the pocket near the end zone in the AFC championship game. (AP Photo/ Gene Puskar)

"We got 'em right where we want 'em," Denver Bronco offensive guard Keith Bishop declared in the huddle.

The statement seemed like false bravado.

The Cleveland Browns had just taken a 20–13 lead on a magnificent 48-yard touchdown pass from Bernie Kosar. Just 5:32 remained in the AFC championship game. The Broncos were starting at their 2-yard line, having mishandled a Cleveland kickoff. One end zone was 98 yards away. The other loomed behind them, with Cleveland's rabid fans howling in the Dawg Pound and making it impossible for the Broncos to hear the calls at the line of scrimmage.

In Denver's last five road games in 1986, they had lost four, averaging under 15 points per game. In this game, they had had the ball twice in the

fourth quarter and had gained a total of 15 yards. They had only 216 yards all day and hadn't sustained a drive, scoring on two field goals and a touchdown set up by a fumble recovery. And for all his obvious athletic talent, quarterback John Elway had not yet proven himself to the NFL at large.

But his teammates, like Bishop, believed in their leader. Elway, playing with a sprained left ankle, smiled at his team and said, "If you work hard, good things are going to happen."

And so "the Drive" began.

Relying on hand signals to combat the noise, Elway started off with a handful of plays sent in by the conservative coach Dan Reeves. That gained some breathing room, but the clock was starting to become a factor, and Denver was still only on its

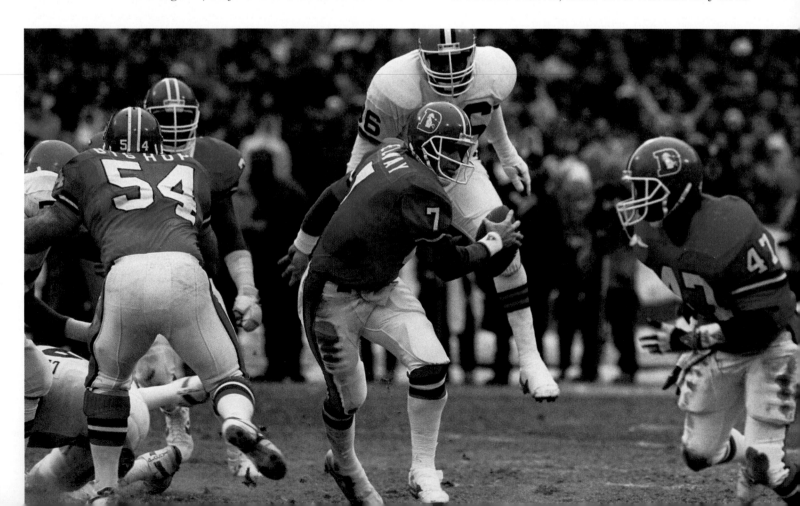

15. This was the moment when Elway lived up to the hype that had made him the number-one overall pick in the 1984 draft.

On second-and-7, Elway took off out of the pocket, scrambling for 11 yards. Just over two minutes left. Now Elway let loose. He connected with Steve Sewell for 22 yards and Steve Watson for 12. The two-minute warning had arrived, but Elway was now in Cleveland territory, at the 40.

Cleveland's defense rallied with a stop and a sack. Facing third-and-18, Elway called for time. The next play almost went horribly awry—with Elway in the shotgun, Watson went in motion, but the snap was mistimed and deflected off the receiver. Still, Elway gained control of the ball, kept his cool, and found Mark Jackson turning in 20 yards down the left sideline. First down.

Now the momentum was all Denver's. Another pass and Elway's scramble brought the Broncos to third-and-1 from the Cleveland 5 with 39 seconds

remaining. The fans were hurling dog biscuits and bones onto the field. Nothing, however, could distract the quarterback. When Jackson cut from left to right, he left behind a cornerback and found a brief opening in the Browns' zone. Elway gunned it to him. "I felt like a baseball catcher," said Jackson of his sliding catch for the touchdown. "That was a John Elway fastball, outside and low."

The Dawg Pound was left whimpering. The game went into overtime, and after Cleveland went three and out, Elway went right back to work. He began at his own 25 this time and gained 50 yards in two completions. After a few running plays, Rich Karlis drilled a field goal, and Denver headed off to the Super Bowl, leaving Cleveland behind.

"When you've got John Elway on your team, you've always got a chance," said Reeves. "Always."

Broncos wide receiver Ricky Nattiel (84) catches a touchdown pass. (AP Photo/ NFL Photos)

Broncos placekicker Rich Karlis (3) follows through on his overtime field goal to give Denver a 23–20 victory. Holding the ball is Gary Kubiak (8). (AP Photo/Al Behrman)

8 | PANTHERS VS. RAMS, 2004

Given Jake Delhomme's flair for late-game theatrics, what happened in the Carolina Panthers' 2003 divisional playoff game against the St. Louis Rams was almost predictable. But that doesn't make it any less remarkable.

After years as an NFL outcast—going undrafted, getting waived, being relegated to a taxi squad, then exiled to NFL Europe and then a third-string role in New Orleans—Delhomme had come to Carolina in 2003 just looking to compete for the starting job. He didn't get it, but in the season opener he took over from Rodney Peete at halftime and threw three touchdowns to overcome a 17–0 deficit, the last coming in a fourth-down situation with just 16 seconds left. Despite having only a 59.2 completion percentage and just nine touchdowns to 16 interceptions, Delhomme led seven game-winning scoring efforts in the fourth quarter or overtime, and the Panthers—1-15 in 2001 and 7-9 in 2002—went 11-5, tying league records for most wins by three points or less (seven) and most overtime victories (three).

St. Louis had won 14 straight at home, but Carolina snatched a 10–9 halftime lead and expanded it to 23–12 in the fourth quarter. The Panthers looked like they would be avoiding a nail-biter for a change, but after they missed a field goal, the Rams

Panthers quarterback Jake Delhomme looks for a receiver during the NFC divisional playoff game against the Rams. (AP Photo/Charles Rex Arbogast)

St. Louis Rams head coach Mike Martz (right) talks with Carolina Panthers coach John Fox before the game. (AP Photo/Bill Boyce)

scored a touchdown, completed the two-point conversion, and then recovered their onside kick.

Carolina got a reprieve when Rams coach Mike Martz, typically an aggressive play caller, suddenly turned conservative, electing to go for a tie on a field goal instead of the win after reaching the Panthers' 15. Martz's lack of confidence in quarterback Mark Bulger stemmed in part from Bulger's two interceptions that quarter. "I was really concerned about throwing it into the end zone and having a ball tipped or bumped," Martz said. "I thought if we got this thing into overtime, we would win the game."

But he put more pressure on a defense that was already exhausted, having allowed 385 yards, including 222 yards rushing. Carolina, of course, felt right at home in overtime. They almost won immediately, moving to the Rams' 23. But they were called for delay of game and missed a 45-yard kick.

"Just look at this hair," Carolina head coach John Fox said afterward, pointing to his silver mane. "I've never seen a game quite like that, and there were . . . peaks and lows as [big as] you can have in a football game."

Jeff Wilkins, who was 5-5 on the day, then fell just short on a 53-yarder for the Rams. "Fifty-three yards—right around there is my cutoff point. I just think I didn't hit it, and I must have gotten under a little bit."

On the Rams' next drive, rookie Ricky Manning Jr. intercepted Bulger. The Panthers went nowhere on their first two plays, and the game went to a second overtime—making it the fifth-longest playoff game in NFL history.

Facing third-and-14 from their 31, Carolina called "X-Clown," a new play just added that week to free up star receiver Steve Smith on a route that would get him off the line without getting bumped. The play worked to perfection.

"I just beat the safety [Jason Sehorn], and Jake threw one of those pretty balls in the last minute, like he always does," Smith said.

Smith caught the ball in stride and ran the rest of the way for a 69-yard touchdown. Game over. Just like that. "We've been in so many close games that we just believe we're going to win," said Delhomme.

Carolina wide receiver Steve Smith (89) celebrates while scoring on a touchdown pass from Delhomme. (AP Photo/Charles Rex Arbogast)

9 | JETS VS. RAIDERS, 1968

Jets quarterback Joe Namath (12) gets a pass off in the first quarter of the AFL championship game on December 29, 1968, as Oakland's Ben Davidson (83) attempts to knock it down. (AP Photo)

The New York Jets hated the Oakland Raiders. And the feeling was mutual. When the teams played, Oakland attacked New York's offense with cheap hits and late shots. They did this to everyone, of course, but against the Jets, the Raiders narrowed their focus to one target: Joe Namath.

Broadway Joe was the AFL's glamour boy, and the Raiders were a bunch of gritty players who resented his flamboyance. They would shove his face in the mud until he choked, and they fractured his cheekbone and punched him in the groin when the refs weren't looking. Since Namath had come into the AFL, Oakland had beaten New York six times in seven tries—emphasis on the word "beaten." That season they had already won the infamous "Heidi" game—storming back in the final 65 seconds of play to a 43–32 triumph after NBC had switched to a regularly scheduled program about the little Swiss girl before the game was completely over.

The Shea Stadium field was a wreck for the AFL championship game—churned up but with no give—and the weather was freezing and windy. The Jets eked out a 13–10 halftime lead, but at a typically punishing price: Namath's bruised coccyx

and sore right thumb got banged up again, and his left ring finger was dislocated. Oakland's Ben Davidson drove a knee into Namath's head, giving him a concussion, and later Ike Lassiter administered a body slam that left the quarterback so disoriented that he didn't know where he was.

Oakland quarterback Daryle Lamonica opened the third with passes of 37 and 40 yards for first-and-goal from the Jets' 6. But New York firmed up, and Oakland settled for a field goal. Namath proved that he couldn't be intimidated with a 14-play touchdown drive that recaptured the lead.

The fourth quarter began with a bang: Lamonica bombing to receiver Fred Biletnikoff, who beat Johnny Sample for 57 yards to New York's 11. But again the Jets stood their ground. Oakland's field goal made it 20–16. Then Namath threw a risky pass that was intercepted, and the big, bad Raiders quickly shut up the New York crowd with a touchdown for a 23–20 lead.

Namath, however, avenged himself immediately. On first down at his own 32, he saw Oakland's secondary playing prevent defense to avoid getting beat deep. He zipped a quick 10-yard pass to George Sauer, showing the Raiders that he had the time and patience for a sustained drive. Both cornerbacks, afraid to let Namath peck away, had crept up to the line. Keeping both running backs blocking for extra protection, Namath sent three receivers deep and lofted it deep and wide, across to the right sideline, where Don Maynard sprinted past George Atkinson.

Maynard looked over his left shoulder, to where the pass should have been, but the wind carried it past that point and over his right shoulder. Maynard swirled around and made a spectacular catch before being shoved out of bounds at Oakland's 6.

Oakland expected New York to pound the ball in on the ground. It's what the Jets usually did inside the 10—in fact, a regular at Bachelors III, the bar Namath co-owned, had grumbled about this risk-averse play-calling. Namath remembered that and called a play-action pass instead, sending four men into the end zone. The first three were covered, but Namath found Maynard free and zipped a hard sidearm past three defenders. It was low, but Maynard slid and snared it. "Not many quarterbacks can hit their fourth receiver," Sauer said.

In three plays, Namath had taken his team 68 yards and right back into the lead, 27–23, but he had struck so quickly that Oakland had 7:47 left. No television networks dared to turn away this time. Lamonica brought Oakland to the Jets' 26 before stalling. On fourth-and-10, Oakland made the wrong call, skipping a field goal that would have brought them within one; Jets right end Verlon Biggs sacked Lamonica. "I had doubts about us being able to get back into position for another field goal later on," Oakland coach John Rauch said after.

With just over two minutes to go, Lamonica passed his way to New York's 24. The Raiders were back in field goal position. Unfortunately, however, they still needed a touchdown.

Lamonica called for a short pass in the flat to Charlie Smith, a play the Raiders had practiced all week and saved for a moment like this. But Biggs pressured Lamonica again, and the pass hit off Smith's fingers and fell to the ground. The play was not, however, a harmless incompletion: New York linebacker Ralph Baker saw that Smith was actually behind Lamonica, meaning the play was a lateral. He scooped up the loose ball, ending the threat.

Smith, a rookie, didn't realize what had happened. "I didn't think it was a lateral, so I didn't bother to chase it," he said.

The Jets had finally slain the Raiders, and they had done it with the kind of dramatic and unpredictable play that Oakland had always seemed to use to vanquish them. Now it was time for the Super Bowl and the heavily favored Baltimore Colts. After beating Oakland, Namath felt so confident about a victory over Baltimore that he guaranteed it.

But for many Jets, this was the game that mattered most.

Jets head coach Weeb Ewbank is carried off the field by his players. (AP Photo/NFL Photos)

10 | THE SNOWPLOW KICK, 1982

High above all the football memorabilia in the hall at Gillette Stadium's Patriot Place is a most unusual item. A John Deere tractor with a sweeper attached hangs from the ceiling.

There would be so much snow on the ground after a storm on December 12, 1982, that the New England Patriots promised $10 and a free ticket to anyone willing to shovel out the seats in the stands. On the field earlier, however, there wasn't much action. Slowed by the storm that had started shortly after the game commenced, the Patriots and Miami Dolphins had battled to a scoreless standstill. With 4:45 left in the game, the Patriots finally got down to the Miami 16. Both teams had already missed field goals, and coach Ron Meyer wanted to make sure that nothing went wrong for kicker John Smith, so he called on Mark Henderson to save the day.

Henderson was a recovering drug addict who had gone to jail for burglary. He was out on a work release program and working with the stadium's maintenance crew. "Nobody wanted to run the tractor," Henderson recalled of the responsibility of sweeping snow from the sidelines. "I knew I was the low man on the totem pole, obviously, so I volunteered. At the end of the day, everybody wished they had volunteered."

Having called time-out, Meyer hunted down Henderson, who was jogging in place to keep warm, and sent him out to clear a spot for the holder and the football.

"Matt Cavanaugh, the backup quarterback who was the holder, saw me coming and started clapping his hands," Henderson said. "He showed me the spot he wanted cleared. I just swerved over to the 23-yard line with my tractor."

Miami coach Don Shula was outraged—but helpless, because there was no written rule against the use of the tractor. (This became known as "the Snowplow Game," but it was a tractor, not a plow, that was used.) "I wanted to go out there and punch him out," Shula said years later. "I should have laid down in front of the snowplow."

With sure footing secured, Smith put the ball between the uprights for a 3–0 lead.

At the two-minute warning, Henderson took a kind of victory lap, clearing the sidelines once more—and spraying snow in the faces of Miami's players as they came to curse him out. "I gave 'em a real thank-you," Henderson said.

The Patriots later gave Henderson a game ball with the score, date, and phrase "Clean Sweep" on it. But they kept him away from the media to avoid further angering Shula. After the season, the influential Miami coach, who was on the NFL's rules committee, pushed through a rule banning such vehicles from the field during games.

Henderson, meanwhile, finished his sentence and has stayed clean ever since. He was brought back to Foxboro Stadium in 2001 before the last regular-season game—which happened to be against the Dolphins—to reenact his moment of glory at Foxboro Stadium. When Henderson rode out on his tractor, he received a standing ovation.

Mark Henderson, a convict on work release from the Massachusetts Correctional Institution, clears snow during the third quarter of a December 13, 1982, game between the Patriots and the Dolphins. In the fourth quarter, he will clear an area on the field from where the Patriots' John Smith will attempt a field goal. (AP Photo/Mike Kullen)

THE *HEIDI* GAME, 1968

"Congratulations," Lucy Ewbank told her husband long-distance over the phone. She had just watched Weeb Ewbank coach his New York Jets to a seemingly huge win over the Oakland Raiders.

"For what?" he asked.

"On winning," she replied.

"We lost the game," he told her.

It wasn't that Lucy Ewbank didn't understand football. It was that she, like the rest of the nation, had been watching the game on NBC.

In this heated battle between the AFL's two top teams—a prelude to their championship game showdown—New York's Joe Namath had passed for 381 yards and a touchdown while Oakland's Daryle Lamonica threw for 311 yards and four touchdowns. The bitter rivals also amassed 19 penalties for 238 yards.

With 1:05 left, New York's Jim Turner kicked a field goal for a 32–29 lead.

But the game was running long, so NBC's supervisor of broadcast operation control, Dick Cline, threw a switch, and on the East Coast, when the network came back from commercials, football had been replaced by *Heidi*, the premiere of a made-for-TV movie about a little girl in the Alps. (The movie was supposed to run at 7:00 p.m. EST, so viewers in other time zones saw the game's end.)

NBC was contractually obligated to make the change, but the executives also figured that this fifth lead change was the last one. Had they been right, the game would have quickly been forgotten. Instead, with 42 seconds left, Lamonica fired a 43-yard touchdown to halfback Charlie Smith for a 36–32 lead.

The Jets hoped for one last shot at a comeback but instead fumbled the football away, and an unknown named Preston Ridlehuber grabbed it and scored. Oakland had won, 43–29, in one of football's most frantic finales.

Equally frantic were football fans, especially in New York—the 10,000 irate phone calls to NBC crashed not only the network switchboard but the entire phone exchange. "I knew something big had happened," says Cline, who still directs sporting events for NBC and CBS, "because we didn't get any phone calls at all. And we couldn't call out."

With NBC's phones out of commission, the telephone company, the *New York Times*, and even the police department were all bombarded by angry callers demanding that something be done. By then it was too late. At 8:20, the network ran a crawl explaining that Oakland had won.

NBC president Julian Goodman was forced to publicly apologize, somewhat absurdly declaiming that the move was a result of "a forgivable error committed by humans who were concerned about the children who were expecting to see *Heidi*."

Cline later dismissed that as PR nonsense. The network, he said, had no choice. "I had it in print," he said. "In fact, the vice president of my division told me that if I had taken it on my own and stayed with the game, I would have been fired."

The relationship between football and television would never be the same. From then on, the sport would become top priority. All other programming would just have to wait on the sidelines.

Browns fullback Jim Brown, after slicing through the New York Giants line at the 35-yard line, breaks loose on his 65-yard touchdown run on the first play from scrimmage in a 1958 game against the New York Giants. Unable to hold Brown is Giants defensive back Carl Karilivacz (center). (AP Photo/HH)

SUMMERALL IN THE SNOW, 1958

New York Giants owner Wellington Mara peered down from the press box. He could barely see his kicker, Pat Summerall, through the wet snow falling from the sky in Yankee Stadium in December 1958.

The Giants were tied with the Cleveland Browns, 10–10, but with the Browns one game up in the standings on the season's final day, a tie would give them the Eastern Division title for the second straight year, sending them to the NFL championship and leaving New York out in the cold.

"He can't kick it that far," Mara speculated aloud. "What are we doing?"

Offensive coach Vince Lombardi was furious. Sure, Charlie Conerly had thrown three straight incompletions. Lombardi wanted to try one more pass rather than a seemingly impossible kick, but head coach Jim Lee Howell overruled him.

When Summerall arrived in the huddle, Conerly was shocked, barking, "What the f*** are you doing here?"

So much for a vote of confidence.

The Giants had faced elimination for three straight weeks and won each time, including a 19–17 comeback over defending champion Detroit the previous game. This game didn't seem likely to come down to the final moments when sophomore running back Jim Brown ran 65 yards for a touchdown on Cleveland's first play. But the Giants had tied the game at 10–10 in the fourth and now had a chance to win.

The Giants had traded for Summerall that season despite his 45 percent average with Chicago; he also played tight end and defense and even returned kicks. But he had been awful early on, missing seven of his first 10 attempts along with two extra points. He had settled down, but then injured his leg and hadn't practiced all week. He had hit one field goal in the first half but missed a 33-yarder in the fourth.

The final drive had stalled on third down when running back Alex Webster, who was open deep, lost sight of the ball in the snow and dropped the pass from Charlie Conerly. So Howell gave Summerall one more chance.

With quarterback Charlie Conerly (42) holding the ball, Giants kicker Pat Summerall boots it from the 49-yard line in a play good for three points. (AP Photo)

RIVER CITY RELAY, 2003

At birth, Summerall's right foot faced completely backward; the doctor broke his bones to turn the foot around when he was six months old, enabling him to learn to walk. But his mother was told that he wouldn't be able to run or play on that foot.

Now Summerall and his right foot came on the field.

Because of the snow, no one knows exactly how long the kick really was. It has been recorded at 49 yards, but players and reporters estimated anywhere from 45 to 55. It was far. "I could barely see the goalpost," Summerall recalled later.

The snap was perfect, and Summerall let fly. He knew instinctively that he had the distance, but as the ball weaved toward the side he wasn't sure it would remain on line. It disappeared into the snowy night, and Summerall didn't know he had made it until he heard the cheering and celebrating in the distance. The Giants led, 13–10.

An ecstatic Summerall floated back to the sideline, where Lombardi greeted him, not in joy but in disbelief that he had been wrong, saying, "You know, you son of a bitch, you can't kick it that far."

But he could, and he did.

The kick's impact lasted long after the ball cleared the goalpost. The Browns were disheartened and lost to New York in a tiebreaking playoff, 10–0, sending the Giants on to face the Colts in the championship game. And after the season, Summerall's celebrity earned him his first radio job. He made the most of that opportunity too.

New Orleans had only one chance to make the playoffs in 2003, and that was to win each of their last two games. In the first of those two crucial contests, the Saints trailed the Jacksonville Jaguars 20–13, stuck at their own 25-yard line with just seven seconds left.

They were too far away for a Hail Mary. They needed something special, something unique.

Quarterback Aaron Brooks passed to Donte Stallworth at midfield; he broke one, then two, then three tackles to reach the Jaguars' 34. Then Stallworth turned and tossed the ball to Michael Lewis, who raced to the 25 before pitching it to Deuce McAllister, who went only to the 20, where he flipped it to Jerome Pathon. Brooks, who had hustled all the way downfield, then took out the last man from Jacksonville, and Pathon scored the touchdown.

This was a modern miracle, NFL-style. Except that it wasn't—football isn't a fairy tale, and happy endings aren't guaranteed. John Carney hadn't missed an extra point in almost four seasons, and he had missed just one since 1996. Yet this one went wide, leaving the Saints in disbelief. "Oh my God, how could he do that," wailed New Orleans radio man Jim Henderson. The Saints gained lasting fame for the 75-yard touchdown, which became known as the River City Relay. But the final score, 20–19, belonged to the Jaguars.

IMPROBABLE CATCHES

All I know is, when I caught it, I just started making moves. Unfortunately, you don't know what kind of moves you make until you watch the film. — Donald Driver, Green Bay Packers wide receiver

1 | BRADSHAW TO SWANN — SUPER BOWL X

Dallas cornerback Mark Washington tries to prevent Pittsburgh wide receiver Lynn Swann from making a catch. (AP Photo/NFL Photos)

Lynn Swann. Even the name implies elegance and grace. And in Super Bowl X—a game pitting two of the league's most celebrated defenses against each other—Swann's lissome athleticism not only won the game for the Steelers but provided the NFL with its first truly great Super Bowl, one destined to live forever in lore and highlight films.

What made Swann's performance truly astonishing was that he had suffered a concussion in the AFC championship game against Oakland and then sat out a week of practice, unable to hold on to any passes when he came back. "I wasn't sure if I'd be able to perform," he said afterward.

Swann caught only four passes in Super Bowl X, but three were works of true beauty, and two were crucial to Pittsburgh's triumph.

In the first quarter, Pittsburgh was trailing 7–0 and had yet to throw a pass in the first nine plays. From the Dallas Cowboys' 48, quarterback Terry Bradshaw sent Swann deep on a fly pattern down the sideline. He got just ahead of cornerback Mark Washington, but Washington came back, and Swann had to leap up and over him, twisting his body to bring in the pass and then land with perfect precision on his toes to stay in bounds. His 32-yard gain set up Pittsburgh's game-tying touchdown.

His next catch didn't lead to a score, but it was so spectacular that it became the defining image of the game and of his career. With the first half winding down, Swann again went deep. Bradshaw's pass was slightly underthrown, and this time Washington stayed with Swann in the air. The ball was tipped and falling fast, but Swann somehow kept it alive, stretched out, and made a nearly indescribable recovery, what he called "a juggling, tumbling 53-yard catch while I was horizontal to the ground." Years later, he admitted, "I still don't know how I caught it." (Roy Gerela missed a field goal afterward.)

Then, in the fourth quarter, with Pittsburgh nursing a 15–10 lead and under four minutes to go, Bradshaw decided to gamble. On third-and-4 from his own 36, he knew the Cowboys would be looking for a short pass. He called for the opposite. And naturally, his target was Swann, who was running a deep post pattern, nothing fancy. Bradshaw was nearly caught by an unexpected blindside blitz, but he stepped up and, just as he was smashed to the ground and knocked unconscious, launched a nearly perfect pass to Swann all the way downfield. Washington again stuck to Swann, but the receiver got inside of him, turned back over his left shoulder, and brought the ball in without breaking stride as he raced into the end zone. That 64-yard touchdown pass would be the difference-maker as Pittsburgh would finally finish off Dallas, 21–17.

Swann became the first wide receiver to win the Super Bowl MVP. In *Sports Illustrated*, Dan Jenkins summed it up best by saying that Swann seemed to "[spend] the day way up there in the crisp sky, a thousand feet above Miami's Orange Bowl, where neither the Dallas Cowboys nor even a squadron of fighter planes could do anything to stop him."

2 | STARR TO MCGEE — SUPER BOWL I

Packers wide receiver Max McGee (85). (AP Photo/NFL Photos)

Max McGee was old. Max McGee was achy and hurt. Max McGee was done. McGee had been catching passes for the Green Bay Packers since 1954, peaking with 51 receptions in 1961. But the numbers had dropped, slowly at first, then precipitously, and in 1966, at the age of 34, McGee caught a mere four passes.

So when the Packers won the NFL championship and faced off against the AFL's Kansas City Chiefs in what would become known as Super Bowl I, McGee—and everyone else—presumed that he would spend the day on the sidelines. In fact, McGee broke curfew to go out carousing with a couple of lovely young stewardesses the night before the big game. He got back at breakfast time and was so hungover that he told starting wide receiver Boyd Dowler, "I hope you don't get hurt. I'm not in very good shape."

Of course, on the game's second play, Dowler separated his shoulder. Coach Vince Lombardi hollered for McGee . . . even though he had younger players who had done more all season. The forgotten man had forgotten his helmet in the locker room, but it didn't matter—it turned out McGee wasn't done after all.

Later in the quarter, McGee ran a down-and-in inside pattern on Kansas City cornerback Willie Mitchell and beat him into the open field. But Bart Starr threw a bad pass behind him. No problem—as Mitchell dove for the ball, McGee reached behind him and made a one-handed grab . . . then raced in for a 37-yard touchdown, the first score in Super Bowl history.

In the third quarter, McGee starred in another touchdown drive, catching an 11-yarder, a 16-yarder on a curl against a double team on third-and-11, and finally, a 13-yarder that he brought under control as he entered the end zone. In the final quarter, McGee made one more big catch, a 37-yarder to set up another touchdown in the Packers' 35–10 rout.

McGee finished with seven receptions for 138 yards. "Max should have been named player of the game," halfback Paul Hornung said. "I told Bart [the MVP] that a hundred times, and he agreed with me. That was the greatest performance by a guy who was out of shape."

Packers running back Elijah Pitts (22) follows guards Fuzzy Thurston (63) and Jerry Kramer (64) on the famed Packers sweep. (AP Photo/NFL Photos)

McGee makes a juggling touchdown catch. (AP Photo/NFL Photos)

3 | MONTANA TO RICE — SUPER BOWL XXIII

Pinpointing Jerry Rice's greatest performance is like trying to decide which was Shakespeare's best play.

Even limiting the options to Super Bowl performances doesn't help much—Rice won the MVP, tied a record with 11 catches, set one with 215 yards, and had four of the longest five plays on the day in his first Super Bowl in 1989. In his last Super Bowl with Oakland, in 2003, Rice caught five passes for 77 yards, including a 48-yard touchdown pass, all at the age of 40. That game solidified his hold on the records for most Super Bowl receptions, yards, and touchdowns over a career. He also became the only person to catch touchdown passes in four Super Bowls.

While that first Super Bowl may have featured Rice's gaudiest numbers, it was Joe Montana leading San Francisco's comeback drive that became the defining image of that game. But in each of Rice's two other Super Bowls—Super Bowl XXIV and Super Bowl XXIX—he caught three touchdown passes, something no other player has accomplished even once.

Both performances inspired awe, but while he had more catches in the later game (10 in Super Bowl XXIX versus seven in XXIV), the first was more memorable. It was the biggest rout in Super Bowl history and the 49ers' fourth Super Bowl in the 1980s, matching the 1970s Steelers. It was also the first time anyone had caught three TD passes in a game, and with 148 yards receiving (compared to 149 in XXIX), Rice averaged a whopping 21.1 yards per catch.

Beforehand, Denver safeties Dennis Smith and Steve Atwater snarled that Jerry Rice and company had never been hit like they were about to get hit. Rice shut them up on the first series of the game,

catching a 20-yard touchdown pass from Montana on which he smashed into Atwater inside the 10-yard line and waltzed into the end zone standing up.

"It was the chance of a lifetime," Atwater acknowledged later. "I tried to take him out."

Rice was neither intimidated nor impressed. "One thing about our receivers today was we made up our minds we were not going down on the first hit. It felt awfully good."

Having delivered the opening blow, Rice also ended the first half with a big play that essentially finished off Denver. With the 49ers up 20–3, Rice ditched Smith on a post pattern and made a 38-yard touchdown pass look easy. (Rice also averaged over 15 yards per catch on his nonscoring receptions.)

The scoring in the second half started the same as the first. After an interception of Denver's John Elway, Montana sent Rice on a deep post on first down, connecting for a 28-yarder. It was a touchdown for the record books, as Rice became the first person to catch three in one Super Bowl.

"I watch the league all the time, and there's no one who compares to his consistency," proclaimed Montana later. "It's impossible to cover Jerry Rice one-on-one. Jerry got to the post more than anyone in history. . . . Somehow he always got behind the safety. I don't know how he did it, but I was happy he did."

"Jerry seemed almost inhuman to me," said teammate Matt Millen. Imagine how the Broncos felt.

49ers wide receiver Jerry Rice (80) dives into the end zone for a touchdown. (AP Photo/Phil Sandlin)

Rice shakes off Denver Broncos defender Dennis Smith. (AP Photo/ Ed Reinke)

4 | BRADY TO BRANCH — SUPER BOWL XXXIX

Deion Branch pulls in a fourth-quarter pass over Eagles cornerback Sheldon Brown (24) and in front of Roderick Hood (29). (AP Photo/ Carlos Osorio)

Branch tries to elude Hood. (AP Photo/ Elaine Thompson)

The spotlight in Super Bowl XXXIX in 2005 was on two larger-than-life figures: quarterback Tom Brady of New England and wide receiver Terrell Owens of Philadelphia. Neither player disappointed: Brady, who had won the Super Bowl MVP in the Patriots' two previous wins, produced his highest passer rating of all at 110.2; Owens was less than seven weeks removed from surgery on a fractured fibula and torn ankle ligament, yet he played nearly the entire game and caught nine passes for 122 yards.

But the Super Bowl MVP was almost smaller than life. Deion Branch, a 5'9" wide receiver who had spent his whole life—even back in middle school—hearing that he wasn't big enough to play the position, had looked like he was proving the league wrong with 43 catches in his rookie year and 57 the following season; with 10 catches for 143 yards in Super Bowl XXXVIII, Branch was becoming a star.

But in the second week of the 2004 season he injured his knee and needed arthroscopic surgery. Coach Bill Belichick opted not to put him on injured reserve, and Branch made the move pay off, returning in the Patriots' 10th game with six catches for 105 yards. Branch also scored two touchdowns in the AFC championship to help bring his team back to the Super Bowl, where he showed that he was ready to surpass his previous year's performance.

He caught a 16-yarder on the Patriots' first play. Later, with New England trailing 7–0 and in a crucial third-and-3 from the Eagles' 30, he caught a seven-yarder to keep the game-tying drive going.

"I could feel my confidence growing during the game," Branch said. "I wanted the ball."

But Branch's biggest contributions came on the third-quarter drive in which New England broke a 7–7 tie. Belichick put him in the slot where he would face man coverage instead of the zone. On third-and-6, he crossed the middle and caught a short pass that he turned into a 27-yard pickup. Soon it was third-and-10, so Brady again turned to Branch over the middle, where he got inside cornerback Sheldon Brown and pulled in the pass for 15 yards. Then with Philadelphia blitzing, he burned cornerback Matt Ware on a corner route to go 21 yards down to the Eagles' 2, setting up a touchdown. And in the fourth quarter, Branch's 19-yard catch—on which he seemed to climb up and over Brown to secure the ball—helped set up the field goal that would ultimately prove the margin of victory.

All told, Branch finished with 11 catches for 133 yards (of Brady's 236 yards passing), tying the Super Bowl record for receptions. When combined with his 10 from the previous year, he had set another record for most catches over consecutive Super Bowls.

"He's a very dynamic player," Brady said after the game. "I was looking to find him today. He was getting open and doing some great things out there."

The player dubbed "the human Venus flytrap" by the *Boston Globe* after the game was named MVP, the first receiver to earn the award since Jerry Rice back in 1989.

5 | THE 1974 AFC PLAYOFF GAME AND THE SEA OF HANDS

Raiders running back Clarence Davis (28) manages to catch a game-winning touchdown amid a "Sea of Hands." (Oakland Raiders)

field, but the Dolphins' defender had fallen too; untouched, Branch quickly got up and ran the rest of the way for the score. Yet Miami had roared back in four plays with a touchdown for a 26–21 lead.

With just two minutes remaining, Stabler again marched downfield, with Oakland fans hoping for a miracle. With under a half-minute to go, Oakland reached the Dolphins' 8, with first-and-goal. On first down, Stabler scrambled left and looked for a receiver. But he was feeling the pressure from Miami defensive end Vern Den Herder. Seeing his quarterback in trouble, Davis, a running back not known as a particularly good pass catcher, started coming back toward Stabler. As Den Herder grabbed Stabler's ankles, the quarterback spotted Davis—on his way down, his knees just barely off the ground, he tossed a weak floater toward his man. But both Charlie Babb and Mike Kolen were guarding Davis, and the pass looked like it might be picked off.

All three men went airborne. Kolen and Babb each seemed to get a hand on the ball, yet somehow it was Davis—given the disparaging nickname "Hands of Wood"—who got both hands on it and pulled the ball in. Just like that, the Raiders had scored. Just like that, the Dolphins were done.

"It was a dumb play," Stabler admitted afterward, since he had the time and downs to try again. But he had been rescued by Davis in what became known as "the Sea of Hands." "It was a great catch."

In the early 1970s, the Miami Dolphins ruled the NFL. They went to three straight Super Bowls, winning the latter two. And in 1974 they seemed poised to retain their throne. But in a classic battle—NBC Sports' top play-by-play man, Curt Gowdy, called the 1974 AFC playoff game between the Oakland Raiders and the Miami Dolphins "the greatest game I have ever seen"—and on a play that seemed absolutely destined to fail in so many ways, Oakland Raiders Ken Stabler and Clarence Davis thwarted their plans.

There were 26 seconds left. The Dolphins had controlled the game—they had led or been tied for nearly 56 minutes. With under five minutes left in the game, Oakland had snatched the lead on Cliff Branch's remarkable 72-yard touchdown reception. He had fallen as he caught the ball 45 yards down-

Raiders head coach John Madden gives the ref an earful as he decides the spot of the ball during the AFC divisional playoff. (AP Photo/ NFL Photos)

IMPROBABLE CATCHES

6 | STAUBACH'S HAIL MARY —
1975 NFC PLAYOFFS

It was Captain Comeback versus the Purple People Eaters.

With the final seconds ticking away on the divisional playoff game and the Dallas Cowboys' 1975 season, Roger Staubach—who had become known for his last-gasp heroics—commandeered the field. Minnesota had just taken a 14–10 lead, and Dallas needed a touchdown against the heralded Minnesota defense, which had played brilliantly and brutally all day.

Staubach took his team from their 15 to midfield in nine plays, the most crucial moment coming when he found Drew Pearson on fourth-and-16 to keep the drive alive. Pearson had been frustrated all day because only one pass (an incompletion) had come his way.

But Staubach grew desperate as the clock hit the half-minute mark. He called what Pearson later said was "a sandlot play not in the playbook."

Using the Cowboys' new innovation—the shotgun formation—Staubach pump-faked to the left, then turned and fired deep to Pearson, who was flying down the right side. But Staubach had lost his grip after the fake, and his pass was floating short. That was especially problematic because Pearson had streaked past cornerback Nate Wright. So the receiver had to stop and reach back for the ball—which he almost missed, catching it after it slipped through his hands by squeezing the ball between his hip and elbow. He also collided with Wright, who fell to the ground, helpless as Pearson ran in for the game-winning touchdown. (The Vikings claimed pass interference to no avail.)

After the game, sportswriters were asking Staubach for details of how he completed the pass while getting knocked down under pressure. His answer, based on his Christian upbringing, gave the play eternal life. "I closed my eyes and said a Hail Mary," Staubach said.

Pearson, who didn't even know what a Hail Mary was at the time, later said that the NFL has been filled with great plays like that. "It's the name that has kept it alive. It has become part of American folklore."

Cowboys quarterback Roger Staubach (12) looks for a receiver in first-quarter action. (AP Photo)

Staubach eyes possible receivers as the Vikings' Jim Marshall (70) looms. (AP Photo)

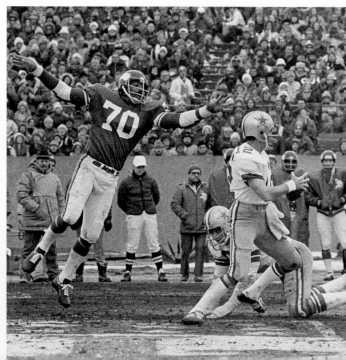

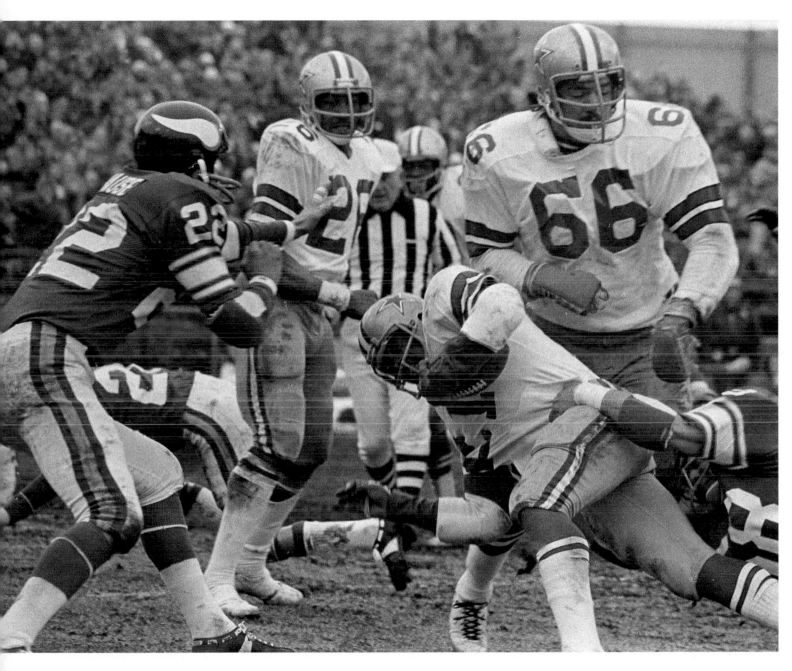

Dallas back Doug Dennison is tackled by Viking Alan Page as the Cowboys' Burton Lawless (66) towers over the action. (AP Photo)

7 | AIKMAN TO IRVIN (TWICE!) — SUPER BOWL XXVII

Cowboys wide receiver Michael Irvin (88) catches a 19-yard touchdown pass. (AP Photo/ NFL Photos)

Irvin beats Bills cornerback Nate Odomes (37) into the end zone for a 19-yard touchdown. (AP Photo/NFL Photos)

Troy Aikman to Michael Irvin. Bam. Touchdown. Troy Aikman to Michael Irvin. Bam. Touchdown. And just like that, in the space of 18 seconds of playing time, Dallas destroyed any hope Buffalo may have had for a Super Bowl victory.

Through nearly the entire first half of Super Bowl XXVII, the underdog Buffalo Bills had fought to stay close to the Dallas Cowboys. With just over two minutes to play, they had sliced the Dallas lead to 14–10.

Aikman had been rattled by the Bills' pressure and was dumping off short passes.

Irvin, meanwhile, had never scored a postseason touchdown. Before the Super Bowl, he had said, "Well, I'm waiting for the perfect game, see, and now it's here."

He picked the perfect time too. After Emmitt Smith ran for 38 yards to the Buffalo 19, the Cowboys turned to Irvin. The Pro Bowler—who once said, "My biggest asset is my ego"—knew that the blitzing defense left him in single coverage, and he told the coaches that he could beat any Buffalo man one-on-one. "You can't do that," he said of the notion of trying to stop him without help. He was right.

When Nate Odomes played eight yards back, Irvin raced at him, then faked to the outside before slanting hard in to the middle. Odomes was spun around, and Irvin cruised in for a touchdown.

On the first play of the Bills' next possession, Leon Lett knocked the ball loose from Thurman Thomas, and Jimmie Jones recovered for Dallas on the Bills' 18. Picking up where they left off, the Cowboys called Irvin's number again. He burned cornerback James Williams by faking inside and going out on a post-corner play, leaping, catching the ball, and then lunging past Odomes to get back into the end zone.

Suddenly, the game was 28–10. The rout was on, and a dynasty was born.

8 | SIMMS TO MORRIS TO SIMMS TO MCCONKEY AND SIMMS TO BAVARO TO MCCONKEY — SUPER BOWL XXI

Six members of the New York Giants caught more passes than Phil McConkey in Super Bowl XXI, but McConkey wasn't complaining.

McConkey was just happy to be there. After all, the Giants had cut the 5'10", 170-pound 29-year-old after training camp—he lacked the speed and athleticism and size they needed. But coach Bill Parcells later brought him back from Green Bay to help out on special teams and fill in at receiver, where he caught just 16 passes during the final 12 games.

In the Super Bowl, the voluble and enthusiastic McConkey incited Giants fans by running around the sidelines waving a white towel. (After the

game, he would run into the stands to celebrate with those New Yorkers.) He would catch just two passes, both in the second half, but they were both instant classics. In the third quarter, McConkey returned a punt 25 yards to set up a field goal for a 19–10 lead. The next time around, quarterback Phil Simms called for a flea-flicker.

McConkey's job was to go in motion left to right and head deep while Simms pitched the ball to, and caught it back from, running back Joe Morris. The play completely froze the Denver Broncos defense. New York's Bobby Johnson was wide open in the end zone, but Simms—in the middle of a magical 22-25 day passing—didn't see him. He did see Mc-

Giants wide receiver Phil McConkey stirs the crowd up during Super Bowl XXI against the Denver Broncos. (AP Photo/ Lennox McLendon)

Conkey alone at the Broncos' 20. "When I caught it, I thought, 'Oh my God, I'm going to score a touch-down in the Super Bowl,'" he said.

He didn't—not then anyway. But as he raced toward the end zone he was also heading toward a place in the highlight films—after bursting past one Bronco, only former Giant Mark Haynes remained, poised to tackle McConkey. The receiver leaped into the air and tried hurdling the defender, only to find himself flipped up and over before he landed dramatically at the 1-yard line. The Giants scored on the next play.

"I thought the flea-flicker just ended the game," said Simms.

Still, McConkey would get his touchdown—and he would do it because of hustle and effort more than speed or size. In the fourth quarter, Simms fired a pass to tight end Mark Bavaro in the end zone. But he zipped it too hard, and Bavaro—who was in the air, surrounded by three defenders—botched it. The ball squirted away and fell toward the ground, but McConkey, who had gone unnoticed on the play, dove in at the last second and caught the ball for the score. "It's something you dream about, scoring a Super Bowl touchdown," he said. "When it happens, you think about every push-up you ever did, everybody who ever helped you."

McConkey (80) flips through the air as he is stopped just short of the end zone after catching a Phil Simms pass. (AP Photo/Rob Kozloff)

Simms looks for a receiver. Coming in at right is Denver's Andre Townsend. (AP Photo/Reed Saxon)

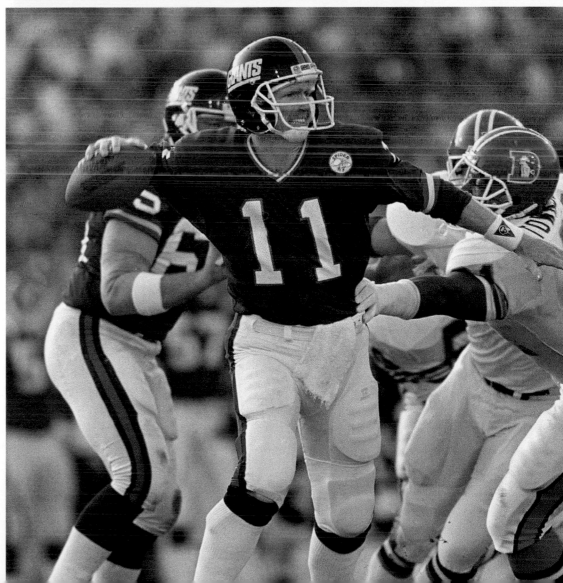

9 | WILLIAMS TO SANDERS — SUPER BOWL XXII

Everybody may get their 15 minutes of fame, but few have done more in that time frame than Ricky Sanders. Most players would be thrilled to catch five passes for 168 yards and two touchdowns in any game, much less in a Super Bowl. Sanders went one step further—he did all that in just one quarter of Super Bowl XXII.

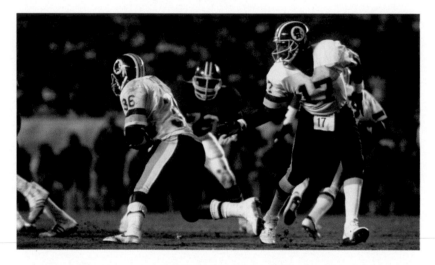

Redskins quarterback Doug Williams (17) hands off to running back Timmy Smith (36). (AP Photo/NFL Photos)

Sanders had started his pro career in the United States Football League, catching passes from Jim Kelly. After a starring role there, he ended up joining the Redskins in 1986. He caught just 14 passes for 286 yards that year but fared better in 1987, catching 37 passes, despite missing four games. His final regular-season game featured eight catches for 164 yards, and he snared six for 92 in the first playoff game. But he had been the forgotten man in the NFC championship game, used only on one running play and two kick returns.

When "the Quarter"—as the second marking period of that Super Bowl is known in Washington—got started, the Redskins trailed the Denver Broncos, 10–0. Sanders had fumbled a kickoff, though Washington recovered.

The Redskins started the second quarter at their own 20. Sanders's defender, Denver cornerback Mark Haynes, was up close. Sanders was supposed to run a short route, but he saw that Haynes wasn't totally set after a quick count. "I ran a five-yard hitch, he came up tight, and I took off," Sanders said. Quarterback Doug Williams hit Sanders at midfield, and the receiver, who had been a track star in high school and a running back in college, then used his speed to outrun the Broncos the rest of the way for a stunning 80-yard touchdown that was, at the time, a Super Bowl record.

Later in the quarter, Washington running back Timmy Smith tore off a 58-yard touchdown run. So on their next possession, the Redskins knew the Broncos would be wary of the run. After Sanders caught a 10-yard slant pass to bring the team to midfield, he went in motion on the next play and took off on a post pattern as Williams ran a play-action fake. "We'd set 'em up with the run," said Sanders. "The pass was a sucker play, off a good run fake. When the free safety came up, I knew I had him."

Indeed, once Tom Lilly got burned, Sanders was wide open deep to haul in another bomb from Williams, this one for 50 yards. He finished the quarter with five catches and the game with nine catches for 193 yards, averaging 21.4 per catch. But even then, Sanders wasn't through. At the Redskins' celebratory visit to the White House, President Ronald Reagan, football in hand, was at the podium giving a speech when he suddenly asked, "Where's Ricky Sanders?"

Sanders raced to the front of the stage, and Reagan tossed him one more pass. Not surprisingly, Sanders caught that one too.

Broncos linebacker Jim Ryan (50) has the angle on Sanders (83). (AP Photo/NFL Photos)

10 | EVERETT TO ANDERSON FOR AN NFL SINGLE-GAME RECORD — 1989

Most weeks, Willie "Flipper" Anderson was the Los Angeles Rams' secondary receiver. The second-year pass catcher would finish 1989 with just 19 catches through the first 11 weeks, and 12 of those had come in one game. Quarterback Jim Everett's main target was Henry Ellard, who was on pace to catch 100 passes.

But in week 12, Ellard had a hamstring injury and spent the day on the sidelines. The Rams, closing in on a playoff spot, had no choice but to turn to Anderson. The result was a hard-fought overtime win, but also an unbelievable performance that landed Anderson in the record books.

After catching just 11 passes off the bench his rookie year, Anderson, a late second-round draft pick out of UCLA, had worked so hard in 1989 that the Rams' coaching staff held him up as an example. An injury to Aaron Cox thrust him into the starting lineup, and he stayed, taking some defensive attention away from Ellard by quickly establishing himself as a deep threat. He was neither overwhelmingly fast nor particularly precise on his routes, but he was relentless, even when there was a man—or two—on him. "He's got a Charles Barkley attitude," Everett said. "Every ball belongs to him."

Everett took to the air constantly against New Orleans in the Superdome on November 26, throwing 51 times and completing 29 for 454 yards. Again and again, he found Anderson on long routes. "The Saints had probably practiced all week on defending Henry, and since he was out, they may have relaxed out there a bit," said Anderson.

After Cleveland Ram Jim Benton, with 303 yards in 1945, and Detroit's Cloyce Box, with 302 yards in 1950, the 300-yard barrier had been out of reach for decades. Then, in 1985, Stephone Page of Kansas City—who happened to be best friends with Ellard—set a new mark with 309 yards.

Anderson nearly didn't make it himself. Everett's two interceptions had undermined the Rams offense, and they trailed the Saints, 17–3, late in the game before scoring twice—the second touchdown, fittingly, coming on a 12-yard catch by Anderson.

That gave him 13 catches for 296 yards for the day . . . impressive, sure, but a feat likely to be remembered only by family and die-hard Rams fans.

In overtime, however, Anderson was the entire show. The Rams gained 35 yards on a pass interference call against cornerback Robert Massey—who had been burned by Anderson all day (yardage that wasn't, of course, credited to the receiver)—and another 14 on Anderson's 14th catch. That play gave Anderson the record by one yard, but he wasn't done yet.

On the game's next-to-last play, Anderson and Aaron Cox—who caught just five passes that day—ran the same pattern. "When I looked back at film of that game, I see that Aaron was 10 steps ahead of his man and Flipper was double-covered," Everett said later. It didn't matter—he chose Anderson. "Sometimes you feel like you're throwing a football through the tire of a Hyundai, but that day, with Flipper, it felt like throwing a ball through the tire of a John Deere tractor."

Anderson brought in the pass for a 26-yard gain, setting up the game-winning field goal on the next play. It was a win that the Rams would need to make the playoffs as a wild-card team, en route to just their second NFC championship game of the decade. Anderson finished the day with 15 catches for 336 yards, a number no one has come close to since. "I never dreamed of a day like this," he said. "Jim Everett and I got into a click. I was kind of unconscious out there, because it all came so naturally."

AMAZING RUNS

An athlete cannot run with money in his pockets. He must run with hope in his heart and dreams in his head. — Emil Zátopek, Czechoslovakian runner and winner of four Olympic gold medals

1 | BIGGER THAN LIFE:
JOHN RIGGINS IN SUPER BOWL XVII

Joe Gibbs decided to go for broke. His Washington Redskins trailed the Miami Dolphins, 17–13, early in the fourth quarter, and three running plays had netted just nine yards. Yet with the Dolphins expecting a punt, Gibbs decided to repeat the running play—"70 Chip"—that he had called on third down. With two tight ends and a lead running back providing extra blocking, the play was supposed to give a big back just enough of a hole to bust through.

That big back was John Riggins. Riggins had an outsized persona—in the days leading up to the Super Bowl he had appeared at a media session in camouflage pants with an elephant gun belt buckle and then shown up at a party in white tie, top hat, and tails. But he ran like the son of Larry Csonka and the grandson of Bronko Nagurski. He was a true workhorse—he had led the league in carries and in three playoff games had rushed 98 times for 444 yards. He had been carrying the ball all day against Miami too.

Paul Zimmerman in *Sports Illustrated* would write that Riggins "grab[bed] modern NFL football by the scruff of the neck and toss[ed] it a few decades back into a simpler era—big guy running behind bigger guys blocking."

Redskins running back John Riggins (44) eludes a tackle by the Dolphins' Don McNeal (28). (AP Photo/File)

Riggins loses the ball after a fourth-quarter run. (AP Photo)

Washington quarterback Joe Theismann (7) holds the game ball at the end of the game. (AP Photo)

The Dolphins called time-out, hoping to catch their breath. But they didn't catch anything. Riggins ran off the left side and gained the needed yard. Then, pumping his knees, he overwhelmed cornerback Don McNeal—whom he outweighed by perhaps 50 pounds—and accelerated away from the entire Dolphin defense. Riggins, who had been a speedster in his youth, hit the end zone 43 yards downfield, pulling away from safety Glenn Blackwood.

It was a stunning display of speed and power, and it gave the Redskins the lead at 20–17. On their next drive, Riggins carried the ball on the first five plays, and eight of 12 overall, as Washington scored again to win, 27–17. Riggins finished with a Super Bowl record 38 carries for a record 166 yards—and the MVP Award.

"You look at the play-by-play, and you'll see: Riggins off-tackle left, Riggins off-tackle left, then maybe a little Riggins off-tackle right, an occasional pass by me, then Riggins left, Riggins left, and one more Riggins left," quarterback Joe Theismann said afterward. "I imagine if we were still out there we'd still be running Riggins left." But thanks to his 43-yard outburst, the Redskins weren't out there anymore—they were inside celebrating.

2 | THE LONGEST RUN IN SUPER BOWL HISTORY: WILLIE PARKER IN SUPER BOWL XL

Steelers quarterback Ben Roethlisberger (7) hands off to running back Willie Parker (39). (AP Photo/David J. Phillip)

Parker makes a 75-yard run chased by Seahawks defenders LeRoy Hill (56), Michael Boulware (28), Bryce Fisher (94), Lofa Tatupu (51), and Etric Pruitt (35). (AP Photo/Mark Humphrey)

Eluding his pursuers, Parker dives into the end zone, completing the longest touchdown run from scrimmage in Super Bowl history. (AP Photo/Michael Conroy)

The media spotlight focused on a Pittsburgh Steeler running back in the days leading up to the Super Bowl, but it turned out to be trained on the wrong one. Jerome Bettis made a great story—the beloved superstar who hoped to win the big one before retiring—but second-year halfback Willie Parker was the one to turn the game around with a single run. He would run for over 1,200 yards that season, but only after enduring a stint as a bench-warmer in college before Pittsburgh signed him as an undrafted free agent.

Pittsburgh was clinging to a 7–3 lead over Seattle as the second half started. After a dropped pass on first down at their own 25-yard line, quarterback Ben Roethlisberger handed off to Parker on a play called "Counter Pike." Every lineman nailed someone from Seattle, but it was Alan Faneca, the

team's Pro Bowl left guard, who delivered the key blow, eliminating linebacker LeRoy Hill. Safety Michael Boulware ran in to save the day, but dove and missed Parker completely. The speedster took off, with another safety, Etric Pruitt, left to eat his dust.

"The play was blocked so well," offensive co-ordinator Ken Whisenhunt said later. But Parker's flash made the difference. "If Jerome's running it, we probably get 15 to 20 yards. When Willie's running it, we get a touchdown."

Given that Seattle came back soon after with an interception and a touchdown, Parker's score proved crucial in what was eventually a 21–10 win. And since his 75-yard score was one yard longer than Marcus Allen's run in Super Bowl XVIII, Parker also landed in the record book with the longest run in Super Bowl history.

3 | THE RECORD THAT WILLIE PARKER BROKE: MARCUS ALLEN IN SUPER BOWL XVIII

The game was already pretty much in hand for the Los Angeles Raiders—who led Washington, 28–9—when Jim Plunkett pitched out to Marcus Allen on the Raiders' own 26 as the third quarter ended. But that was okay: the play looked insignificant as Allen headed out to the far left, an extra helping of defenders waiting to smother him.

Allen had been respectable in his first full season (the previous one had been strike-shortened), gaining 1,014 yards, but he had averaged only 3.8 per carry, and his longest run was just 19 yards. The only category in which he led the league was fumbles, with 14.

But in this Super Bowl, Allen was giving the NFL a preview of the Hall of Fame career he would have. He had a solid 51 yards on 11 carries in the first half, then scored on a five-yard run that faked out three different defenders. Now he showed

everything he had on this one play. He suddenly cut back, and instead of reversing completely to go wide right, he spotted an opening up the middle and tore through it on a diagonal. From Washington's perspective, it was as if he had disappeared, only to reappear untouched in the end zone, 74 yards away.

"I was just picking myself up off the ground," Raider right guard Mickey Marvin said. "Then I looked around, and a rocket went through."

Allen's record-setting run helped him break John Riggins's single-game rushing record from the previous year—he would finish with 191 yards and an MVP as Oakland swaggered to a 38–9 victory.

"This was the greatest run that I ever had against a team that I coached," said Washington's linebacker coach Larry Peccatiello later. "That was seven points that should have been a five-yard loss."

Raiders back Marcus Allen (32) runs with the ball after taking a handoff from quarterback Jim Plunkett. (AP Photo)

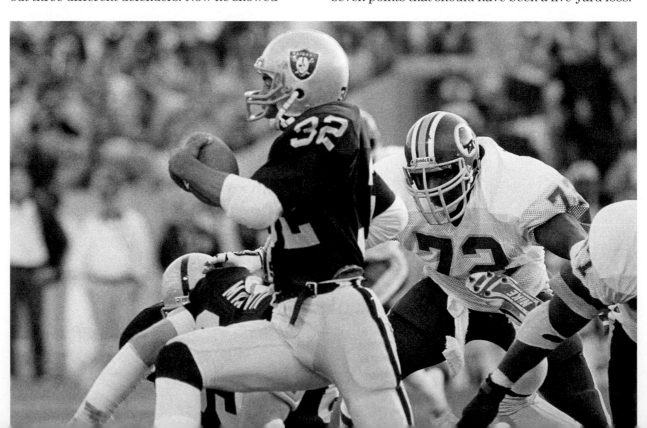

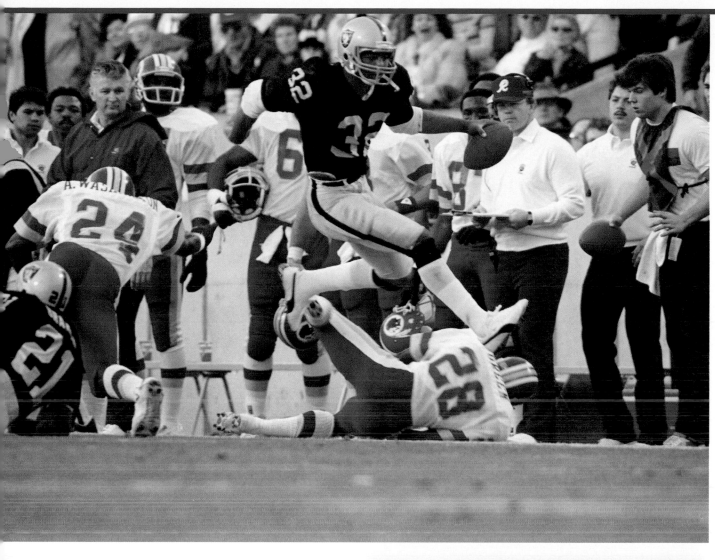

Allen high-steps his way down the sideline past Washington Redskins defenders Anthony Washington (24) and Todd Bowles (28). (AP Photo)

Allen gives the number-one sign and holds up the Super Bowl trophy in the locker room. (AP Photo)

4 | 2,000 YARDS IN A SEASON: O. J. SIMPSON IN 1973

Think back to a time when O. J. Simpson was simply "the Juice," the game's most electrifying, unstoppable running back.

In 1971 Simpson, in a part-time role, ran for a respectable 742 yards on 183 carries. As Buffalo's main man the next year, he led the league with 1,251 yards on 292 carries. But in 1973 he outdid himself, literally, scoring more in one season than he had in the previous two combined. More importantly, he broke two of the legendary Jim Brown's records in one game, stunning the football world and ensuring his own iconic status.

Running behind his "Electric Company" front line, Simpson gained a record 250 yards in the season's first week. He would churn out eight 100-yard games in the next 11 as the Bills, who had won only eight games total over the three previous seasons, finished 9-5. Simpson saved the best for last. He garnered 219 yards in a win over New England in the 13th week, then went to New York, the nation's media capital, to play the Jets.

Brown had set a single-season record of 1,863 yards. Simpson entered freezing, snowy Shea Stadium just 60 yards shy of that mark. He gained 30 on the second play from scrimmage. The record fell on Buffalo's second drive, and officials briefly stopped the game to give him the ball. (On that very same play, Simpson also broke Brown's mark for most carries in a season.) His teammates congratulated him, then told him to go get more. Although he fumbled on the very next play, he immediately took off after a new plateau: the 2,000-yard mark.

Before Simpson, 2,000 yards in a season had seemed unthinkable—and after him no one would do it again in a 14-game season. Simpson, who averaged a whopping 6.0 yards per carry, did it with ease, running for a gain of seven halfway through the fourth quarter, to finish with 2,003 yards. That run also gave him 200 yards on the day, making him the first person in NFL history to have three 200-yard games in one season. As his teammates put Simpson on their shoulders to carry him off, even New York Jets fans stood and cheered.

Afterward, the Jets had a special press room set up for Simpson to bask in the spotlight. Instead, he brought in his entire offense and introduced them individually to the media. "These are the cats who did the job all year long," he said.

O. J. Simpson (32) celebrates as he is carried off the field. (AP Photo)

Simpson leaves Jets defensemen in his wake as he breaks the NFL rushing record with more than 2,000 yards for the season. (AP Photo)

5 | RUSHING FOR SIX TOUCHDOWNS IN A GAME: ERNIE NEVERS IN 1929

In pro football's early days, there were three unstoppable runners—superstars who helped forge the modern game and the NFL. Two of those men remain household names among sports fans—Jim Thorpe and Red Grange—yet it was the third man, halfback Ernie Nevers, who put on one of the most mesmerizing single performances in league history.

On Thanksgiving in 1929, Nevers's Chicago Cardinals faced off against their crosstown rivals, the Chicago Bears, who had Red Grange in their backfield. The Bears had held the Cardinals without a touchdown in four consecutive battles. "This was a game we just had to win," Nevers wrote later in his autobiography, *Football Hero*. "We were in the throes of deep frustration. . . . Someone had to do something about it."

That someone would have to be Nevers. After all, he had scored all 19 of his team's points the previous week against Dayton. Comiskey Park was blanketed with snow, so head coach Dewey Scanlon ditched his double-wing offense in favor of an inside game. Nevers pounded up the middle relentlessly, and with record-setting results.

In the first quarter, he scored on a 20-yard touchdown run. By halftime, he had three touchdowns and the Cardinals led, 20–0. He added another score in the third and two more in the fourth.

Final score: Cardinals 40, Bears 6. Since that day, just two other players have scored six touchdowns in a game, Cleveland's Dub Jones in 1951, who ran for four and caught two, and Chicago Bear Gale Sayers in 1965, who ran for five and returned one kick. But Nevers is the only player to run for six touchdowns, making this the longest-lasting NFL record.

And here's the kicker: Nevers also went four for six in booting extra points that day. So he was responsible for every point on the board. As George Halas, the Chicago Bears' founder and coach, later acknowledged, the final score was really Nevers 40, Bears 6.

Ernie Nevers, Cardinal star, squirms his way along the ground for a gain in the game between the New York Giants and Chicago Cardinals on Thanksgiving Day 1929 at the Polo Grounds. (Bettmann/Corbis)

Ernie Nevers of the
Duluth Eskimos,
before he joined the
Chicago Cardinals.
(AP Photo/Pro Foot-
ball Hall of Fame)

6 | PROPELLING CHICAGO TOWARD THE PLAYOFFS: WALTER PAYTON IN 1977

It had been a decade since the Chicago Bears had a winning season, and nearly 15 years since they had reached the postseason. With the team scuffling along at 4-5 before facing the first-place Minnesota Vikings on the Sunday before Thanksgiving, 1977 was looking like the same old same old.

To make matters worse, Walter "Sweetness" Payton, their lone bright spot, was suffering from the flu—he had spent the latter half of the week in bed. "I didn't think I could do too much," he said afterward.

Talk about underestimating yourself. Payton was a third-year back who had opened the season with a 160-yard game and who had already had his first 200-yarder that season against Green Bay. His signature stiff-legged stride was already gaining attention before this game. Now it would carry him into the record books.

Payton gained 29 yards on the very first play. He finished the first quarter with a reasonable day's numbers—13 carries for 77 yards. His second quarter was almost as good as he added another 13 runs for another 67 yards. Every run but two was to the right side, but Minnesota just couldn't stop him. Most important in that span was his one-yard run for a touchdown and a 7–0 Chicago lead. His yardage also helped set up a field goal for Chicago's only other score of the day.

The 5'11", 204-pound Payton kept pounding the right side of the Vikings defense to finish the third quarter with 34 carries and 192 yards. O. J. Simpson's two-year-old record of 273 yards in a game seemed safe—especially when there were just five minutes left and 63 yards still to go. But everything changed with another run over the right tackle—this time Payton broke free and tore down the sideline, fighting off several Vikings en route to a 58-yard gain. Two plays later, on his 40th carry, a run to the right side gave him the single-game rushing record, with 275 yards.

On the entire afternoon, Chicago passed for only 23 yards. But with Payton churning out that yardage, Minnesota never had time to get back in the game—the Vikings' lone score in the Bears' 10–7 win came on a blocked punt.

"He's the best back in football," said Vikings coach Bud Grant after the game.

Payton's performance inspired the Bears, who won the rest of their games to finish at 9-5 and reach the postseason for the first time since 1963. Payton finished with a league-best 1,852 yards and the MVP Award. His record would stand for nearly a quarter-century, and it still ranks fourth on the all-time list.

After setting the record, Payton was famously asked what was the best way to get him. "Well," he said, "the night before the game I'd kidnap Walter Payton."

It might have been the most sensible approach.

Walter Payton (34) runs for three yards in the first quarter of a November game against the Vikings. (AP Photo/ Fred Jewell)

7 | SETTING A ROOKIE RECORD:
EARL CAMPBELL IN 1978

Earl Campbell had a lot to prove as a Heisman Trophy winner and a number-one draft pick. He started proving it almost immediately, helping turn around a moribund Houston franchise with one strong game after another. But nothing could top his *Monday Night Football* appearance in late November 1978.

The Miami Dolphins struck first, with Bob Griese firing a 10-yard touchdown pass. But the Oilers came right back, and Campbell chugged through the line for a 1-yard run over Miami's safety Charlie Babb to cap the drive. Still, Campbell didn't make much of an impression in the first half, gaining just 44 yards. But he kept churning those powerful thighs, and eventually the defense caved in. He scored on a six-yard run in the third to give Houston a lead, and on a 12-yard run in the fourth he put his team back on top, 28–23, with less than five minutes to go.

Campbell now had 118 yards and three touchdowns on 27 carries; the quintessential workhorse, he had run the ball on nine of Houston's last 13 plays. A very good day indeed. But it would be his final run that made this game special.

With 1:22 left in the game, the Oilers started at their own 19. Campbell was exhausted, but his team called on him again, hoping he could dig deep for a couple of more carries and grind out one more first down.

Campbell took a pitchout, spotted a hole, and cut outside.

"Before [quarterback Dan] Pastorini tossed me the ball," Campbell said, "I would have sworn I couldn't run anymore at all. Even after I was through the hole and I saw [teammate] Tim Wilson hit his man, I didn't think I could make it to the other end of the field. Then I saw pure sideline, and I decided to keep running until somebody knocked me down."

"About five people had an angle on him, and two of them were cornerbacks, and they couldn't catch him," recalled his coach, Bum Phillips. Campbell raced 81 yards for a touchdown, wrapping up a big win for his team and gaining a total of four scores and 199 yards for the day. (The Oilers, who hadn't reached the playoffs since joining the NFL in the 1970 merger, would go on to finish 10-6, and they beat both Miami and New England in the playoffs before falling to Pittsburgh.)

"That's the kind of thing that made him great," Phillips said of the late-game heroics. "When everybody else was getting worn down, Earl was still running."

Houston running back Earl Campbell (34) jumps his center, Carl Mauck (55), to pick up three yards before he is hit by Miami's Bob Matheson (53) and Doug Betters (75) in the first quarter of an Oilers-Dolphins game on November 20, 1978. (AP Photo)

Campbell (34) turns the corner in the second quarter as he breaks the tackle of the Dolphins' Tim Foley (25). (AP Photo)

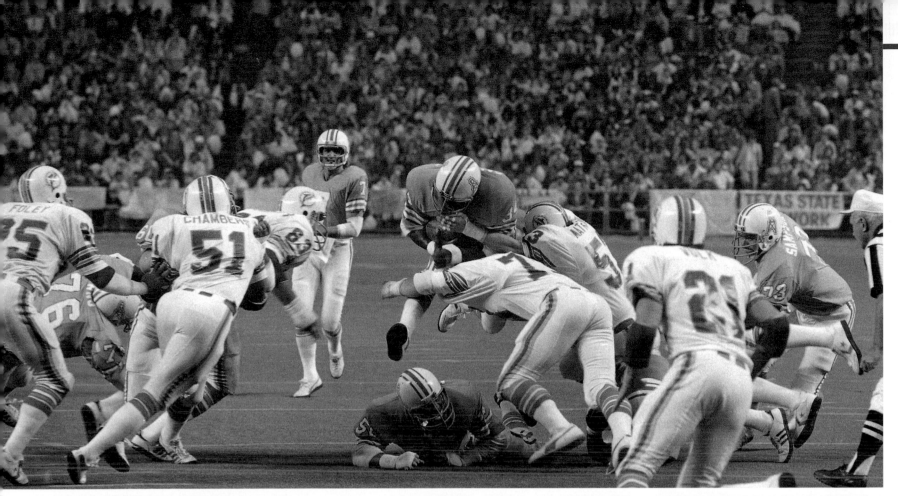

8 | SETTING A GAME RECORD:
ADRIAN PETERSON IN 2007

Adrian Peterson had been in the NFL for just eight games when he fulfilled his boast that he wanted to be the best ever. The Minnesota rookie had already rushed for 224 yards in a game, but against the San Diego Chargers he would make that look like an off day.

The 2007 Chargers, a team bound for the AFC championship, had a strong running defense, one that was geared toward stopping Peterson. That plan worked well . . . for half the game. After 30 minutes of play, San Diego led, 14–7, and Peterson had netted just 43 yards.

The second half was a different story, beginning with Peterson's game-tying 64-yard touchdown early in the third quarter. From that point on, he was unstoppable. He became the first rookie ever to have two 200-yard games, and he put the game away with a 46-yard touchdown run in the fourth to make it 28–17. Then, with under a minute to play, he ran for three yards on a play that gave him 296 for the day. That was one more than the single-game mark set by Jamal Lewis in 2003. (Peterson also finished the day with 315 total yards, more than San Diego and more than eight of the 16 other teams playing at the same time.)

Afterward, Peterson said he wasn't even aware that he was approaching the history books. "I was out playing ball," he said. "I wasn't thinking about the record at all."

Adrian Peterson hurdles San Diego Chargers linebacker Carlos Polk (52) as Vikings guard Steve Hutchinson, left, blocks Chargers defensive tackle Ryon Bingham (97). (AP Photo/Tom Olmscheid)

Peterson rushes for extra yardage in the first quarter against the Chargers on his way to an NFL record. (AP Photo/ Jim Mone)

9 | A 99-YARD TD DASH:
TONY DORSETT IN 1983

Tony Dorsett holds an NFL record that can never be broken.

On *Monday Night Football* against Minnesota in 1983, Dallas found itself backed up just inches from its own end zone. Desperate for some breathing room, the Cowboys called on fullback Ron Springs to power up the middle. Unfortunately, Springs was on the sideline, thinking another formation had been called with Dorsett as the single back, so the Cowboys went to the line with just 10 men.

When Danny White took the snap, he turned and handed off to the one man behind him, Dorsett. And the Vikings, perhaps thrown off by the lone back setup, had not pinched their defense to the inside. So when Dallas center Tom Rafferty and

guard Herb Scott cleared out a hole, Dorsett burst through, outrunning a Minnesota cornerback, faking out a safety, getting a crucial downfield block from receiver Drew Pearson, and stiff-arming one final defender.

After more than 99 yards, Dorsett finally reached the sanctuary of the opposite end zone. No one else had ever run so far from scrimmage. No one else can ever run farther. But when Dorsett came to the bench afterward and was told by a Dallas executive that he had just set an NFL record, Dorsett was too beat to care. "I'm like, man, I'm not worried about no NFL record," Dorsett recounted later. "I'm trying to get to the bench, sit down, and get me some nice oxygen."

Cowboys placekicker Rafael Septien (right) pats teammate Tony Dorsett on the head after his record-setting 99-yard touchdown run. (AP Photo/Jim Mone)

Dorsett drops the ball after the touchdown is signaled as surprised Minnesota fans watch him complete a 99-yard run from scrimmage in the fourth quarter of a Cowboys-Vikings game, setting a new NFL record. (AP Photo/ Jim Mone)

10 | FROM THE OUTFIELD TO BACK-TO-BACK TD RUNS: BO JACKSON IN 1987

In October 1987, the baseball season ended. Fans of the Kansas City Royals were quite thrilled with Bo Jackson, their rookie outfielder who hit 22 home runs. But Jackson would go long in an even more impressive manner at the end of November.

Switching sports and excelling in both was the kind of thing that only Bo Jackson could do. And he did it in unsurpassed fashion: in his fifth pro game, on his 25th birthday, before a national *Monday Night Football* audience.

Playing running back for the Los Angeles Raiders, Jackson scored early in the second quarter on a 14-yard pass catch. He also broke off several nice-sized runs. But Jackson entered NFL lore that night because of two very different plays.

At the end of the second quarter, he stunned Seattle with his speed. Jackson, who could run the 40-yard dash in 4.125 seconds, beat everyone to the sidelines and then outran the entire Seattle defense team for a 91-yard score. He then earned bonus points with the audience when he kept going through the end zone and into the locker room.

Then, in the third quarter, he showed off his power. Seattle's loudmouth linebacker Brian Bosworth had made disparaging remarks about Jackson. Now Jackson made him eat his words. From the Seattle 2-yard line, Jackson took a handoff and ran straight at Bosworth. He lowered his shoulder and drove the defender backward into the end zone and onto the ground. Touchdown Jackson. "He just flat ran my butt over," Bosworth confessed after.

By the end of Oakland's 37–14 rout, Jackson had gained 221 yards on just 18 carries, and America knew for sure that Bo knew football.

Bo Jackson (34) runs over Seattle's Kenny Easley (45) for a 12-yard gain. (AP Photo/Barry Sweet)

Jackson (34) follows Dokie Williams (85) for a four-yard gain in the first quarter of a regular-season game against Seattle. (AP Photo/Barry Sweet)

Gale Sayers could do more on one play than most people could in an entire game. He could also do more in one game than most people could in a season.

Take, for example, his performance on December 21, 1965, perhaps the greatest one-man show in NFL history, and especially the punt return that capped it off.

This game at Wrigley Field against San Francisco was played on a sloppy, muddy field. And by the time Sayers caught the fourth-quarter punt, he knew that the entire 49er defense was geared toward stopping him.

With the game a blowout—the Bears would win 61–20—coach George Halas pulled Sayers from the backfield in the fourth quarter. But he was just one touchdown shy of tying the league record and one touchdown shy of setting a new record with 21 touchdowns in a season. So Halas sent Sayers back in to return another punt.

He caught it back at his 15. And then he took off. If the mud didn't stop him, then San Francisco surely couldn't. On this play, he cut right, broke a tackle at the 15, then tore through three 49ers; after a stretch of open field, he saw three more defenders converging on him. Somehow Sayers, without ever slowing down, moved horizontally across the field—it seems he might even have moved backward—to elude the defenders, then accelerated to another gear, leaving them in his wake. By the end of his 85-yard romp, he was so alone he could trot in.

"He had this ability to go full speed, cut, and then go full speed again right away," says Chicago Hall of Fame linebacker Dick Butkus, who came into the league with Sayers. "You could never get a clean shot on Gale. Never."

With that one punt return, Sayers achieved both records. He also managed to score on a run, a pass, and a kick all in one game. (It has been done just six times—three of those times by Sayers—in history.) And if Halas had left him in, there would have been more. "I could have scored eight touchdowns," Sayers said years later. "There was no doubt in my mind."

Still, the 336 all-purpose yards on just nine rushes, two catches, and three punt returns was plenty impressive. In fact, when it was all over, Chicago gave Sayers his second game ball of the season, something the Bears had never done before. (He had earned one earlier for a four-touchdown game.)

"It isn't often that the Bears break a tradition," said Halas, who had founded the team. "But this is the greatest exhibition I have ever seen by one man in one game."

Fleet-footed Chicago Bears halfback Gale Sayers (40) eludes San Francisco 49ers tacklers and runs 80 yards for a touchdown in the first quarter. (Bettmann/Corbis)

THE KICKOFF RETURN

Return men didn't win MVP Awards in the Super Bowl. It was just that simple. For thirty years, starting with the very first game in 1967, there had been no punts and just three kickoffs returned for touchdowns—and all had been by the losing team.

But in Super Bowl XXXI in 1997, Desmond Howard changed all that. Right when it seemed that the New England Patriots were threatening the Green Bay Packers, Howard buried New England with a record-setting 99-yard kickoff return.

"I knew that sooner or later I was going to scorch 'em," said Howard, who had been put on the expansion list after 1994 by Washington (where he fell asleep in meetings) and released by Jacksonville in 1995. While Howard hadn't returned any kickoffs for TDs in the 1996 regular season (his longest run was just 40 yards), he had excelled on punts. Busting out with a league-leading three scores off punts—including a 92-yarder—he had finished second in the league with 15.1 yards per punt return. In the playoffs, he had dashed off a 71-yard punt return for a score.

Through much of the first three quarters in the Super Bowl, Howard had been shut down on kickoff returns, gaining just 55 yards total on three tries as the Patriots cut off Green Bay's route up the middle, then guessed right and shut him down outside. Still, his punt returns of 32 and 34 yards proved critical, providing the field position that led to 10 points for the Packers.

But the turning point came right after New England cut Green Bay's lead to 27–21 with 3:27 left in the third. New England's Tom Tupa kicked off right down the middle, right where Howard wanted it. The Packers sent blockers out to push the Patriots to the perimeter; Travis Jervey nailed Marrio Greer, and Calvin Jones took out Tedy Bruschi. Then came the Green

Bay wedge, with 242-pound defensive end Keith McKenzie and 243-pound linebacker Lamont Hollinquest tag-teaming to destroy the Patriots' biggest threat, the 205-pound defensive back Larry Whigham.

That opened a seam, and when Howard got loose near the 40-yard line, Don Beebe nailed defensive back Mike McGruder to set Howard completely free. He fairly flew to the end zone, then turned around and talked trash to all the Patriots on the sideline, who he felt had been doing too much yapping in the days leading up to the game.

New England didn't score again. Patriots head coach Bill Parcells commented after the game: "We had a lot of momentum, and our defense was playing better. But [Howard] made the big play. That return was the game right there. He's been great all year, and he was great again today."

Howard's 244 total return yards tied a Super Bowl record and made him the first return man to win the game's MVP. "Obviously [that play] was a backbreaker," Howard said. "They had just scored, they had the momentum. Then we have my return, and that was basically the game."

Packers wide receiver Desmond Howard (81) returns a kickoff for a touchdown in Super Bowl XXXI. (AP Photo/ Susan Ragan)

DEFENSIVE GREATS

I wouldn't ever set out to hurt anyone deliberately unless it was, you know, important — like a league game or something. — Dick Butkus, former linebacker for the Chicago Bears

1 | BALTIMORE RAVENS
SUPER BOWL XXXV

The story of the Ravens' 2000 defense, arguably the greatest in NFL history, began a year earlier a few hours after Super Bowl XXXIV ended.

All-Pro linebacker Ray Lewis was arrested in a murder case that sprang from a post–Super Bowl celebration gone bad outside an Atlanta nightclub. His attorney successfully argued, however, that this was a case of "wrong place, wrong time" for Lewis, and he got off on a misdemeanor charge in June 2000. His dedication to football energized by the wake-up call, Lewis showed up for the 2000 season bulked up to 250 pounds but as fast as ever.

"He's motivated, has great instincts, runs like hell, and makes a ton of plays," Tennessee Titans general manager Floyd Reese said of Lewis in 1998. "And if you lose a guy like that, you lose a bit of the team's soul."

Their soul intact, the Ravens allowed a record-low 165 points and became the first team to give up less than 1,000 rushing yards in 16 games. Led by Lewis, who was named the NFL's Defensive Player of the Year, the Ravens defense recorded four shutouts during the regular season, then gave up just one TD in three playoff games to roll into Super Bowl XXXV.

And after all that, the best was yet to come.

The Giants found out the hard way that the Ravens were led by one of the game's all-time great linebackers, but his teammates were outstanding in their own right. The Giants offense was stymied,

posting zero points and a paltry 152 yards. They threw four interceptions and punted a record 11 times in 16 possessions.

From start to finish, the Giants were stunned by a defense that was both ferocious and athletic and started six former first-round picks. With All-Pro safety Rod Woodson anchoring the secondary, Lewis controlling the center of the field, tackle Sam Adams anchoring the middle of the line, and ends Rob Burnett and Michael McCrary and linebacker Peter Boulware all providing a strong outside pass rush, the Giants never knew where the next hit was coming from.

"They're on the attack everywhere," coach Jim Fassell could be heard saying on the sideline, sounding like a hapless victim in a horror movie. The Giants, running back Tiki Barber admitted later, were stunned by "the speed of their defense."

"They had a scheme to stop everything we had," added veteran Giants offensive lineman Lomas Brown. "And I have never seen, in all my years of football, such an athletic defense."

Giants quarterback Kerry Collins had thrown for 381 yards and five touchdowns in New York's 41–0 rout of Minnesota at the NFC title game, but he never got anything going against the Ravens. Under pressure from the get-go, he found himself looking in vain for open receivers and throwing off his back foot. "They completely took me out of my rhythm," Collins said. "Everything I tried to get

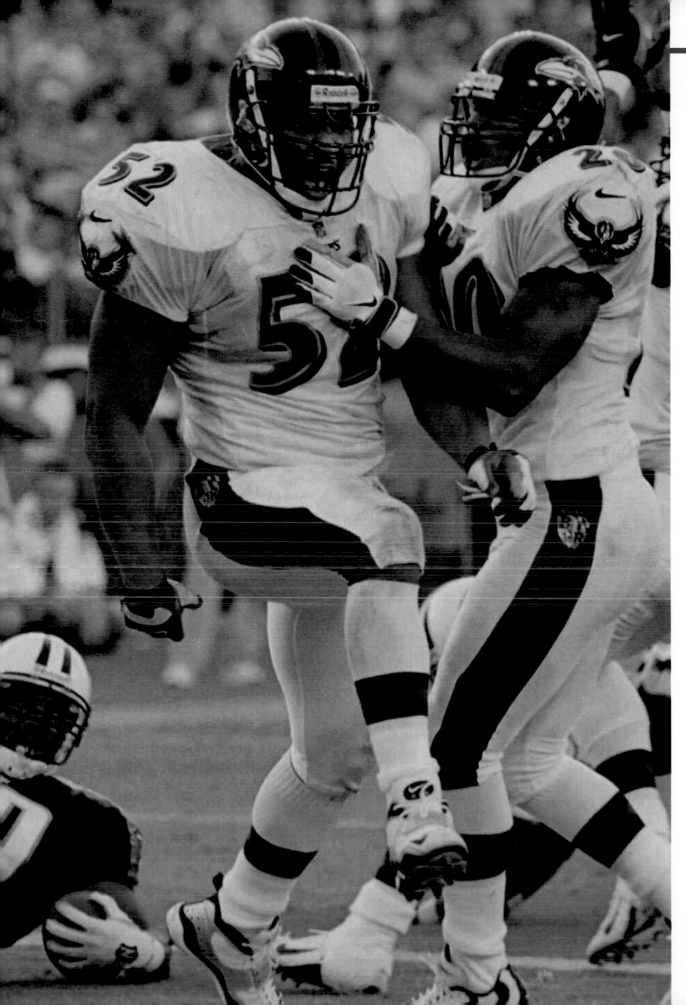

Ray Lewis (52) celebrates with teammate Kim Herring after bringing down Titans running back Rodney Thomas in the end zone for a safety in the third quarter of a 1999 regular-season game. (AP Photo/ Wade Payne)

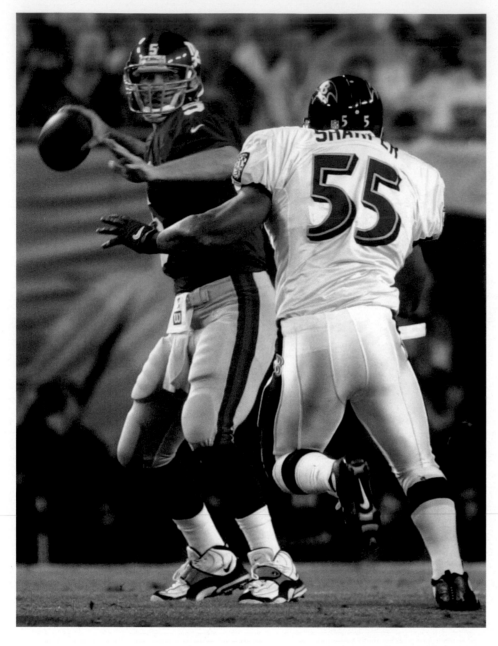

going always seemed to end up in a bad stop."

The Ravens defense was both hard-hitting and seemingly everywhere the Giants wanted to go. It was a joint effort with 10 players contributing at least three solo tackles, three different players breaking through for sacks, and four making interceptions.

"It seemed like there were nine Ray Lewises out there," Giants defensive end Michael Strahan said. "It seemed like [this was a situation where] all 11 guys were better than your 11."

Lewis, for one, was not surprised by the Giants' inability to deal with the Ravens' depth and athleticism on defense.

"The thing is, the Giants just didn't know," he said. "You just don't know until you play us, but our defense is a buzz saw. . . . Without disrespecting anyone else, I truly believe this is the best defense in NFL history."

One thing was for sure. With the possible exception of the 1985 Bears, no defense was more dominant in the Super Bowl.

The Giants, trailing 10–0, didn't reach Ravens territory until near the end of the first half. But an interception by cornerback Chris McAlister quickly ended that threat. Later, linebacker Jamie Sharper crashed into wide receiver Ike Hilliard with such force that it stunned the game's announcers.

The outcome was still in doubt late in the third quarter when cornerback Duane Starks, taking advantage of something he later said he had noticed

Giants quarterback Kerry Collins (5) looks to pass as he is pressured by Ravens linebacker Jamie Sharper (55) in the first quarter of Super Bowl XXXV. (AP Photo/Laura Rauch)

on film, intercepted a pass intended for Amani Toomer on the left side. With a clear field in front of him, Starks raced 49 yards for a touchdown to make it 17–0.

"I studied [Collins's] three-step drop," Starks said. "When he gave me that little extra hop, I knew he was going to throw the ball. I had a positive read. I knew I had the upper hand on that three-step read."

Although the Giants would return the ensuing kickoff for a touchdown, they managed just one first down on their last four possessions and ended up losing, 34–7. Lewis was named Super Bowl MVP for a performance that included five tackles and four pass deflections, one leading to an interception by Sharper. Those weren't huge numbers by Lewis's standards, but his ability to read and react swiftly was instrumental in the Ravens' strategy to ignore the Giants' shift-happy offense.

"We let the Giants do all their shifting and waited for them to come to us," defensive coordinator Marvin Lewis said. "Of course, Ray stuffed everything. He just keeps rewriting the linebacker position."

The game marked a joyous end to Lewis' year of tumult. "The thing about the Man Upstairs," Lewis said, "He doesn't put you through tragedy without bringing you through triumph."

Super Bowl XXXV was a triumph for Lewis, for the Ravens, and for the power of an overwhelming defense.

The Ravens' Duane Starks reacts in the end zone after an interception return for a touchdown in the third quarter. (AP Photo/Tony Gutierrez)

2 | CHICAGO BEARS
SUPER BOWL XX

Bears coach Mike Ditka. (AP Photo/ Charlie Bennett)

By 1985, Chicago's "Monsters of the Midway" had been reborn as a vicious six-headed beast that could strike from anywhere. À la Zeus in *Clash of the Titans*, defensive coordinator Buddy Ryan released the Kraken without mercy.

Ryan's creation, the now-legendary "46 Defense," was designed to put relentless pressure on the quarterback with a variety of unorthodox formations—including both outside linebackers moving to one side of the field and three of four down linemen going to the other. The end result was that quarterbacks got pounded, running backs got stuffed, and the Bears defense, by 1985, became the most brutally dominant in NFL history.

"The 46 Defense, to make it very plain and to the point, is all about pressure," said middle linebacker Mike Singletary, the 1985 Defensive Player of the Year. "We're gonna come at you, and we're gonna hit your quarterback until you get another one in.

It was a nightmare, I know, for quarterbacks."

Years later, Ryan was asked why the Bears' 1985 defense was so dominant. "We had a scheme that nobody knew how to block," he said, "and then we had some great athletes at certain spots."

The front four included end Richard Dent, end-tackle Dan Hampton, and tackles Steve McMichael and William "The Refrigerator" Perry. Singletary anchored a linebacker corps that included Wilber Marshall and Otis Wilson. Safeties Dave Duerson and Gary Fencik also were allowed to crowd the line of scrimmage, sometimes blitzing or helping to stuff the run. Singletary, Dent, Hampton, Duerson, and Wilson all went to the Pro Bowl, while McMichael, Dent, and Singletary earned All-Pro honors.

"We were gonna keep coming, keep you guessing, and we were going to have fun," Singletary said, "because the 46 was as physical and nasty as you want to get."

The Falcons' Gerald Riggs (42) gets a dose of heavy coverage by Bears defenders Mike Singletary (50), Dave Duerson (22), and Steve McMichael in NFL action on November 24, 1985. (AP Photo/Charlie Bennett)

The Bears' William "The Refrigerator" Perry (72) helps a teammate to his feet during a game against the Packers on October 21, 1985. (AP Photo/Charlie Bennett)

It was no secret that Ryan and coach Mike Ditka clashed more than once during their years together. That included the '85 season, despite the team's 18-1 record, but that didn't stop Ditka from being awed by a defense that was unique, talented, and violently dominant.

"I was the coach, but I was a fan," he said. "I marveled like the people in the bleachers. As the season went on, it became relentless."

By the playoffs, the Bears defense was as effective as any in NFL history. They became the only team to shut out two playoff teams in a row, 21–0 and 24–0, against the Giants and Rams. And then, somehow, they got even better in Super Bowl XX at the New Orleans Superdome.

The Bears demolished the Patriots, 46–10, while giving up just 123 total yards, including a record-low seven on the ground. They recovered four fumbles and intercepted two passes while sacking Tony Eason and then Steve Grogan a record-tying seven times. The Patriots ran 21 plays for minus 19 yards in the first half and didn't break into positive yards until the Bears had a 30–3 lead. The Patriots' only points came on an early field goal after a Bears turnover and a fourth-quarter touchdown after Ditka pulled the starters.

"There was never a doubt in my mind we were going to win that Super Bowl," Singletary said. "It was only a question of by how much."

Perhaps the Bears were inspired by a brief speech that Ryan gave the defense the night before the game. "It was an emotional meeting," Duerson said, "and very short. Buddy [who would soon leave to become the Eagles' head coach] came in and said, 'Win or lose, next week you guys are my heroes.' There were tears down his cheeks."

The Bears gave him a standing ovation. The next day they went out and mauled the Patriots. Early on, the Bears got to Eason, who went 0-6 before being relieved by Grogan and becoming the only starting quarterback never to complete a pass in a Super Bowl. "I saw a look of confusion and doubt coming out of the huddle," Singletary said. Added Hampton: "He was a little bit afraid to throw the ball, and a little bit too timid to run it."

On the Patriots' third series, Dent rammed into Eason, knocking the ball loose. Hampton, who had boasted that trying to stop the Bears defense "was like stopping an avalanche," recovered. Next time around, Craig James was met in the backfield, again by Dent, and his fumble was recovered by Singletary. The score was soon 13–3.

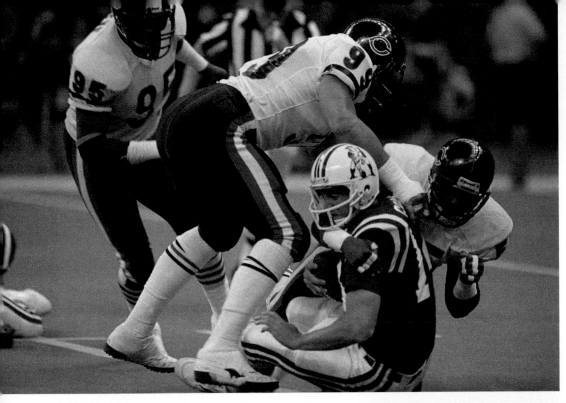

The Bears' Dan Hampton (99) and Otis Wilson sack the Patriots' quarterback Steve Grogan in Super Bowl XX. (AP Photo/Ray Stubblebine)

Bears defensive coordinator Buddy Ryan is carried off the field by the team after Chicago's Super Bowl victory over the Patriots. (AP Photo)

The Bears kept moving Dent around, and he kept abusing the Patriots who tried to block him. "Dent [the Super Bowl MVP] was coming free," Singletary said. "We knew we could be effective with different stunts until the well ran dry. It never did."

The Patriots didn't seem to know what hit them. "It was like trying to beat back the tide with a broom," Pats guard Ron Wooten said. "I'm not embarrassed, I'm humiliated."

Later, Singletary would vividly sum up the frenzy that took over the defense in Super Bowl XX. "It was Dent, and it was Hampton and Marshall and Otis. Those guys are just barking. They all wanted to hit the quarterback. And I'd say, 'Wait, the guy is bleeding at the mouth, bleeding at the nose. You don't have to kill the guy.' And they'd say, 'We don't care, he's the quarterback. We're going to get him. That's what we do.'"

After the final gun, the Bears followed tradition and hoisted Ditka on their shoulders. Then the Bears broke with tradition (as was their style) and put a second coach on their shoulders—the man behind the NFL's most fanatical defense, the one and only Buddy Ryan.

3 | PITTSBURGH STEELERS
SUPER BOWL IX

Going into Super Bowl IX in New Orleans, Minnesota's "Purple People Eaters" were probably more familiar to the average sports fan than Pittsburgh's "Steel Curtain." That was about to change.

Before, during, and after the Steelers' first appearance on the Super Bowl stage, the Steel Curtain's colorful cast of characters put together an introductory performance that would long be remembered. The defense that would help the Steelers win four Super Bowls in five years was loud, funny, hard-hitting, mean, and, most of all, dominating on the field.

It started with defensive tackle "Mean Joe" Greene, the NFL Defensive Player of the Year, telling the world that the Steelers' real meanie was linebacker Jack Lambert. "He's so mean he don't even like himself," he quipped.

It continued on the field, where the Steel Curtain closed around quarterback Fran Tarkenton—who threw two interceptions—and the Vikings offense, limiting them to an all-time low 119 total yards and nine first downs, also a record for futility. The Vikings' only score came on a blocked punt, and their offense also gave up an embarrassing safety in a 16–6 loss.

The Steelers' ability to play smash-mouth football was apparent over and over again, especially on one of the Vikings' two best scoring opportunities. Tarkenton found John Gilliam open on a long pass at the Steelers' 5-yard line, but safety Glen Edwards hit the receiver in the mouth with his arms. The ball popped loose, and cornerback Mel Blount alertly made the interception, preserving what was then just a 2–0 lead.

"Glen Edwards made what was, in my opinion, one of the all-time hits," Blount said. Linebacker

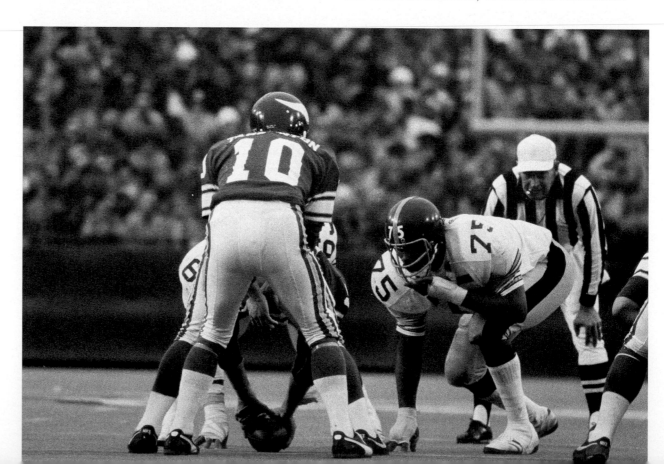

Steelers tackle "Mean Joe" Greene (75) gets ready to rush in at Vikings quarterback Fran Tarkenton (10) during Super Bowl IX. (AP Photo/ Harry Cabluck)

Tarkenton goes back
to pass. (AP Photo/
NFL Photos)

Jack Ham said, "Edwards and Gilliam had a little feud going. That play may have [made the difference]."

Greene and fellow tackle Ernie Holmes kept switching the angle of their attack, using stunts unveiled in the playoffs by defensive line coach George Perles. The defense that held the Raiders to 29 yards on 21 carries in the AFC title game made it so hard on the Vikings' interior line that Lambert, Ham, and Andy Russell were free to commit mayhem. Vikings All-Pro running back Chuck Foreman and Dave Osborn were the victims, gaining 17 net yards on 20 carries.

"Their defense outplayed us," Vikings tackle Ron Yary said. "They beat us with their line, they beat us with their linebackers."

No one typified the Steel Curtain's toughness—both physically and mentally—better than defensive end Dwight White, who combined with fellow end L. C. Greenwood to bottle up the mobile Tarkenton and help make his life miserable on this particular Super Sunday. The 6'4" White played despite catching pneumonia and losing 18 pounds in the hospital in the week leading up to the game. He would return to the hospital for 10 days after Super Sunday, but he was a key factor in several big plays, including a swatted pass that Greene intercepted.

"Doctors told me I might suffer some serious consequences if I got a negative reaction after playing," White said. "But this is the Super Bowl, and I wasn't going to pass it up."

Steelers coach Chuck Noll was amazed by White's ability to contribute. "He was weak," he said. "I figured he'd take part in the pregame workouts, and then he'd keel over and we'd drag him off. But it didn't happen that way. . . . White showed the attitude this team had through the playoffs. He symbolizes the attitude of the whole defensive unit, the whole football team."

With the Steelers leading, 9–0, in the fourth quarter, Greene made the Steel Curtain's final big play. After a Steelers fumble and a pass interference call, the Vikings had the ball at the Pittsburgh 5, but Foreman ran into a wall on the next play and fumbled. Greene emerged with the ball.

Minutes later, the Vikings would score their only TD on a blocked punt, making Greene's fumble recovery that much bigger. "That was the biggest defensive play of the day," Noll said. "They tried to run a counter play, and Greene knocked the ball out of Foreman's hands."

"I'm proud of this football team," Noll added. "It's especially fitting in a championship game that our defense shut out the [NFC] champions."

It was no wonder that after the game *Sports Illustrated* wrote, with just the slightest hyperbole: "And now, for an encore, the Pittsburgh Steelers defense will pick up Tulane Stadium and throw it into the middle of Bourbon Street. L. C. Greenwood or perhaps Mean Joe Greene will swallow what is left of Fran Tarkenton in a crawfish bisque."

The Vikings' Chuck Foreman (44) puts his hands on his hips as he watches teammate Dave Osborn get stormed by Pittsburgh's Ernie Holmes and L. C. Greenwood (68). (AP Photo/ Ed Kolenovsky)

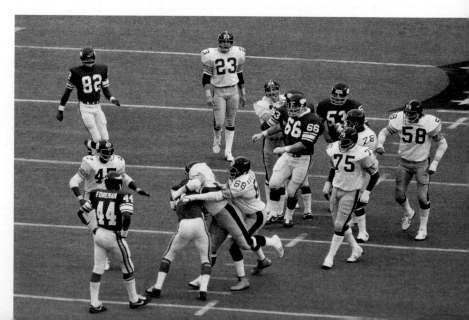

Greene (75) gets ready to block a Tarkenton pass. (AP Photo/Harry Hall)

Mel Blount (47) indicates the Steelers are number one as he and teammates Joe Greene (75) and Andy Russell (34) leave the field after stopping the Vikings attack. (AP Photo/HC)

4 NEW YORK GIANTS
1958 TIEBREAKER PLAYOFF

The New York Giants' Sam Huff in 1961. (AP Photo/NFL Photos)

Browns fullback Jim Brown busts through the Eagles' line, sweeps wide for four yards, and breaks a record during this NFL game on October 4, 1965—his 106th career touchdown tops the mark held by Green Bay's Don Hutson. (AP Photo)

In his second year as a pro, Cleveland's Jim Brown dominated the NFL, leading the league with 1,527 yards, 10 touchdowns, and 127.3 rushing yards per game in what was then a 12-game season. Still considered by some today the greatest running back in NFL history, Brown was always the focus of middle linebacker Sam Huff whenever the Giants faced the Browns.

Everyone else saw it the same way. "It was Huff-Brown," said Browns defensive end Paul Wiggin. "That was the title of it."

The 6'1", 230-pound Huff was a proud man, a fierce warrior, and he learned early on what it meant to take on the 6'2", 232-pound Brown. In 1957, Brown's rookie year, Giants defensive coordinator Tom Landry told Huff, "He's your man. It's up to you to stop him."

Landry also warned Huff that Brown would soon be the game's greatest player, something Huff already knew from a college game in which he had been knocked out trying to tackle the then-Syracuse star. "Every other fullback I know was taught to run with his knees high," Huff said. "Jimmy shuffles his feet as he runs and has them planted firmly on the ground when you hit him. It's like running into a tree. If he ran any harder, he'd kill a few of us."

Try as they might, the Giants had little success stopping Brown in the regular season. Brown gained 113 yards in one game and 148 yards in the other, highlighted by 58- and 65-yard touchdown runs. Nevertheless, the Giants won both games—21–17 in the earlier game, then 13–10 in the season finale—to leave both teams 9-3.

That forced the two NFL powers to face each other a third time a week later in a special playoff game to determine which team would face the Colts in what would become a legendary NFL championship game. So the intensity had reached a fever pitch when Brown and Huff took the field on a bitterly cold day in New York.

For once, that turned out to be bad news for the supremely talented Brown and, by extension, the Browns. Not only did the Giants dish out a beating to Brown while holding him to a career-low eight yards on seven carries, but they shut out the Browns and held them to seven first downs in a 10–0 triumph for one of the NFL's great defenses.

On one play, Huff, Jim Katcavage, and Andy Robustelli combined to blast Brown on a sweep, forcing a fumble that the Giants recovered. "That's the only time I've seen Jim Brown woozy. It was

Jim Brown (32) makes another try to crack the Giants' line in an October 27, 1963, game in Cleveland. (AP Photo)

Jim Brown in 1965. (AP Photo/ NFL Photos)

the best lick I've ever seen," Browns defensive back Bernie Parrish said. Another time, Huff and Dick Modzelewski belted the league's greatest running back. "He got up and went back to the huddle, but he didn't know where he was," Huff said.

Brown, knocked out of the game, later gave Huff his just due. "I don't know that anyone ever hit me harder than Sam Huff," Brown said. "Especially in that playoff game, he had my number on a couple of plays."

Remembering that game and their New York–hyped rivalry, Brown would say, "I always say Sam got famous from tackling me. He was a great player."

With Brown slowed, the Browns were no match for the Giants defense. Milt Plum was sacked six times for 52 yards and intercepted three times. Brown's only big run of the day, good for 20 yards to the Giants' 4 in the third quarter, set up a definitive series. Brown was stuffed on the next play, Plum was then thrown for a 12-yard loss by Huff, Rosey Grier, and Katcavage, and Huff intercepted Plum's next pass to preserve the shutout.

"Jim Brown was the greatest player that ever touched a football," Huff said, and that just made this one triumph all the sweeter.

5 | NEW YORK GIANTS
1990 NFC CHAMPIONSHIP GAME

Joe Montana faded back to pass from his own 23 with less than 10 minutes remaining in the fourth quarter of the 1990 season's NFC championship game. The legendary quarterback and his San Francisco 49ers—winners of seven straight post-season games—seemed to be just minutes from another Super Bowl and their anticipated shot at an unprecedented "three-peat."

Sure, the New York Giants, owners of the league's best defense, had come up with a new 3-4 look that had limited Montana to a subpar 190 yards passing on the day, its constant pressure forcing him to dump off short passes and stopping nearly every third-down play. But still, Montana's one big play—a 61-yard touchdown bomb to John Taylor—seemed like it might be enough. San Francisco held a 13–9 lead, the Giants had not reached the end zone once all day, and they hadn't beaten the 49ers in their last four meetings, dating back to 1987. One more drive and the Giants might be finished, especially if Montana could put points on the board.

The offensive line sent New York's defensive end Leonard Marshall sprawling to the turf. When Marshall picked himself up but was knocked down again, Lawrence Taylor took over the effort. At 31, the 6'3", 240-pound linebacker equivalent of Montana was slowing down—his 10.5 sacks was his lowest total since 1983—yet number 56 remained the team leader, in sacks and in persona. And he was still there at the biggest moments. On this play, he forced Montana out of his pocket, sending the quarterback on the run. So when the persevering Marshall got up once more, he saw that the quarterback still had the ball. Boom. Then he didn't.

Marshall blindsided Montana at the 16 with a resounding thud, knocking the ball loose and knocking the superstar from the game. Montana later said it was the hardest hit he'd ever received. "My ribs and chest hurt so bad that I didn't know my hand was broken," he said. "Normally, when you get the wind knocked out of you, you can usually breathe a little bit of air out. But I couldn't even get a breath out. And I was thinking, 'Oh God, I'm gonna die here, I know it. Something is seriously wrong.'"

Even though this hit came right after ex-Giant Jim Burt nailed New York quarterback Jeff Hostetler on a play that New York players thought was dirty, Marshall maintained that he was just going for the sack. "It was a good, clean hit, just a football hit, but I knew I hurt him bad," Marshall said. "I knew he wasn't going to be back. I could hear him moaning." While the hit was clean, even some of the Giants wondered if the emotion behind the blow was payback for Burt's hit on Hostetler, who overcame a sore knee to remain in the game. "It probably wasn't a dirty hit, but because Jim Burt was [once one of us], we were upset," linebacker Carl Banks said. "When [Marshall later] hit Joe, we thought he killed him."

The 49ers recovered Montana's fumble, but the Hall of Fame quarterback known for his fourth-quarter heroics was done for the day. The two-time defending Super Bowl champion 49ers had a pretty good backup in Steve Young, however, and their coveted three-peat was still doable.

It would take another big hit by the determined Giants to secure victory. After a Giants field goal cut the deficit to 13–12, the 49ers had the ball on the Giants' 30 with 2:36 left. This time, tackle Erik Howard rammed his helmet into the ball carried by tailback Roger Craig, forcing a fumble that line-backer Lawrence Taylor recovered.

Seven plays later, Matt Bahr's fifth field goal gave the Giants a 15–13 victory and a trip to the Super Bowl. The 49ers' dynasty was derailed.

"Everyone said we couldn't stop the 49ers," Marshall said. "But no one is invincible. We played physical, aggressive football, and we did it for 60 minutes. We were relentless."

That same day, the Bills put on an equally dominant display of defense in the AFC title game against Los Angeles, intercepting the Raiders five times and holding them to three points. But that effort was overshadowed by the Bills' 51-point explosion.

The Giants went on to beat the Bills in Super Bowl XXV by a score of 20 to 19. Their hard-hitting, talented defense secured a place among the NFL's all-time best. And it all started with that hit on Montana.

49ers quarterback Joe Montana (16) warms up. (AP Photo/Greg Trott)

Giants linebacker Lawrence Taylor (56) runs after recovering a 49ers fumble in the fourth quarter of the NFC championship game. (AP Photo/ Rich Pedroncelli)

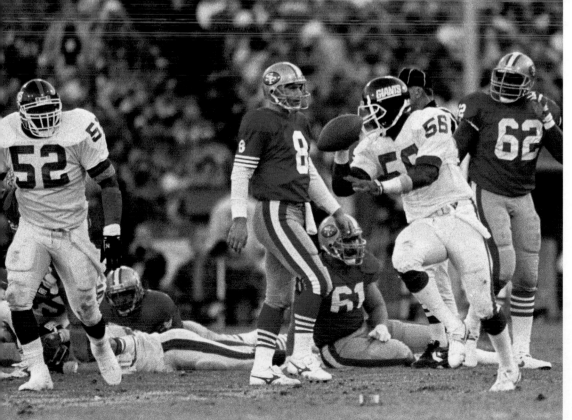

6 | LOS ANGELES RAIDERS
SUPER BOWL XVIII

The Raiders' Howie Long (left) battles the Redskins' George Starke on the line during the first half. (AP Photo)

Redskins quarterback Joe Theismann is sacked by the Raiders' Rod Martin (53) in Super Bowl XVIII. (AP Photo)

Super Bowl XVIII turned out to be a rematch of the October 2, 1983, regular-season game in which the Redskins offense pushed around the Raiders and won a 37–35 shootout. Only these weren't the same Raiders: after trading for cornerback Mike Haynes from the Patriots, the Raiders had paired him with cornerback Lester Hayes for the last five games of the regular season.

Haynes and Hayes. It had a nice ring to it. More than that, the pairing of what many believe was the greatest cornerback tandem in NFL history transformed the Raiders defense from really good to great going into the playoffs—a dramatic upgrade that shocked the Redskins. Haynes and Hayes together not only shut down other teams' top receivers but gave the Raiders the freedom to overplay the run and the short pass while attacking the quarterback, all at the same time.

In the Super Bowl that meant that wide receivers Art Monk, Charlie Brown, and Alvin Garrett were minimized. That, in turn, limited what QB Joe Theismann and tailback John Riggins could accomplish. And that left the league's number-one-rated offense sputtering and out of sync. The Redskins, who averaged 33.8 points, were lucky to get nine against the Raiders.

"We couldn't get off the line of scrimmage," Redskins GM Bobby Beathard said. "They were big, physical corners who could run. We had never played against someone like that. That changed our whole game plan."

Riggins, the hero of the previous Super Bowl, had finished the season first in touchdowns and fifth in rushing yards. In this Super Bowl, he could only grind out 64 yards on 26 carries. Quarterback Joe Theismann won the league's MVP that year, but he found few open targets, completing just 16 of 35 passes while throwing two interceptions.

The cornerbacks freed safety Mike Davis to crowd the line of scrimmage, where he supported the front seven against the run and made seven tackles. That freed linemen Howie Long, Reggie Kinlaw, and Lyle Alzado, along with a variety of blitzing linebackers, to attack the quarterback. The result was six sacks against the renowned offensive line known as "the Hogs."

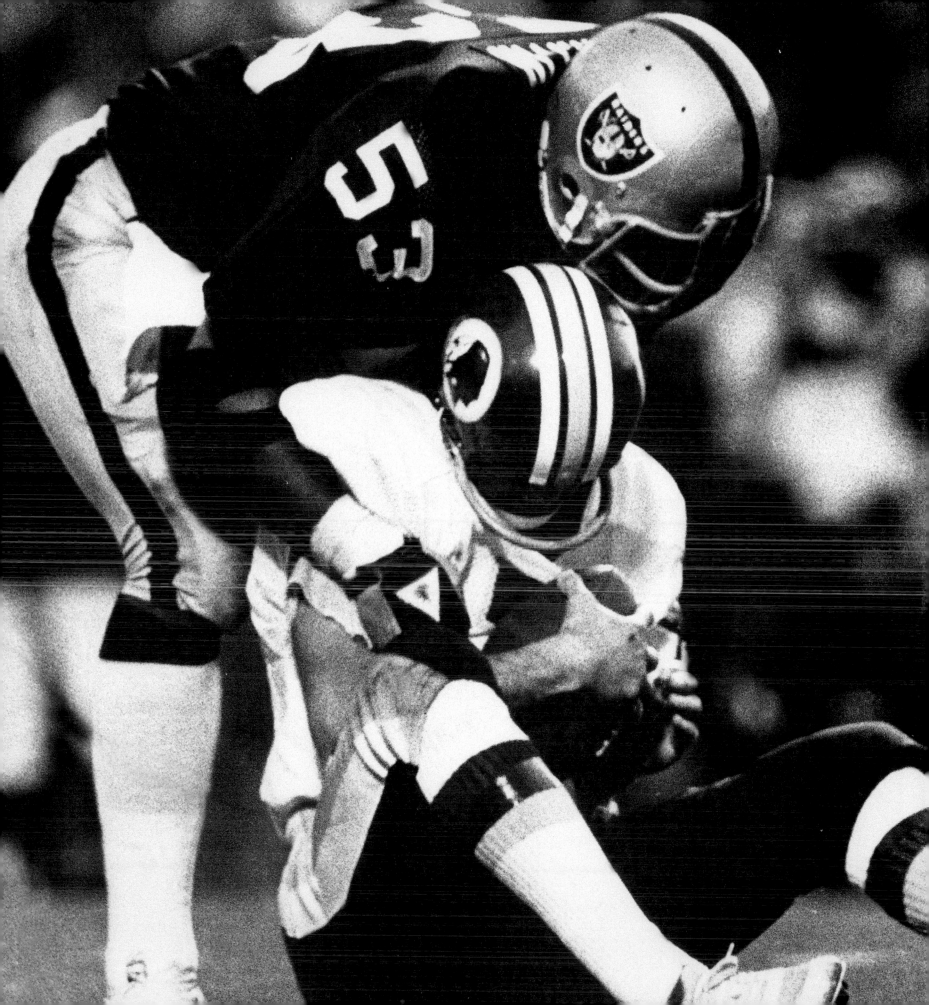

"No matter what formation they lined up in," Haynes said, explaining the beauty of the Raiders' in-your-face coverage combined with an attacking front-seven (or front-eight) defense, "in the end it just came down to man-to-man, very basic stuff. 'You take that guy, I take this one.' My kind of football."

Raiders running back Marcus Allen, who carried the ball 20 times for a then-record 191 yards and two TDs, certainly deserved the Super Bowl MVP Award, but he knew what the addition of Haynes meant to the defense. "It was the greatest steal of all time [Haynes for two draft picks]," Allen said years later. "Now you have two strong guys in there. Where do they throw the ball?"

Hall of Fame cornerback Willie Brown, then a Raiders assistant coach, didn't care. "Let 'em do whatever they want to do. Teams cannot throw the ball on us," he said.

As a result, the Raiders' legendary swagger was on full display during and after Super Bowl XVIII, trouncing the Washington Redskins 38 to 9.

"Our front seven came up with our own nickname this week," Long said. "We're 'the Slaughterhouse Seven.' We've never had a hog before that tasted so good."

"By the fourth quarter, we'd been in man-to-man coverage about 95 percent of the time," Hayes said. "That's because the Smurfs [the nickname earned by the Redskins receivers because they only ranged in height from 5'7" to 5'10"] can't function with tight, physical man-to-man coverage."

Theismann barely scrambles away from the Raiders' Mike Davis (36) during the first quarter. (AP Photo)

Raiders running back Marcus Allen (32). (AP Photo)

Raiders quarterback Jim Plunkett (16) is sacked by the Redskins. Plunkett lost the ball on the play. (AP Photo)

7 | TAMPA BAY BUCCANEERS
SUPER BOWL XXXVII

Somewhere in Las Vegas, the oddsmakers were sitting slack-jawed in disbelief. The Oakland Raiders, who had the league's best offense and the MVP in quarterback Rich Gannon, had been favored to win Super Bowl XXXVII. Then they were blindsided by a Tampa Bay Buccaneer defense that seemed to know what they were going to do before they did.

Of course, maybe everyone should have seen that swarm of Buccaneer defenders coming. After all, Tampa Bay had the league's best defense. They had made 31 interceptions and recovered 16 fumbles during the season, then added eight more turnovers to the collection in two playoff wins. "We're a quick, physical, smart team, and those big [offensive] linemen don't affect us like they do other teams," said cornerback Ronde Barber.

But the secret weapon was head coach Jon Gruden, who had been ditched by Oakland owner Al Davis after four seasons. Gruden had created the offense that Gannon tried in vain to run in the Super Bowl, and he knew its every wrinkle. "They were jumping our routes before our receivers even made their breaks," Raiders running back Tyrone Wheatley said.

The 39-year-old coach even got involved during practice, playing the part of Gannon to show the defense exactly what to expect, right down to the pump-fakes that the Bucs defense ignored all day.

"Jon Gruden was Gannon. Nobody can be like Gannon like Gruden can," said defensive coordinator Monte Kiffin, a holdover from former coach Tony Dungy's staff. "He taught Gannon. He was in Gannon's head."

"It's uncanny how the plays we ran in practice showed up, same formation, same motion," said All-Pro strong safety John Lynch, who called one play out loud before the snap, making an adjustment that led to an interception by teammate Dexter Jackson.

Add it all up and the Raiders never had a chance. Remarkably, the Raiders didn't seem to anticipate that Gruden would know their every move, and they didn't even change many of their audible calls. The Bucs turned five interceptions into three touchdowns that fueled a 48–21 triumph for Gruden and his defense.

Super Bowl MVP Dexter Jackson had two interceptions, as did Dwight Smith, who returned both of his picks for touchdowns, including a 50-yarder to finish off the scoring with two seconds left. Derrick Brooks also returned an interception for a touchdown. Simeon Rice had two of the Bucs' five sacks as Tampa Bay romped to a 20–3 halftime lead, then scored two quick third-quarter touchdowns.

"We were just absolutely terrible. It was a nightmarish performance," Gannon said. The interceptions and the TD returns were both Super Bowl records that may never be broken. In addition, the Bucs limited the Raiders to 19 yards rushing, 269 total yards, and just 11 first downs. The Raiders had just 62 total yards in the first half—the second-lowest total in Super Bowl history—and more than half their total yards came long after the outcome was decided.

"There was nothing they could do to us," Bucs defensive tackle Warren Sapp said. "Nothing."

Tampa Bay corner-back Dwight Smith (26) celebrates his 50-yard interception return for a touchdown in Super Bowl XXXVII. (AP Photo/ Lawrence Jackson)

Buccaneers tight end Ken Dilger (85) goes airborne as Raiders cornerback Charles Woodson takes out his legs. At right is the Raiders' Anthony Dorsett (33). (AP Photo/Mark J. Terrill)

8 | NEW YORK GIANTS
2000 NFC CHAMPIONSHIP GAME

Giants defensive coordinator John Fox. (AP Photo/Mark Lennihan)

"It was the match, and the fire has been burning since then," Fassell said after the Giants won their seventh straight game to reach the Super Bowl. "I think we shocked a lot of people, but we didn't shock ourselves."

The us-against-the-world Giants were out to shock and awe the Vikings. They succeeded by putting great pressure on young quarterback Daunte Culpepper. Playing in only his second playoff game, Culpepper rarely got time to find his star receivers. And they weren't open anyway.

"The big key was getting in Culpepper's face," said cornerback Jason Sehorn. "They put so much pressure on him, he was running for his life."

Defensive coordinator John Fox was not surprised that his athletic front four were able to bother the mobile Culpepper. "I thought our front seven, and our front four in particular, could put a consistent pass rush on, even with a mobile quarterback," he said.

Sehorn, who mainly covered deep threat Randy Moss, pointed out that the Giants got in the receivers' faces as well. "We did not give them free releases down the field," Sehorn said. "Receivers don't like to get hit, and we hit them all day long."

An early interception by Emmanuel McDaniel, who muscled the ball free from Vikings receiver Cris Carter for a touchback in the first quarter, set the tone. "When he made that play, I told him, 'You don't know how big that interception was. Cris Carter is one of the biggest of the big-time players,'" Giants secondary coach Johnnie Lynn said.

The most one-sided beating in NFC championship history left Vikings coach Dennis Green in shock.

"There's just no way you think you're going to go out and not score any points," Green said. "There's just no way you think you're going to go out and not be able to protect your quarterback or not be able to run the ball. So there's really nothing that took place that we were prepared for."

Actually, few NFL followers were prepared for the success the Giants enjoyed in 2000–2001. Many scoffed at coach Jim Fassell when he guaranteed that the Giants would make the playoffs after a loss to Detroit left them 7-4. Instead, the bold prediction seemed to light a fire under the Giants.

The Giants held the Vikings to just nine first downs and 114 total yards, the third-lowest total in NFL postseason history, while handing Green his first shutout loss in eight years in Minnesota. Culpepper was sacked four times, threw three interceptions, and finished with just 78 passing yards.

Defensive end Michael Strahan thought the shock factor worked in the Giants' favor after the team went 7-9 in 1999 and looked in trouble at 7-4 in 2000. Once the Giants built some momentum, they came together so tightly that even the Vikings' seemingly potent offense was in trouble.

"The sweetest thing was not how we played after last year, but the way we came back from 7-4 this year and won every game since then," Strahan said. "No one thought we would get this far when we were 7-4."

Certainly, none of the Vikings thought the Giants defense could be that good. "Forty-one-to-doughnut," Moss said. "I think that [was] the worst defeat I've ever been in in my life."

Vikings wide receiver Cris Carter is stopped by Giants linebackers Mike Barrow (left rear), Jessie Armstead (98), and safety Shaun Williams (36). (AP Photo/Bill Kostroun)

Vikings quarterback Daunte Culpepper (11) is sacked by the Giants' Cedric Jones (94) in the second quarter of the NFC championship game. (AP Photo/Amy Sancetta)

9 | DALLAS COWBOYS
SUPER BOWL VI

Dallas had a superior scheme, superior players, and a superior desire to win an NFL championship after excruciatingly close calls in Super Bowl V and in two '60s title games against Green Bay. It was no wonder that a defense featuring tackle Bob Lilly, linebacker Chuck Howley, and a shutdown secondary (Mel Renfro, Cliff Harris, Cornell Green, and Herb Adderley) held the Dolphins to a record-low 185 total yards and a harmless field goal.

"[Our offense got] destroyed," Shula said afterward. "They were a great defensive team."

The Dolphins would be all but unstoppable a year later in their glorious 17-0 season, but on this day star running backs Larry Csonka and Jim Kiick managed just 40 yards apiece—a critical component in the Dolphins' inability to move the ball. "The Flex [Defense] is the reason why Csonka did nothing against us," Cowboys safety Charlie Waters said.

The Flex shifted the positioning of two of the Cowboys' four linemen a yard off the ball, while Cliff Harris moved in from free safety to stop the run, creating a puzzle that neither the Dolphins nor any other team solved during the playoffs. The Cowboys gave up just 17 points in three victories. They did not allow a TD in the Super Bowl or the NFC title game against the 49ers.

The mobile Lilly set a record by sacking Bob Griese for a 29-yard loss. A 41-yard interception return by Howley set up a TD for Dallas, which scored

The Dolphins didn't know it going into Super Bowl VI, but the NFL's second-most-prolific offense in 1971 never had a chance.

In their first Super Bowl, they were facing the Cowboys' "Doomsday Defense" during its early years; this was the flex alignment that coach Tom Landry had invented and Miami coach Don Shula called "revolutionary." Just as important, the Dolphins were facing a team with a playoff hunger bordering on desperation.

Dallas head coach Tom Landry watches from the sidelines during Super Bowl VI. (AP Photo/NFL Photos)

Cowboys defensive tackle Bob Lilly (74) attempts to hold back Dolphins offensive center Bob DeMarco. (AP Photo/ NFL Photos)

Lilly (74) chases Dolphins quarterback Bob Griese (12). (AP Photo/ NFL Photos)

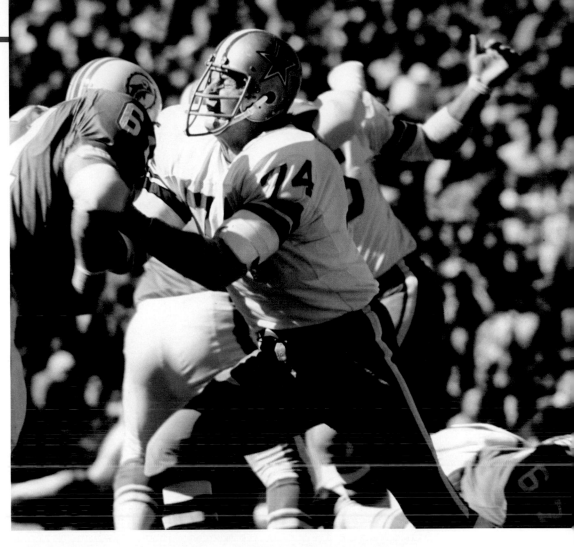

10 points off the defense's big plays. The Dolphins failed to gain a first down in the third quarter and got past midfield only once in the second half.

When it was all over, the Cowboys had captured their first NFL title by a lopsided score of 24 to 3. The emotion that fueled the defense's dominance came spilling out in a decidedly un-Landry-like display of joy.

Wrote Bob St. John of the *Dallas Morning News*: "Free at Last. . . . The Cowboys have been accused of being an unemotional team after sound victories over Minnesota and San Francisco to get here. Emotions flowed this time, though perhaps the greatest picture of all was when All-Pro Bob Lilly, who has lived and died many times through it all, lit up a victory cigar. Backslapping . . . frenzy . . . madness. But it was fine madness."

A fine madness and a fine defense.

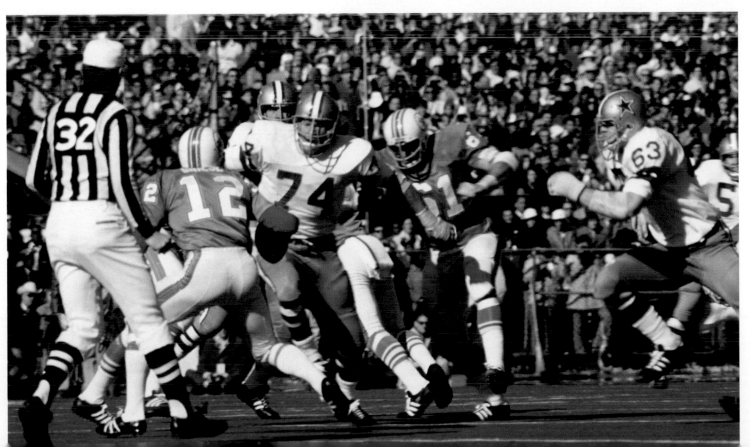

10 MIAMI DOLPHINS
1982 AFC CHAMPIONSHIP GAME

Jets quarterback Richard Todd (14) goes down at the hands of Dolphins defensive end Kim Bokamper. (AP Photo)

A lot of people were upset that Dolphins coach Don Shula, with NFL approval, opted not to cover the Orange Bowl's field with a tarp after rainstorms hit Miami in the week leading up to the 1982 AFC title game. Dolphins linebacker/end A. J. Duhe would not be one of them.

Storms that dropped 3.7 inches of rain turned the uncovered field into such a quagmire that the game would be dubbed the Mud Bowl. That negated the cutting ability of Jets running back Freeman McNeil—who had led the league in rushing that strike-shortened season—and made it tough for both offenses.

The end result was a tense, low-scoring defensive battle that was 0–0 at halftime. Jets quarterback Richard Todd would end up the goat, throwing five interceptions in a vain attempt to overcome the loss of McNeil's offense. Duhe, who had just two previous career interceptions, would be the unlikely hero. He intercepted three passes in the second half: one set up the game's first score, and he returned another 35 yards for the game-clinching TD.

"It was a meaningful day for all of us," Duhe said later. "We had a pretty good scheme defensively. We had put together some defensive combinations to take away [receivers] Wesley Walker and Jerome Barkum. I happened to be involved in a couple plays that had coverage involved with those guys."

While Shula may or may not have envisioned

such a muddy field when the rains came, the Dolphins defense still deserved credit for a rare playoff shutout. Doug Betters, Bob Baumhower, and Kim Bokamper effectively kept Todd from scrambling, and the Dolphins, who led the league in pass defense and interceptions, wisely bumped the Jets' receivers at the line of scrimmage, further ruining their routes in the muck.

"That's one thing [defensive coordinator Bill] Arnsparger stresses every day," cornerback Don McNeal said. "It's especially effective on a muddy field. It makes a receiver slip, and it throws his timing off."

Duhe's first two interceptions came when he dropped into coverage over the middle. The third was a freaky play on a freaky field and ended with him dashing into the end zone, sending the Dolphins to Super Bowl XVII. "That was probably my best play," he said. "They tried to cut me and throw a little swing pass out in the flats. I protected myself and batted the ball up, and that's where history was made."

The game ended on a score of 14 to 0. The scoreless Jets were furious with Shula and the Dolphins for letting the field become saturated, believing the decision was a deliberate attempt to negate their running attack. Jets coach Walt Michaels was fired soon after the game and never returned to the NFL. Asked years later how disappointing the Mud Bowl was, he would say: "Are you kidding me? How much more did I coach in the NFL after that?"

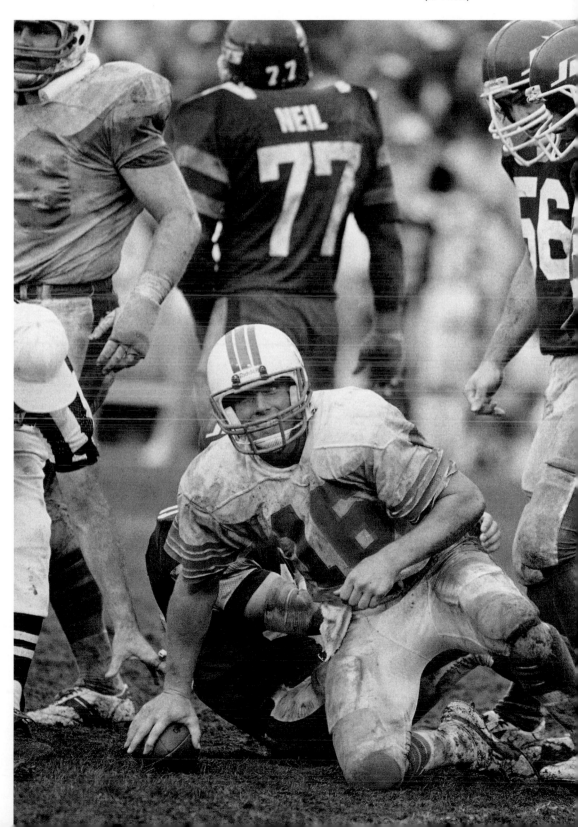

Dolphins quarterback
David Woodley (16).
(AP Photo)

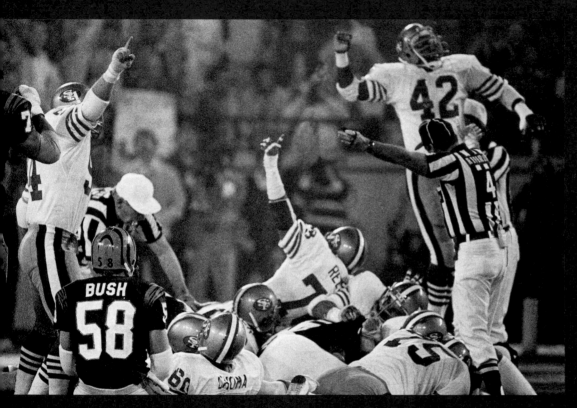

1. San Francisco 49ers
Super Bowl XVI

Bengals center Blair Bush (58) watches as the 49ers react after they stop a Bengals drive within the 1-yard line in Super Bowl XVI. (AP Photo)

San Francisco had what seemed like a comfortable 20–0 halftime lead in Super Bowl XVI. Then leaks started springing up.

First Cincinnati scored on an 83-yard drive to start the second half. Soon after, on a third-and-23, receiver Cris Collinsworth burned cornerback Eric Wright for a 49-yard gain, and the Bengals followed that with another big play when Pro Bowl fullback Pete Johnson smashed through the defense for two yards on fourth-and-1 from the San Francisco 5. The 49ers were in such disarray that they had only 10 defenders on the play: linebacker Keena Turner was on the sidelines, having misheard the call.

Now the Bengals had first-and-goal from the 3. A touchdown would close the gap to 20–14. Given the 49ers' total of just four yards of offense in the quarter, this was the game's critical moment. San Francisco stacked the defense with six linemen, four linebackers, and hard-hitting safety Ronnie Lott.

On both first down and second down, Johnson slammed up the middle. He got to the 1, but no farther—on one play, linebacker Jack Reynolds nailed him so hard that Reynolds himself was "groggy and dazed" after. On third down, the Bengals tried something different, a swing pass to Charles Alexander. But backup linebacker Dan Bunz stopped him just inches from the goal line, knocking the screws loose from his own face mask in the process.

"I never saw him coming," Alexander said. "He arrived as soon as the ball arrived. I had no chance to get my feet down for some second effort."

The Bengals gave it one more try on fourth down. Everyone knew the ball was going back to Johnson, a 252-pound bull who was perennially among the league leaders at putting the ball in the end zone. "Once he gets past the line of scrimmage, he's tough to stop," Reynolds said. Johnson barreled forward, but Reynolds, assisted by Bunz, had one last big stop. The drive had come up empty. Later, Cincinnati would make it 20–14, but not until there were five minutes gone in the fourth quarter.

The 49ers would win their first Super Bowl by less than one touchdown, 26–21.

2. Green Bay Packers
1966 NFL Championship

Beyond Vince Lombardi, the symbols of the Green Bay Packer dynasty feature the offense—their famed "Run to Daylight" sweeps by Paul Hornung or Jim Taylor and Bart Starr's passing or his Ice Bowl quarterback sneak.

But the team's backbone was its defense, which was nearly always first or second in points allowed. While the unit's greatest games were the 1961 and 1962 championships, in which it held the Giants to a total of seven points, its toughest stand—and greatest moment—came against Dallas in the 1966 NFL title game. The game would determine who would be the first team to represent the league against the upstart AFL in the first-ever championship game, a role Lombardi coveted.

Green Bay had been in charge the whole game, but Dallas was constantly nipping at its heels, with quarterback Don Meredith throwing a 68-yard touchdown bomb to pull the Cowboys within 34–27. When Dallas stopped the Packers offense, the Cowboys, who had more overall yardage on the day, made one last charge. Meredith steered his team to a first down at the Green Bay 2 with 1:52 on the clock.

Four tries to tie the game. Dan Reeves attacked the middle and gained one yard, but on second down Dallas went offside and was moved back to the 6. Green Bay adjusted and stopped the pass. But Meredith hit tight end Pettis Norman on third down to put Dallas back on the 2. One more play. Score or go home.

Meredith called a play named "Fire 90 Quarterback Roll Right," in which he rolled out with the option to pass or run. Meredith took a chance by heading to the closer sideline, a move that limited his maneuver-ability but gave him more blockers. Green Bay's Pro Bowl linebacker Dave Robinson, who had guessed an off-tackle run was coming, adjusted and took off after Meredith.

"He played it perfectly," Meredith said. "He came in with his hands up high, screening off my receivers until he got close enough, and then he dropped his arms around me. I couldn't do anything but flip the ball into the end zone and hope someone in a white jersey would catch it."

"I tried to pin both his arms, but all I could get was his left," Robinson said. "Under Lombardi, you always try for perfection, and if I had played this one perfectly, I would have had both of his arms. This way he got the ball away."

Tom Brown was one of the less heralded members of the Packers defense—he was mostly known for one failed season playing major league baseball—and he had fallen down on Meredith's previous touchdown pass. But this time he stayed with the play and picked off Meredith's pass. The Packers were heading on to the next game.

"We got together and said we couldn't let the offensive team down," linebacker Lee Roy Caffey said of that last stand. "They had played such a beautiful game. For the first time, down there on the 2, we knew we could stop them."

Green Bay head coach Vince Lombardi is carried off the field after the Packers win the 1965 NFL championship. (AP Photo)

3. New York Giants
Super Bowl XXI

The Denver Broncos already had a 10–7 lead in Super Bowl XXI. Now they were pushing for more, shoving the New York Giants back on their heels. John Elway had come up with a 54-yard bomb and several big third-down passes. The Broncos had first down at the Giants' 1. No team had ever overcome a 10-point deficit in the Super Bowl, so a score would loom large.

It was, as New York's defensive coordinator Bill Belichick later said, the game's "critical juncture."

Elway tried to bootleg in on first down, but he was no match for the great LT. Racing across the field, Lawrence Taylor hunted him down from behind to drop the quarterback for a one-yard loss. "Hell of a play," Denver coach Dan Reeves said.

Next, the Broncos went inside with a trap for Gerald Willhite. But when nose tackle Erik Howard was taken out, linebacker Harry Carson read the play, charged in, and, with help from defensive end Eric Dorsey, shut the door on Willhite. Rather than mix things up with a pass, or at least a different look, Denver went with the predictable, reviving a pitchout they had used successfully against New York from the 4 in the regular season.

"I expected that play again, and that's what they called," linebacker Carl Banks said. When Sammy Winder took the toss, he was met behind the line by Banks, Carson, and cornerback Perry Williams. Another four yards in the wrong direction.

"I didn't have time to square up and make a form tackle," Banks said. "I just got my head in there and made the hit. I had zigzags in my eyes for the rest of the half."

When Denver's Rich Karlis missed a field goal, the Broncos sagged. "We could have been way ahead," coach Dan Reeves said. "That was huge."

4. Kansas City Chiefs
1969 AFC Divisional Playoff Game

The New York Jets looked like a dynasty in the making. The defending Super Bowl champs trailed Kansas City, 6–3, in the fourth quarter of the 1969 AFC divisional playoff game, but a pass interference call had just given Joe Namath and company first down from the Chiefs' 1. Going one yard and gaining the lead, with four plays, seemed eminently doable for the league's third-most-prolific offense.

But Willie Lanier, one of the game's greatest middle linebackers (and the first African-American starter at the position), was having none of it. The perennial All-Pro stepped once more into the breach, exhorting his teammates to stand firm. "They're not going to score," he yelled again and again.

5. Dallas Cowboys
Super Bowl XXVII

The Chiefs defense was the best in the league in yards and points allowed, with future Hall of Famers in Lanier, fellow linebacker Bobby Bell, lineman Buck Buchanan, and cornerback Emmitt Thomas. "We were probably a team that proved the axiom that you can't win without great defense," said linebacker Jim Lynch.

The Jets tried running twice, but the Chiefs stacked up Matt Snell and then Bill Mathis. On third down, Namath tried something different, rolling out, hoping to pass to Snell in the end zone. But Bell and safety Jim Kearney had Snell double-teamed. With Lynch nearly upon him, Namath threw the ball away. The Jets had to settle for a field goal. The game was tied, but it was the Chiefs who had the momentum. Moments later, Kansas City quarterback Len Dawson completed a 61-yarder and a 19-yarder to put Kansas City back ahead, this time for good. "The Jets thought they were gonna repeat," Bell said. "We shut 'em down."

The Dallas Cowboys very well might have blown the Buffalo Bills out of Super Bowl XXVII no matter what. But through much of the first half, it was a tight battle.

By the second quarter, Dallas led, 14–7, when Buffalo got a first down at the Cowboys' 4. A score here would tie the game and give Buffalo—losers of the last two Super Bowls—much-needed confidence.

Fullback Carwell Gardner plowed through the defense to the 1. The Bills tried a counter play for Thurman Thomas that had already produced a two-yard touchdown run. But linebacker Vinson Smith nailed him for no gain, leaving Thomas limping off the field. Kenneth Davis came in as a replacement, took a handoff, and burst toward a hole near left tackle. Quarterback Jim Kelly began raising his arms to signal the touchdown he saw coming. But rather than diving in low, Davis charged right at linebacker Ken Norton, who wrapped him up 18 inches from the promised land.

The Cowboys read the call in from the Buffalo sidelines and knew a pass was coming, so they switched up their defense. Defensive end Tony Tolbert drilled Kelly as he was rolling out; Kelly barely got his pass off, a floater to the end zone, where Dallas safety Thomas Everett was waiting to intercept it. "We had a play called, but not for that defense," admitted coach Marv Levy afterward. The Bills had no answer for the Cowboys defense—or their offense—the rest of the game, falling in the end, 52–17.

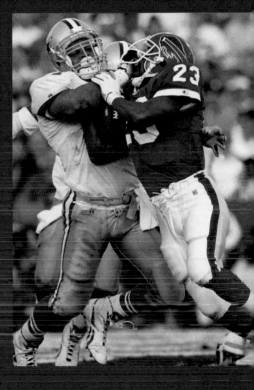

The Cowboys' Ken Norton (left) stops the Bills' Kenneth Davis (23) at the goal line in the first quarter of Super Bowl XXVII. (AP Photo/Eric Risberg)

Kansas City Chiefs' linebacking legend Willie Lanier. (AP Photo/NFL)

THE GREAT QUARTERBACKS

The heartbeat of a football team is the quarterback position, and I think everyone who has any intelligence about the game understands you must have consistency at that position to be a championship team. — Philadelphia Eagles quarterback Ron Jaworski

1 | JOHNNY UNITAS

Johnny Unitas and head coach Don Shula in 1964. (AP Photo/ NFL Photos)

When he was 10 years old, Johnny Unitas and his sister, Shirley, were both bitten by the family dog. Each required 21 rabies shots, and the painful procedure, described in the book *Johnny U*, punctured skin all over their young bodies.

Unitas refused to cry, telling his sister, "It's only a needle."

Even at that early age, Unitas had a thick skin.

It served him well as he found himself questioned, criticized, and rejected time and again in his struggle to prove that he belonged on a football field.

Unitas grew up in poverty, and fatherless after his dad died of kidney failure when Unitas was just five. He was nearly kicked off his high school team before he took his first snap because he was deemed too small. Along with the fear that Unitas might get hurt playing with bigger kids, his coaches wondered if he could be successful in a sport where strength and durability were so important. But after he uncoiled that magical arm, nobody mentioned his size again.

Until he tried to play college ball. Unitas was rejected by Notre Dame, again because of his slight build. He had grown to 5'11", but weighed only 137 pounds.

But the University of Louisville, coming off a losing season and lacking the financial resources for extensive recruiting, was willing to take a chance on a high school kid whose prowess had spread by word of mouth. Unitas wound up playing his collegiate ball there and did well enough to be picked by the Pittsburgh Steelers in the ninth round of the 1955 draft, the 102nd player taken. But with three weeks remaining in training camp, he was cut for being too slow, not only physically but mentally in terms of picking up the offense.

Said Pittsburgh's coach, Walter Kiesling, of Unitas, "He'll never be anything."

Desperate to play football, Unitas settled for earning $6 a game as the quarterback of the Bloomfield Rams, a semipro team, while keeping his day job on a construction crew.

"I always thought I could play pro ball," Unitas said. "I had confidence in my ability. You have to. If you don't, who will?"

Given a second chance by the Baltimore Colts, Unitas went from semipro to All-Pro to all-time, becoming one of the greatest quarterbacks in NFL history.

He had come a long way from the meager days of his youth. In the opinion of Minnesota Viking

Johnny Unitas at a rookie training camp with the Steelers in 1955. (AP Photo/NFL Photos)

coach Norm Van Brocklin, Unitas was driven to the top by his memories of growing up at the bottom of society.

"We should have won," said Van Brocklin of a 1965 game between the Vikings and the Colts, "but Unitas is a guy who knows what it was to eat potato soup seven days a week as a kid. That's what beat us."

That and supreme confidence. Asked if the possibility of throwing an interception affected his play-calling, Unitas said, "When you know what you're doing, you're not intercepted."

He will always be best remembered as the star of what became popularly known as "the Greatest Game Ever Played," the 1958 NFL championship battle between Baltimore and the New York Giants.

In what was the Super Bowl of its day, the Colts won, 23–17, in the first sudden-death game ever played. Unitas's heroics in two unforgettable drives, one to tie the game in regulation time and the other to win it in overtime, transfixed the nation, made Unitas an instant superstar, and generated unprecedented interest in pro football, leading to its eventual emergence as the national pastime.

Unitas was known for his stoic demeanor on the field. Touchdown pass or interception, his facial expression was the same.

"You get emotional at weddings and funerals. Football is just a game," he said.

Unitas's favorite target, receiver Raymond Berry, said that what made the quarterback exceptional "was his uncanny instinct for calling the right play at the right time, his icy composure under fire, his fierce competitiveness, and his utter disregard for his own safety."

Punishment and pain, two occupational hazards for every quarterback, were endured by Unitas without a crack in that stone face. The kid who bravely withstood the sting of a needle withstood a lot more as an adult without flinching.

But Unitas wasn't about to be a mere punching bag. He found ways to counterpunch.

"A guy broke through the line, hit [Unitas], pushed his head in the ground," teammate Bubba Smith told ESPN. "He called the same play, let the guy come through, and broke his nose with the football. I said, 'That's my hero.'"

On one occasion when Don Shula was coaching the Colts, he sent in the field goal unit on fourth down. Unitas waved them off, went for the touchdown, and got it.

"Don't do that to me again," Shula told Unitas when he came off the field.

"No," Unitas replied, "you've got that wrong. Don't do that to me again."

Unitas wound up winning three titles with Baltimore: 1958, 1959, and 1971, the last in Super Bowl V. In all, the Colts played in five championship games, including two Super Bowls, in the Unitas years.

Unitas played 18 seasons, 17 with Baltimore and a final year with the San Diego Chargers long past his prime, before retiring at 40.

Was he the best who ever played?

Hall of Fame quarterback Sid Luckman thought so. "Better than me," Luckman said. "Better than Sammy Baugh, better than anyone."

Among his accomplishments is an NFL record that may never be broken. Unitas threw a touchdown pass in 47 straight games, a mark that compares in degree of difficulty to Joe DiMaggio's 56-game hitting streak.

Three days before his death from a heart attack in 2002 at the age of 69, Unitas sent a birthday card to his sister Shirley.

On it Unitas had written, "Don't forget to take the time to smell the flowers. Watch out for the bees."

Johnny Unitas (left) and wide receiver Raymond Berry (right) in the early 1960s. (AP Photo/NFL Photos)

2 | JOE MONTANA

Notre Dame quarterback Joe Montana with head coach Dan Devine. (AP Photo/WFH)

49ers owner Eddie DeBartolo Jr. (right) congratulates coach Bill Walsh (left) and quarterback Joe Montana in the locker room after their Super Bowl XIX win over the Dolphins. (AP Photo)

Tom Landry didn't become one of the greatest coaches of all time by making mistakes. But he made a big one in the third round of the 1979 draft by skipping over the name at the top of his chart. It was a quarterback, and the Dallas Cowboys already had Roger Staubach (about to play his last season). "We don't really need another quarterback," Landry said.

But who wouldn't need or want Joe Montana?

The San Francisco 49ers were more than happy to take Landry's leftovers, grabbing Montana to launch one of the great careers in league history.

"I don't even think," said 49er owner Eddie DeBartolo Jr., "that [coach] Bill Walsh, with all his foresight and with all his brilliance, could ever have realized what we were in the midst of when we took a chance on that skinny kid from Notre Dame. It changed our lives forever."

Montana played for the 49ers for 12 full seasons, led them into the postseason nine times, and won four Super Bowls before finishing up his career with two seasons and two more playoff appearances with the Kansas City Chiefs.

"Montana was in a zone . . . for about six years," said Jim Mandich of the Dolphins radio network.

Or maybe longer. His mother, Theresa M. Montana, told *Sports Illustrated* that her son was already making daredevil moves while still an infant.

"He used to wreck his crib by standing up and rocking," she said. "Then he'd climb up on the side and jump to our bed. You'd hear a thump in the middle of the night and know he hit the bed and went on the floor."

Landry should have known better than anybody what Montana was capable of on a football field.

At Notre Dame, he was known for pulling off fourth-quarter rallies, but none was more impressive than the one that occurred in Dallas. It was New Year's Day 1979, the Cotton Bowl, the Fighting Irish vs. the University of Houston. Notre Dame was trailing, 34–12, midway through the fourth quarter. With Montana at the controls, the Irish scored 23 points in about seven and a half minutes to win, 35–34, the winning points the result of a Montana touchdown pass with two seconds to play.

Arguably Montana's most memorable performance as a pro came in a 1989 rally he led on football's biggest stage. It was Super Bowl XXIII, and the 49ers were on their own 8-yard line, trailing the Cincinnati Bengals, 16–13, with just over three minutes to play.

Montana proceeded to lead his squad down the field, finishing with a 10-yard, game-winning touchdown pass to John Taylor.

The quarterback's heroics became known as "Montana Magic."

"Joe Montana," said receiver-turned-broadcaster Cris Collinsworth, "is not human."

Walsh didn't credit Montana's ability to the supernatural, merely to skills that were "inherent, instinctive, genetic."

Even when he was finishing up his career in Kansas City, Montana retained his trademark sharpness. At the age of 37, he led the Chiefs to a 27–24 victory over the Pittsburgh Steelers in a first-round playoff game.

"He carved us up," said Steelers defensive back Rod Woodson, "like it was Thanksgiving."

The end came for Montana at 38, and he wasn't happy about it.

"In sports," he said, "you play from the time you're eight years old, and then you're done forever."

Done but, in the case of Montana, never forgotten.

Montana makes a pass in Super Bowl XXIII. (AP Photo/ NFL Photos)

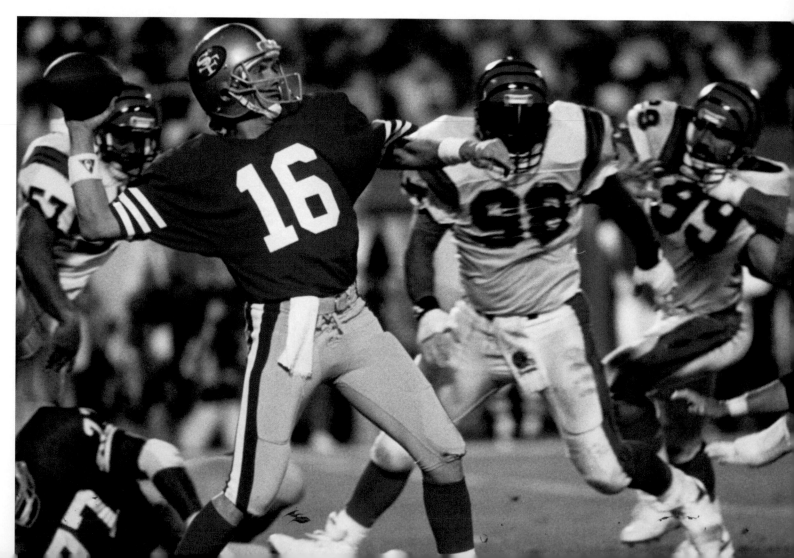

Wearing his Hall of Fame jacket, Montana
waves to the crowd during a game in 2000.
(AP Photo/Greg Trott)

3 | TERRY BRADSHAW

Terry Bradshaw signs a multi-year contract with the Pittsburgh Steelers in the city's new Three Rivers Stadium. Looking on are (from left) his father, William Bradshaw; Steelers vice president Dan Rooney; and Robert Fugh, his lawyer. (AP Photo/Harry Cabluck)

Dallas Cowboys linebacker Thomas "Hollywood" Henderson once said that Terry Bradshaw was so dumb that he "couldn't spell 'cat' if you spotted him the 'c' and the 'a'."

Bradshaw responded by proving he could spell R-I-N-G-S.

Bradshaw was the first pick in the 1970 draft, selected by the Pittsburgh Steelers, then a franchise that had been woefully inept throughout most of its existence. Bradshaw, however, gave the Steelers an extreme makeover after struggling his first two seasons, leading Pittsburgh to four Super Bowl triumphs.

One might think that a Steelers fan, rooting for a team that had never even won a division title and that considered a .500 season something to brag about, might show some patience with a young quarterback.

Think again.

Bradshaw had been an All-American at Louisiana Tech. But when he threw 46 interceptions and only 19 touchdown passes in his first two seasons at Pittsburgh, the fans let him have it, picking on his Louisiana roots.

Playing off the fact that he was born in Shreveport, they called him "the Bayou Bumpkin" and a lot of other things that made Henderson seem kind in comparison.

"I always wanted everyone to like me," said Bradshaw in the book *No Easy Game*.

> I wanted the city of Pittsburgh to be proud of me. But my first few seasons, I could count the number of people on my bandwagon on one finger. I had people call me a dummy and a hick. I had a lady stop me outside the stadium and tell me I stunk. I heard the people cheer when I got hurt. Rub up against enough briar patches and your hide will get pretty tough. Mine did.

Bradshaw knew how to tame the crowd.

"The only way to shut everybody up is to win," he said.

With one unforgettable throw, a throw that didn't even hit the mark, Bradshaw shut them up. It was a throw that became known as "the Immaculate Reception."

The dispute lingers to this day about who first touched the last pass thrown by Bradshaw in Pittsburgh's 1972 first-round playoff game against the Oakland Raiders. But there is no disputing the fact that fullback Franco Harris wound up with the ball in his hands and raced into the end zone to score the deciding points in a 13–7 Steelers victory.

They advanced no further in that postseason, but two years later, with the reins firmly in Bradshaw's hands, Pittsburgh began an incredible run that resulted in four Super Bowl victories in six seasons.

Bradshaw guarantees that will never happen again.

"You can chisel that sucker in stone," he said.

There were plenty of stars on those teams, rushers like Harris, receivers like Lynn Swann and

Bradshaw at Louisiana Tech University in 1969. (AP Photo/NFL Photos)

John Stallworth, defenders like "Mean Joe" Greene and Jack Lambert. But Bradshaw's coach, Chuck Noll, made it very clear who was the heart and soul of those Steelers.

"Realistically, the quarterback should just be one-twenty-second of the team," Noll said, "but that's not quite the way it works. Terry is a much bigger part of us than that. He's the one who makes us go. He's the leader out there, the driving force."

It was a drive Bradshaw relished.

"Imagine yourself," he said, "sitting on top of a great thoroughbred horse. You sit up there and you just feel that power. That's what it was like, playing quarterback on that team. It was a great ride."

When the ride was over, after 14 seasons in Pittsburgh, Bradshaw retired and traded his helmet for a headset, becoming a network analyst. That was when he found himself struggling against a new opponent: depression.

After his third divorce, he said, he "could not bounce back." Anxiety attacks resulted in crying spells, weight loss, and insomnia.

Bradshaw was diagnosed with clinical depression. Thanks to therapy and antidepressants, he has been able to get it under control.

Bradshaw is a member of the Pro Football Hall of Fame and has been an actor, both in movies and on TV, author, singer, motivational speaker, and football analyst for nearly three decades.

"I'm happy," he said. "I think I've lived a pretty full life."

Not bad for a Bayou Bumpkin.

Bradshaw playing for Woodlawn High School in Shreveport, Louisiana, in 1965. (AP Photo/ NFL Photos)

Bradshaw turns around to hand the ball off to running back Franco Harris (32) during Super Bowl XIII. (AP Photo)

4 | JOHN ELWAY

When his high school football games were over, teammates and friends of quarterback John Elway headed to a nearby pizza parlor to celebrate or commiserate.

Elway went home.

It wasn't that he was antisocial, but he first wanted to review the game with his dad, Jack.

Jack Elway was more than just a supportive parent. He had been a college quarterback at Washington State and went on to coach at the high school and college levels (including Stanford and San Jose State) and scout for NFL teams. His son was always his star pupil.

John Elway played in his first football game prior to entering the fifth grade. He scored four touchdowns. According to the *Denver Post*, a spectator, who was also a coach, told Jack, "Either every kid on that field is the worst football player I've ever seen or your boy is the greatest player I've ever seen."

The latter proved to be true.

He went on to play in high school, at Stanford, and then in the NFL for 16 years with the Denver Broncos. Elway led Denver to five Super Bowls, winning the last two. He passed for 300 touchdowns and over 51,000 yards. And he is the all-time NFL leader with 47 fourth-quarter rallies.

Elway went into the Hall of Fame in 2004, three years after the death of his father. He used the occasion to pay tribute to the man who had been by his side on the road to Canton.

"My dad wasn't just my best friend," Elway said. "He was my hero, my mentor, my inspiration. He was the keeper of my reality check list, the compass that guided my life and my career, and he taught me the number-one lesson of my life— always make your family proud. Now that he's gone, I thank God every day for letting him see the Broncos win two Super Bowls. My dad didn't so much teach me how to play football, but why to play. He taught me to compete, to never give up, to play every down like it's your last. He taught me to appreciate the game, to respect it, to play it like it was meant to be played. He taught me to enjoy my successes and learn from my failures. And above all, he told me to make sure, when you go out with your offensive linemen, you pick up the tab."

When Elway retired after the 1998 season, his father said, "If I had drawn a blueprint for what you want a son to be, I would have undersold this one. I'm proud of him as a football player, but I'm prouder to be able to call him my best friend."

The Super Bowl victories are considered the highlights of Elway's career, but his former coach, Mike Shanahan, pointed to the first three of their Super Bowl teams, teams that lacked a powerful running game, as another measurement of Elway's greatness.

"I don't think there is anybody," said Shanahan, "who could have brought us to the three Super Bowls with the cast we had other than John Elway."

"I've always joked about Joe Montana not appreciating his Super Bowls nearly as much as I do because he never lost one," said Elway. "We lost three before we got one. I've experienced the highest of highs and lowest of lows. I think, to really appreciate anything, you have to be at both ends of the spectrum."

Other than the Super Bowls, Elway is best remembered by two words: "the Drive." Stuck on his

John Elway scrambles during the third quarter of Super Bowl XXXII against the Green Bay Packers in San Diego. (AP Photo/Ed Reinke)

Elway (right) and
Denver head coach
Mike Shanahan
laugh on the vic-
tory stand after their
Super Bowl XXXIII
victory. (AP Photo/
Amy Sancetta)

own 2-yard line and trailing by seven points with five and a half minutes to play in the AFC championship game in 1987 against the Cleveland Browns, Elway fought his way down the field, getting the tying touchdown with 37 seconds remaining on the 15th play of the Drive. Denver won in overtime to qualify for its first Super Bowl.

"The way he played that drive," said sportswriter Ray Didinger, "is the very definition of clutch quarterbacking."

"John's ability to improvise, to find a way to win, was the greatest I've ever seen," said Gary Kubiak, Elway's backup quarterback who went on to become head coach of the Houston Texans.

"I look at my career, and it's still hard for me to believe the way things turned out and how things happened," Elway said. "I've been so blessed."

And so appreciated by Bronco fans.

"The only thing bigger [than Elway] in Colorado," said Tim Schmidt, a business partner, "is Pikes Peak."

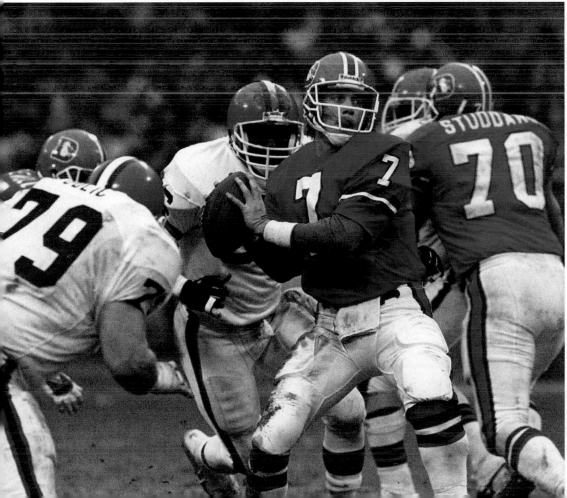

Elway prepares to send the ball downfield in the 1986 AFC championship game against the Browns. (AP Photo)

Elway lunges for the goal line to score a 10-yard touchdown in Super Bowl XXI. At left is the Giants' Harry Carson (53). Denver's Dave Studdard (70) takes out the Giants' Leonard Marshall. (AP Photo/ Phil Sandlin)

5 | TOM BRADY

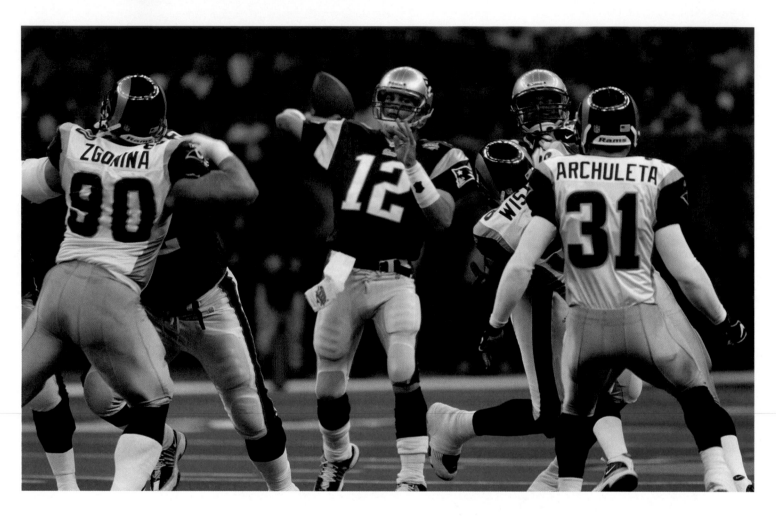

Tom Brady (12) throws in the third quarter of Super Bowl XXXVI as the Rams' Jeff Zgonina (90) and Adam Archuleta (31) defend. (AP Photo/Doug Mills)

What if?

Those are the two most intriguing words in sports. And never more so than in the case of Drew Bledsoe and Tom Brady.

Bledsoe was in his ninth season as the New England Patriots quarterback when he took off on a run down the sideline in the Patriots' second game of the 2001 season.

In pursuit was New York Jets linebacker Mo Lewis, who hit Bledsoe with such force that he ultimately knocked the veteran off the roster, but inadvertently opened the door for a bigger menace to opponents than Bledsoe ever was.

With Bledsoe out with internal bleeding and a collapsed lung, New England coach Bill Belichick had to turn the offense over to Tom Brady, Bledsoe's unproven backup.

Brady had dreamed of such an opportunity for two decades, since he had sat in Candlestick Park as a four-year-old in 1982 and watched Joe Montana throw the touchdown pass to Dwight Clark that launched the San Francisco 49ers' dynasty.

But dreams and reality proved quite different. A quarterback at Michigan, Brady was a full-time starter for only one season.

Brady celebrates with the Vince Lombardi Trophy after the Patriots' 32–29 victory over the Panthers in Super Bowl XXXVIII. (AP Photo/Dave Martin)

Michigan quarter-
back Tom Brady
passes in the second
quarter of a 1998
game against Penn
State. (AP Photo/
Duane Burleson)

"How high do you want to draft a guy who they're really trying to replace as a starter at college?" said Belichick on selecting Brady in the 2000 draft.

Not too high, as it turned out. The Patriots took him in the sixth round with the 199th pick.

"Don't lose hope yet," Brady's father, Tom Sr., told him, according to *Sports Illustrated*, as player after player was called before him. "Even Montana wasn't taken until the third round."

"The thing with Brady was really the traits: his work ethic, his intelligence, his decision-making," Belichick said. "I think a lot of the draft process is [about] not where the player is right now, but where the player will be a year from now, or where he'll be two calendar years from now.

"I don't think I've ever seen a player improve as much as Tom did."

Brady improved so much that, by the time Bledsoe was ready to return, his job had been filled.

Under Brady, New England finished the 2001 regular season 11-3 and went on to upset the St. Louis Rams in the Super Bowl.

"Here's this kid," said sportswriter Ralph Vacchiano, "who just basically got handed this starting job, and he's out on that field like he's in his backyard."

As it turned out, Brady, the man whom sportswriter Peter King refers to as "the total flatliner" for his calm, cool approach, had just begun a glory-filled journey that would take him to the pantheon of NFL quarterbacks. Brady would lead New England to two more Super Bowl victories, giving him three in four years, and appeared headed to his greatest year in 2007 when he threw a league-record 50 touchdown passes in an undefeated regular season. But the Patriots' perfect season was ruined when they were upset by the New York Giants in the Super Bowl.

Still, at least in the eyes of former quarterback Joe Theismann, Brady had earned the right to be linked with Montana, his hero, if not above him.

"I felt that Joe Montana was the greatest quarterback who ever played the game," said Theismann in declaring that Brady had surpassed him. "My criteria is, have you won with different people around you? Have you won at different times in your career? Have you won in different ways?"

In Brady's case, said Theismann, the answer was yes to all of the above.

Brady's appeal has extended far beyond the football field thanks to his good looks and attention to fashion. *GQ* magazine named him one of its 50 historical "icons of cool."

"You see a guy in the locker room, and he's just one of the guys," said Patriots linebacker Larry Izzo of Brady. "Then you go out on the street and it's, like, rock star–type stuff."

"It's just the position," said Brady in trying to deflect the attention. "If I was anybody else on the team, they wouldn't even care."

And, he insists, what he has done in the past will be of little help in the future.

"I don't think there's a lot of carryover from year to year," Brady said. "I don't think anybody cares what you did the year before. I don't care about three years ago. I don't care about two years ago. I don't care about last year. The only thing I care about is this week's game."

Brady is sacked by Giants defensive end Michael Strahan (92) in the third quarter of Super Bowl XLII. (AP Photo/Paul Sancya)

6 | BRETT FAVRE

Brett Favre celebrates his diving touchdown in the second quarter of Super Bowl XXXI. (AP Photo/David J. Phillip)

Through triumph and failure, pain and heartbreak, the glory years with the Packers, the agonizing year with the Jets, and the spectacular comeback with the Vikings, there was one unshakable constant in the career of Brett Favre. When his offense lined up for its first snap of the game, Favre was standing behind the center.

In 2010, his 20th season in the NFL, Favre extended his record for the most consecutive starts at any position to 297 games until a shoulder injury finally sidelined him. It was a streak that began in 1992.

"His record for most consecutive starts will never be broken," said Cincinnati Bengals quarterback Carson Palmer. "It's one of the most amazing records in sports. I guarantee you, he gets an im-

mense amount of respect from every quarterback in the NFL for that record."

Favre has broken more records than a tornado surging through a music store. Look at any significant statistical category for an NFL quarterback—passes attempted, passes completed, passing yards, touchdown passes, wins—and you'll find Favre's name at the top of the list. He also led the Green Bay Packers to two Super Bowls, winning Super Bowl XXXI against the New England Patriots in 1997 but losing the following year to the Denver Broncos.

But it's the consecutive-games mark that best defines Favre. It demonstrates his durability, determination, and passion for the game.

The 41-year-old quarterback shrugs off his accomplishment, saying, "At this point, I'm pretty grateful for every game played."

His ability to fight through any adversity to get on the field didn't begin when he turned pro. Heading into his senior year at Southern Mississippi, Favre was involved in an auto accident in July and injured so badly that 30 inches of his small intestine had to be removed.

He lost 40 pounds, but incredibly, when Southern Miss opened the season, there was Favre, a month after his operation, in the starting lineup and leading his team to a 27–24 upset of Alabama en route to an 8-3 season.

Said Favre's coach, Curley Hallman, of his quarterback's performance against Alabama, "Brett was larger than life."

The same could be said of his performance on December 22, 2003. Just a day after his father, Irwin, died, Favre suited up to face the Oakland Raiders on *Monday Night Football*.

He passed for 311 yards and four touchdowns. And that was in the first 30 minutes.

"What he did in the first half—four touchdowns and no interceptions—shoot, it should probably go down as one of the best one-half performances ever," said Reggie McKenzie, the Packers' director of pro personnel. "If this isn't the best, I don't know what is."

Favre looks to throw during Super Bowl XXXI. At right is Aaron Taylor (73). (AP Photo/Dave Martin)

"You can put as many superlatives in there as you want," Green Bay offensive tackle Mark Tauscher said, "and I still don't think that would cover it. [Imagine] the things that had to be going through his mind. What a champion he is. I think that's the best way to say it."

"I know that my dad would have wanted me to play," Favre said. "I love him so much, and I love this game. It meant a great deal to me, to my dad, to my family. I did not expect this kind of performance, but I know he was watching tonight."

Favre was also able to play through the difficult days after his wife, Deanna, was diagnosed with breast cancer.

"I remember," she said on Fox News, "getting in bed one night with my bald head, looking at him, saying, 'I bet you never thought you would sleep with a bald girl.'

"But he was great. He was so compassionate, so caring, so supportive, encouraging me to rest and let other people help. He was phenomenal."

"Family is obviously the most important thing," Favre said. "There was a time when I thought football was the most important."

Favre is pressured by Broncos defensive tackle Keith Traylor (94) during Super Bowl XXXII. (AP Photo/Elaine Thompson)

Favre is escorted off the field with his wife, Deanna, after the Packers defeated the Raiders on December 22, 2003. Favre's father passed away just the day before. (AP Photo/Paul Sakuma)

7 | TROY AIKMAN

Troy Aikman led his team to three Super Bowl triumphs, one fewer than the record number by Joe Montana and Terry Bradshaw. More than Johnny Unitas, John Elway, and Brett Favre.

Yet in discussions about the NFL's greatest quarterbacks, Aikman's name rarely surfaces.

Why? Because of that number three again, as in triplets. That was the name given to the offensive trio rightly credited with jointly leading the Dallas Cowboys to victory in the 1990s in Super Bowl XXVII (over the Buffalo Bills), XXVIII (Buffalo again), and XXX (Pittsburgh Steelers). Sharing the glory with Aikman, a Hall of Famer, were two others whose busts also reside in Canton, running back Emmitt Smith and receiver Michael Irvin.

Still, in that first Super Bowl, Aikman threw four touchdown passes and was named the game's MVP.

He has no problem sharing the stage.

"I feel wholeheartedly," he said, "that our success was linked together in so many different ways. I think that all three of us . . . pushed aside our egos and selfishness in order for the team to thrive."

There were times when it appeared that Aikman would never get the chance to thrive. His life is best summed up in the title of a book he wrote, *Things Change*.

Born in West Covina, California, he had to wear casts on both feet up to his knees until he was 14 months old because of congenital foot problems.

When the family moved to Oklahoma, Aikman,

coming out of high school with his foot problems long behind him, jumped at the chance to play for coach Barry Switzer at the University of Oklahoma.

But when Aikman realized that Switzer wasn't going to alter his focus on the running game to accommodate his talented quarterback, Aikman was no longer jumping for joy.

"He changed . . . [the offense] a little bit," Aikman told *Sports Illustrated*, "but the only real difference when I played was that we threw the ball 12 times a game instead of seven."

The issue was settled when Aikman suffered a broken ankle and lost his starting job. So things changed again.

For the better.

He transferred to UCLA, where he got the opportunity to unleash his arm and was so impressive that the Cowboys made him the number-one overall pick of the 1989 draft.

But then things changed again. After leading UCLA to 20 wins in 24 games as a starter, Aikman joined a struggling Dallas squad and went 1-15 in his first season.

He had always believed that the key to success on game day could be found in the week leading up to it, so he buried his head in the game plan and continued working.

"He prepared every week in infinite detail," said Wade Wilson, a Cowboy backup quarterback. "He played in the same offense so long, he had to know it better than the coaches, but he was always

Troy Aikman throws during
second-quarter action in
Super Bowl XXX. (AP Photo/
Beth Keiser)

taking notes. He'd come to meetings with all kinds of different-colored pens and write things down like he was hearing them for the first time. Then he'd study it all as if he was preparing for a test and anything less than 100 percent was unacceptable."

That's also the way Aikman regarded his performance on the field.

"If we were out there and a defense stopped us, Troy could deal with that," Irvin said. "He knew they were pros just like us, and they were doing their jobs. But an interception . . . he couldn't take it. He would feel like he hurt his team. It would eat him up. In Troy's mind, the perfect game for a quarterback wouldn't have to have 10 touchdown passes. It would have to have no interceptions."

"The things that stand out are his accuracy and toughness," said broadcaster Pat Summerall, a former player himself. "He hit receivers in stride as well as any quarterback that ever played the game. And you couldn't rattle him. We saw him take unbelievable hits—not all of them sacks, mind you—and get up on the next play and hit [a receiver] for a key first down."

While that toughness fueled Aikman's brilliant career, it also led to its premature ending. After suffering four concussions over a 20-game span, Aikman retired at 34 after 12 seasons.

He had made the most of that time. He was voted into the Hall of Fame on his first year of eligibility, validation that he indeed belongs among the best to ever play the game.

Aikman celebrates the Cowboys' 30–13 win over the Bills in Super Bowl XXVIII. (AP Photo/ Doug Mills)

Aikman scrambles during the first quarter in Super Bowl XXVII. (AP Photo/Susan Ragan)

8 | ROGER STAUBACH

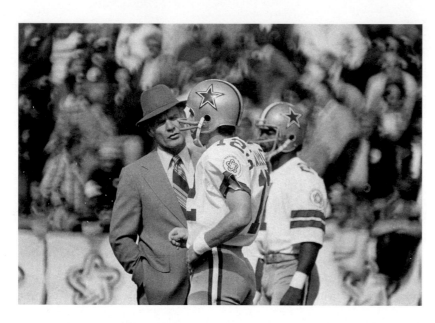

Cowboys coach Tom Landry and Roger Staubach prior to Super Bowl X. (AP Photo)

Since the Dallas Cowboys were known as "America's Team," it was logical that Roger Staubach would be nicknamed "Captain America."

Like the fictional superhero, Staubach would swoop in at the last minute—or more accurately, the last few seconds—to save the day.

Also known as "Captain Comeback" and "Roger the Dodger," Staubach engineered 23 come-from-behind victories, 17 in the final two minutes of the games.

"Roger never knew when the game was over," said Dallas tight end Billy Joe DuPree.

"Staubach was one of those Hemingway-esque heroes who showed grace under pressure," said Steve Sabol of NFL Films.

Staubach also showed an ability that differentiated him from the other great comeback quarterbacks, like Johnny Unitas and John Elway. Staubach was also effective on the ground, blessed with the quickness and elusiveness to have been a running back had he not possessed the arm to be a brilliant quarterback.

That made him a nightmare to opposing defenses, not to mention a one-man highlight reel. Staubach would provide some of the most memorable NFL moments of the 1970s.

Staubach didn't even want to be a quarterback in high school. It was his coach at Cincinnati's Purcell High, Jim McCarthy, who moved him to that position.

"I told him," Staubach said, "'Coach, I don't want to be a quarterback.' I was a receiver and a defensive back. I asked why he wanted me and he told me, 'Because the other guys listen to you.'"

Staubach went on to play for the Naval Academy, winning the Heisman Trophy as a junior. Navy coach Wayne Hardin called him "the greatest quarterback Navy ever had."

He would leave a lasting imprint on pro football as well. The term "Hail Mary" is used in the sport to describe an all-or-nothing, last-second heave by a desperate quarterback.

A Staubach specialty? The expression was coined to describe one of his throws.

It came at the conclusion of a 1975 playoff game against the Minnesota Vikings. Staubach's touchdown pass to receiver Drew Pearson provided the margin of victory in a 17–14 Cowboy win.

"The play never dies," Pearson said. "I can't tell you how many times people have come up to me and told me exactly where they were and what they were doing when it happened. It has become part of American folklore."

Staubach's heroics resulted in four trips to the Super Bowl for Dallas, the Cowboys winning Super Bowl VI over the Miami Dolphins and XII over the Denver Broncos.

"He was a great competitor," said former Colts

and Ravens coach Ted Marchibroda. "Staubach could do it more ways than most quarterbacks."

"Roger Staubach might be the best combination of a passer, an athlete, and a leader ever to play in the NFL," said his coach, Tom Landry.

While Landry and Staubach will be forever linked in Cowboy history, it was not a smooth relationship. Landry was the stern disciplinarian, a master strategist who favored an ironclad game plan. Landry insisted on calling the plays and expected them to be followed.

Staubach could be a mad scrambler on occasion, but there was method to his madness. He wanted to call the plays himself, keeping the option to use his running skill or otherwise improvise when necessary.

"Coach Landry wasn't happy with my scrambling," Staubach conceded. "It caused a running feud between us. But I put up with his play-calling, and he put up with my scrambling."

Staubach played 11 seasons with the Cowboys, retiring at 37 after a series of concussions, and went on to a very successful career in real estate. He was voted into the Hall of Fame in 1985.

No less an authority than Otto Graham, himself one of football's greatest quarterbacks, saw Staubach's greatness.

"I coached the College All-Star Game for 10 years," said Graham. "Of all the quarterbacks in that game, Roger was the best I ever had. He was a great leader. That's the most important thing for a quarterback."

Staubach earned MVP honors in Super Bowl VI after throwing for two touchdowns. (AP Photo/NFL Photos)

9 | PEYTON MANNING

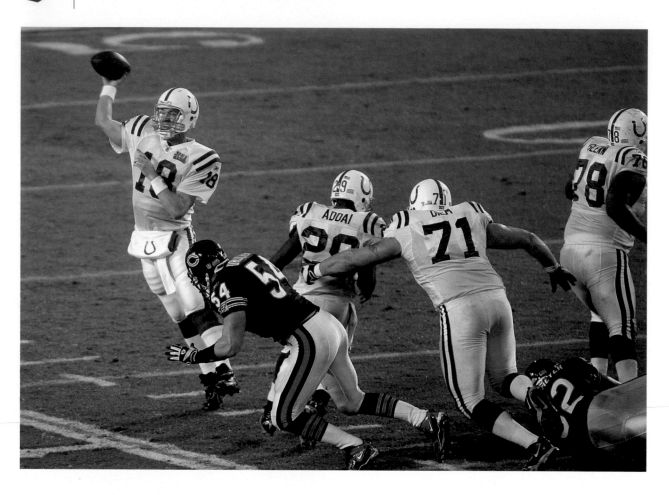

Colts quarterback Peyton Manning (18) unloads a pass against the Bears in Super Bowl XLI. (AP Photo/Paul Spinelli)

Tennessee quarterback Peyton Manning (16) directs a play during their 31–17 win over Ole Miss. (AP Photo/Mark Humphrey)

Eleven-year-old Peyton Manning listened intently as George Fowler, his youth basketball coach, told his players why they had just suffered their first defeat.

"The reason you lost was that you didn't have your minds ready to play," Fowler said.

"The reason we lost," volunteered Manning, "is that you don't know what you are doing."

When Manning told his father, Archie, what he had said while they were driving home, Archie made a U-turn and drove Peyton to the coach's house for the youngster to apologize.

Even at that age, Manning's two sides were evident. There is the polite, personable Manning,

a megastar in the endorsement world. With all the commercials he does, his face is on TV more than a network anchor's.

And there is the highly competitive Manning, so cognizant of strategy that he has made himself into a coach as much as a player. He drives opposing defenses crazy at the line of scrimmage, wildly waving his arms and running up and down the line, all the while barking out signals, many of them phony to throw the other side off, as he looks for the tiniest telltale sign of the defense's intent.

Manning usually finds what he is looking for. Now in his 13th season with the Indianapolis Colts, he has twice led his team into the Super Bowl, win-

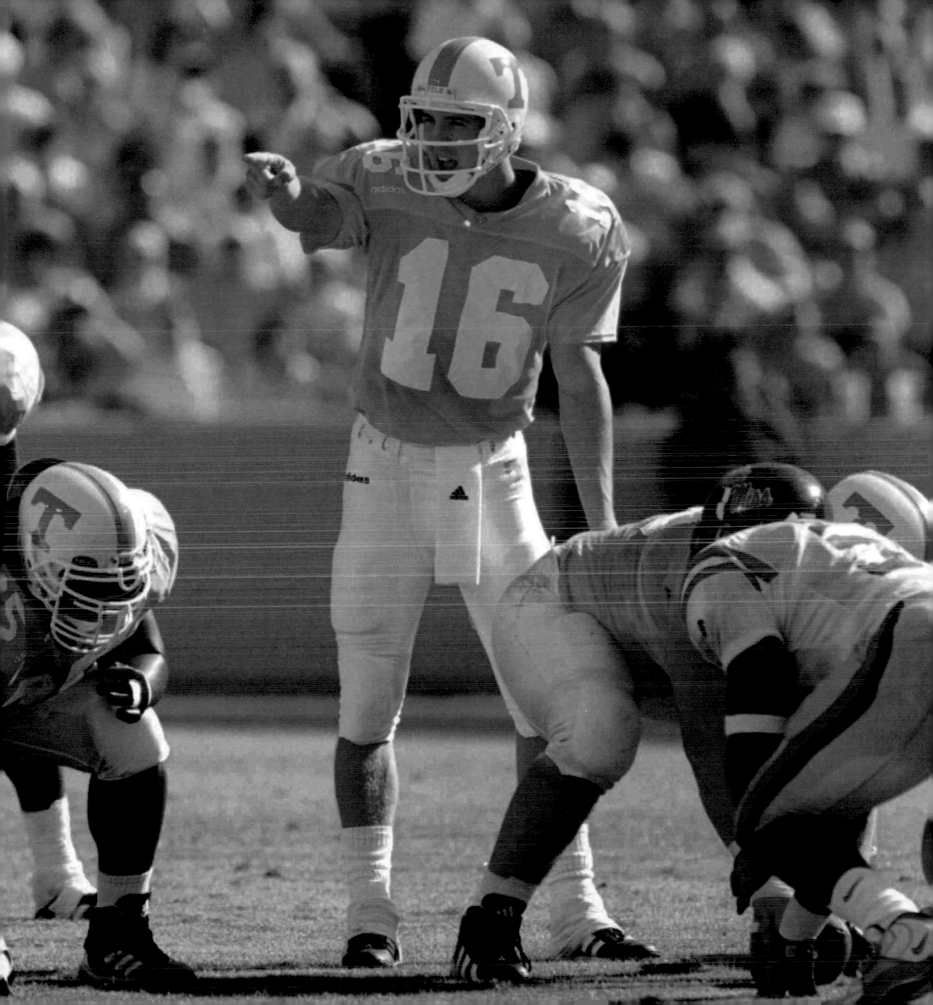

ning Super Bowl XLI against the Chicago Bears. After struggling in his rookie season, Manning has taken the Colts into the postseason every year but one since then, the team's regular-season win total reaching double figures in all 10 of those playoff-bound years.

In 2004, Manning set an NFL single-season record with 49 touchdown passes, a mark subsequently broken by Tom Brady, who threw 50 in 2007.

The great quarterbacks are also judged on their ability to rally their team in the fourth quarter, but this is a criterion Manning dismisses.

"You hear about how many fourth-quarter comebacks that a guy has," he said, "and I think it means a guy screwed up in the first three quarters."

Manning possesses a football mind and a quarterback's arm, but the first attribute usually mentioned when describing him is that work ethic.

"He's probably the hardest-working guy I've been around who has great ability," said his former coach Tony Dungy. "Overachievers work hard because they have to. Peyton has rare talent, but chooses to push himself like he doesn't."

Manning joined the Colts after setting two NCAA marks and 33 school records at Tennessee. Indianapolis made him the overall number-one pick in the 1998 draft.

NFL players, however, are less than impressed with a rookie's press clippings. They want to see how those clippings translate into production on the field.

Manning (right) and coach Tony Dungy talk before the start of a practice held a few days before Super Bowl XLI. (AP Photo/ Michael Conroy)

Peyton Manning (right) greets his brother, Giants quarterback Eli Manning, following a game pitting the brothers against each other in September 2010. (AP Photo/Darron Cummings)

"From the first day, it was his huddle," said Colts offensive tackle Adam Meadows. "Anyone who works as hard as he does gets respect."

If it seems like Manning was born to be a quarterback, that's because he was. As a toddler, he had a football in his hand as often as he had a bottle. Asked at age three what he wanted to be when he grew up, he said, "A quarterback."

What else would you expect from a toddler who watched his father fill that role? Archie was a quarterback at Mississippi, where he was a two-time All-American, and in the NFL for 14 years, the majority of that time with the New Orleans Saints.

Peyton's younger brother, Eli, has also upheld the family tradition. A star at Mississippi, Eli is now the quarterback of the New York Giants.

"I'm proud to be Archie's son," said Peyton. "Being a quarterback, I had my mentor and hero living in the same house."

"I never coached my sons," Archie told the *L.A. Times.* "I never pushed. Sometimes, I think if you do that, you just screw them up. But I was always there if they wanted to ask me anything."

Was there pressure on Peyton to live up to the Manning name?

"Pressure," said Peyton, "is something you feel when you don't know what the hell you're doing."

Manning raises the Vince Lombardi Trophy after the Colts' 29–17 win over the Chicago Bears. (AP Photo/Amy Sancetta)

10 | OTTO GRAHAM

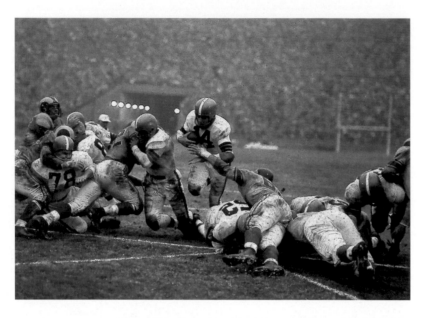

Otto Graham goes over from the 1-yard line for his final score against the Rams in the Browns' 38–14 victory in the 1955 NFL championship game. (AP Photo)

The Cleveland Browns' Otto Graham on the list of all-time great quarterbacks? That might be hard to believe for today's generation of fans, who see Graham as a figure on grainy black-and-white film wearing a funny helmet and playing in an era before the Super Bowl.

In one sentence, however, *Los Angeles Times* columnist Jim Murray stifled the debate as only a Pulitzer Prize winner can.

"Imagine a quarterback leading his team to ten straight Super Bowls today and you have a measure of the kind of man Otto Graham was," wrote Murray.

Not to mention the fact that Graham won seven of those games.

In making the case for his quarterback, coach Paul Brown said, "The test of a quarterback is where his team finishes. By that standard, Otto Graham was the best of all time."

Graham didn't need a football in his hands to demonstrate his talent. He went to Northwestern on a basketball scholarship, was a hoops All-American, and played one year professionally for the Rochester Royals. It was the same year he made his debut with the Browns. Both teams won championships that season.

Even Bo Jackson, called the greatest two-sport star ever, couldn't claim that distinction.

Actually, Graham didn't need any type of ball in his hands to excel. He played not only football and basketball at Northwestern but, as a music major, the piano, violin, coronet, and French horn as well.

Graham gave up music to concentrate on sports and later said that was his one regret.

He had shown potential. At 16, he was the Illinois French horn champion.

For Graham, it was just the first of many championships to come.

Brown first saw Graham when the quarterback led Northwestern to victory over Brown's Ohio State team in 1941. When Brown began assembling the Cleveland team to play in the new All-America Football Conference, he thought of Graham.

"I was getting a naval cadet's pay in World War II when Brown offered me a two-year contract at $7,500 per season," said Graham. "He also offered me a $1,000 bonus and $250 a month for the duration of the war. All I asked was, 'Where do I sign?' Old Navy men say I rooted for the war to last forever."

After the war ended, it was the Cleveland fans who were doing the rooting. Graham was the Browns' quarterback for 10 seasons and led them to a championship game each year. The AAFC was in existence for four seasons. With Graham at the controls, the Browns were that league's champions all four years.

Those who doubted Cleveland could succeed in the rival NFL were silenced when the Browns joined the league in 1950 and won the NFL title in their first season. They were back in the title game each of the next four seasons, winning in 1954 and '55.

In the 1954 NFL championship game, won by Cleveland, 56–10, over the Detroit Lions, Graham threw three touchdown passes and ran for three more.

That season, Graham also made a much-less-publicized but unique and everlasting contribution to the game at all its levels. When he suffered a deep cut on his face that required 13 stitches, a plastic bar was attached to his helmet at halftime to protect his face.

"That's my real claim to fame right there," Graham said. "I was the first guy who ever wore a face mask—college, high school, or pro."

"When you say 'Otto Graham,' people say, 'Yeah, he was a great quarterback, but . . . ' But what?" said *Houston Chronicle* sportswriter John Mc-Clain. "The problem is, they just can't remember seeing him. They didn't have TV."

Graham is stopped at the one-foot line by Washington Redskins guard Gene Pepper in a 1950 contest. Also shown are Browns players Weldon Humble (38), Frank Gatski (22), and Mac Speedie (58), and Redskins players Paul Lipscomb (76) and Jerry Houghton (71). (AP Photo/Julian C. Wilson)

Coach Paul Brown and quarterback Graham are shown in the dressing room after the Browns upended the Detroit Lions, 56–10, in the 1954 National Football League title game. The man on the left is Graham's father. (AP Photo)

7 | TOM MATTE

No position in football is harder to learn than quarterback. And no one ever had it tougher than Tom Matte.

Rather than easing into the role in training camp, his first solo effort was in a playoff game.

Rather than taking over for someone who had proven inadequate, he was replacing a quarterback by the name of Johnny Unitas.

The year was 1965. The Colts, still in Baltimore, were battling for a playoff spot down the stretch when they lost Unitas and his backup, Gary Cuozzo, with one game still remaining in the regular season.

Matte was the third-string quarterback, having played at Ohio State.

The Colts picked up veteran Ed Brown for their final game of the regular season, and he led them to a 20–17 win over the Los Angeles Rams, giving Baltimore a 10-3-1 record and a tie atop the Western Conference with the Green Bay Packers. Matte threw only seven passes in that game, connecting on just one for 19 yards, while also throwing an interception.

Ahead lay a playoff game with the Packers, and because Brown had been signed too late to qualify for the postseason, the fate of the Colts rested on the throwing arm of Matte.

In the book *Johnny U*, Don Shula, then Baltimore's coach, remembered calling Ohio State coach Woody Hayes.

"Tell me about Matte as a quarterback," Shula said.

"Great kid, wonderful young man," Hayes said.

"Yeah, yeah, Woody," Shula said, "but we're trying to beat Lombardi and the Packers here. Were there any negatives you can remember? It might help me prepare."

"Well," Hayes said, "he had a little trouble taking the snap from center."

How reassuring.

Shula put the plays on Matte's wristband, something new in those days, and held his breath.

"It was like a dream," said Matte.

It turned into a nightmare, but that wasn't Matte's fault.

He was only able to complete five of 12 passes for 40 yards, but the Colts scored a defensive touchdown and took Green Bay into a second overtime period, when Baltimore was finally beaten on a controversial Don Chandler field goal.

In those days, the losing teams in the conference championship games met in the Playoff Bowl.

That season the Colts were matched against the Dallas Cowboys. Baltimore won, 35–3, with Matte, the experience of a full game behind him, throwing for 165 yards and two touchdowns. He was named the game's MVP.

"We knew we could run on them, but they seemed surprised we threw the long ball," Matte said. "We said we would all week, but they apparently didn't believe what they read in the papers."

The Colts were thrilled to have Unitas back for the next season.

And Matte?

"I always had a lot of respect for him, and now I have so much more," Shula said. "We'll probably have to keep a Matte offense in our book."

But with Unitas back on the field, that Matte offense stayed in the book.

Colts quarterback Tom Matte (41) lines up behind the center in the 1966 playoff game against the Cowboys. (AP Photo/NFL Photos)

GREAT COMEBACKS

You hear about how many fourth-quarter comebacks that a guy has, and I think it means a guy screwed up in the first three quarters. — Peyton Manning, NFL quarterback

1 | JANUARY 3, 1993
BILLS 38, OILERS 35

The greatest comeback in NFL history, if not all of sports, doesn't top the list just because it involved a record-setting 32-point turnaround in the second half of a win-or-go-home playoff game. It is just as memorable because it was sparked by a backup quarterback and a backup running back who lit a fire under an injury-riddled team that seemed completely outclassed until—defying all odds—"the Comeback" sprang to life on a cold December day in Buffalo.

Although they had gone to the Super Bowl the two previous years, the Bills staggered into the playoffs, going 7-5 in the last 12 games of the 1992 season. The week before they took the field on that windy Sunday in Buffalo, they had lost their Hall of Fame quarterback, Jim Kelly, to injury in a feeble 27–3 loss to the very same Houston Oilers. They had also entered the AFC wild-card game without star linebacker Cornelius Bennett (hamstring), and Hall of Fame tailback Thurman Thomas was limited by a hip pointer.

Throughout the first half, there was no hint that the Bills had learned anything from the beating they had taken the week before. Quarterback Warren Moon, a master of the Oilers' "Run and Shoot," dissected Bills defensive coordinator Walt Corey's six-DB scheme, going 19-22 for 220 yards and four touchdowns. Buffalo backup quarterback Frank Reich, by contrast, generated just three points before opening the second half with a pass that

bounced off tight end Keith McKeller's hands. Oilers safety Bubba McDowell intercepted the deflection and raced untouched for a 58-yard TD.

Just like that, it was 35–3 less than two minutes into the second half, prompting an Oilers radio announcer to say, "The lights are on here at Rich Stadium. They've been on since this morning. They can pretty much turn 'em off on the Bills right now."

Bills coach Marv Levy would say that day and numerous other times over the years: "Did I think we had a chance at that point? Yeah, I thought we had a chance, about the same as winning the New York lottery."

Levy wasn't as frank with Reich. "Trying to encourage him a little bit, I said, 'Frank, you're going to lead the greatest comeback in the history of the National Football League.'" Reich had no reason to dismiss his coach's crazy speculation. Backup or not, he could draw on his own experience at Maryland, where he had once come off the bench at halftime trailing 31–0 and led the Terrapins to a record-setting 42–40 win over Miami.

"Do the math," Reich said years later. "They beat us 27– or 28–3 the week before, and now we were down 35–3. That's [62–6 over six] quarters. I actually think that was part of the key to the comeback. They were feeling now like they couldn't lose, and we were totally humiliated. . . . I wasn't thinking in terms of winning. I was just thinking of taking it one play at a time."

Bills wide receiver Andre Reed (83) and teammate Keith McKeller celebrate Reed's third
touchdown during the fourth quarter. (AP
Photo/Bill Sikes)

And so, from the depths of humiliation, began the Comeback. One play at a time.

On the ensuing kickoff, the wind contributed to Al Del Greco's accidental squib kick, giving the Bills great field position. A 10-play, 50-yard drive ended when running back Ken Davis ran around left end for a one-yard TD, making it 35–10.

In one of several remarkable coaching decisions Levy and his staff would make that day, the Bills tried an onside kick, which Houston failed to anticipate. Special teams coach Bruce DeHaven called for the "Suicide Onside," as it was known, with Steve Christie dribbling the ball 10 yards down the center of the field. Christie recovered his own kick, and the Bills again had the ball at midfield with the wind at their back.

This time Reich and wide receiver Don Beebe did the damage with a 38-yard touchdown. Replays showed that Beebe stepped out of bounds early in his route, but no one saw it. Suddenly the Bills had some momentum, trailing 35–17 with 7:56 left in the third quarter.

Next, Houston's Run and Shoot began shooting itself in the foot against the Bills' normal 3-4 alignment, a change made by defensive coordinator Walt Corey in a desperate attempt to turn the tide. The Bills' energized defense pressured Moon into a pair of incomplete passes.

After a short punt and a 20-yard run by Davis, Reich found Andre Reed uncovered down the left sideline for a 28-yard TD and the Oilers' 32-point lead was down to 11, 35–24.

"When Beebe scored, I was thinking, 'Hmm, can this really happen?'" Reich recalled. "But it was when Reed scored that I think everyone started to think, 'We're going to win this game.'"

Years later, McDowell reflected on a surreal second half that seemed straight out of the *Twilight Zone*. "At any point in time, could somebody just please wake me up?" he told NFL Films. "There's no way that these guys could have come back and beat us."

The Buffalo Bills bench, including receiver Don Beebe (82) and injured quarterback Jim Kelly, behind Beebe and wearing street clothes, celebrates Steve Christie's winning overtime field goal. (AP Photo/Bill Sikes)

Bills cornerback Nate Odoms (37) gets a lift from teammate Henry Jones after intercepting a pass by Warren Moon of the Oilers during the overtime period. (AP Photo/Bill Sikes)

After the kickoff, a Moon pass sailed into the wind and was intercepted by Henry Jones, giving the Bills the ball at the Oilers' 23. Levy then daringly opted to go for it on fourth-and-5 at the 18. Incredibly, Reich and Reed made Levy look like a genius, hooking up for a diving 23-yard catch in the end zone and cutting the Oilers' lead to 35–31 entering the fourth quarter.

"The wind was just enough of a factor [for that decision to make perfect sense]," Reich said. "There were some throws I made in that quarter I'm not sure I could have made into the wind."

The Bills got one more break when Oilers punter/holder Greg Montgomery couldn't handle the snap on a 32-yard field goal try with six and a half minutes left. Davis then burst free for a 35-yard run that set up Reed's third TD. The 17-yard catch put the Bills ahead, 38–35, with 3:08 left.

Del Greco's 26-yard field goal forced overtime in the final seconds, setting up one last fateful decision. The Oilers won the toss, and coach Jack Pardee elected to receive rather than take field position. Cornerback Nate Odomes then intercepted an into-the-wind pass by Moon, who was 7-28 for 151 yards and two interceptions after halftime. Three plays later, Christie's 32-yard field goal made history and set off bedlam in Rich Stadium.

It was another story inside the Oilers' locker room. "We went in that Oilers dressing room, and it was almost like they'd all had frontal lobotomies," John McClain of the *Houston Chronicle* recalled. "They were sitting there like vegetables."

When a reporter asked Oilers cornerback Chris Dishman about the collapse, he corrected him, saying, "The greatest choke in history. 'Collapse' is just being nice."

Reich, who finished 21-34 for 289 yards and four TDs, including eight for 136 yards and three TDs to Reed, had a kinder take. "I'd like to give our team credit," he said. "We had to shut them down on every count. I don't look at it like a choke. I look at it as a miracle from God."

2 | DECEMBER 7, 1980
49ERS 38, SAINTS 35

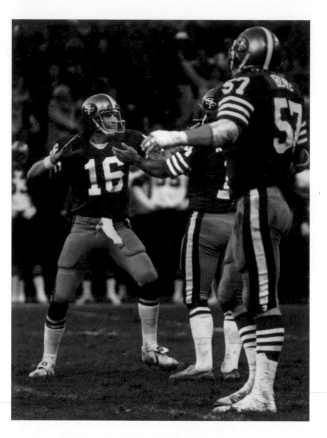

Joe Montana (16) is exultant as the 49ers beat the Saints in overtime, 38–35. (Michael Zagaris)

As sneak previews go, this was one for the ages.

San Francisco was not yet "the Team of the '80s," Joe Montana was not yet "the Comeback Kid," coach Bill Walsh was not yet "the Genius," and the "West Coast Offense" was not yet the trendy way to move the football when the 49ers faced the division-rival Saints on a cool December 7, 1980, afternoon in San Francisco. Far worse for the 49er faithful, their struggling heroes started the second half trailing, 35–7, after a horrific first half in which New Orleans quarterback Archie Manning threw for 248 yards and three touchdowns and the winless Saints administered a demoralizing beating that had even Walsh hoping for little more than a moral victory.

Several 49ers later said that Walsh urged them to finish the game in a "respectable" fashion. With the exception of lineman Archie Reese, the players said, no one really stood up and tried to snap the 49ers (then 5-8) out of what had been a horrible performance on both sides of the ball. Considering that their playoff hopes had already been dashed and the Saints had outgained the 49ers, 324–21, in the first half, the lack of excitement in the locker room was understandable.

But everything changed once the second half began. Montana jump-started the 49ers with a 41-yard bomb to Dwight Clark and then scored on a short run to cap an 88-yard drive for the offense's first TD of the game. (Freddie Solomon's 57-yard punt return had made it 21–7 in the second quarter.) Minutes later, Clark turned a medium-range pass into a 71-yard touchdown, and the 49ers were back in the game, trailing only 35–21.

After three drives failed—but the defense held firm—Solomon scored on a 14-yard Montana pass to end an 83-yard drive, Lenvil Elliott ran for seven yards to tie it, and Ray Wersching's 36-yard field goal in overtime gave the 49ers the victory in what is still the biggest regular-season comeback in NFL history.

After the first of what would be 26 fourth-quarter comebacks in his years in San Francisco, Montana finished 24-36 for 285 yards and two TDs. Elliott gained 125 yards on 20 carries, and Clark had 155 receiving yards on six catches, all numbers that would be reproduced routinely during the rest of the '80s by Walsh's West Coast Offense. Although Montana would receive his just due after the game, much of the credit for the comeback went to Clark and Elliott.

"This was the beginning of things for us," Montana said, reflecting on his remarkable run in San Francisco. "It was a game we could look back at to remind us what we could do offensively. It really built our confidence."

Montana keenly remembered a play that came to typify the 49ers' get-it-done mentality during the '80s, a decade in which they would win four Super Bowls. "Our field all that year was a quagmire because of the rain," he said. "I hit Dwight on a little crossing route, he took the ball, ran it to the sideline, and cut back for a long TD. We were all shocked he could run that fast in the mud. He told us he lost his defender by taking him into the muddiest part of the field."

The 49ers finished 6-10 that season (the Saints were 1-15), but they went on to win 18 NFC West titles and five Super Bowls over the next 18 seasons. As if psychic, Walsh can be heard on tape after the game telling a player: "This is great for the team, great for the franchise."

Indeed, the very next season the 49ers would transform themselves into the team of the '80s. They went 13-3 in the regular season, they beat the Cowboys in the NFC title game that featured "the Catch" (by Dwight Clark), and Montana—now firmly established as the 49ers' leader after that comeback win over the Saints—earned Super Bowl MVP honors for the first of three times.

"There have been, and will be, much better arms and legs and much better bodies on quarterbacks in the NFL," former 49er Randy Cross said, "but if you have to win a game or score a touchdown or win a championship, the only guy to get is Joe Montana."

The Saints were the first to find that out.

3 | DECEMBER 23, 1972
COWBOYS 30, 49ERS 28

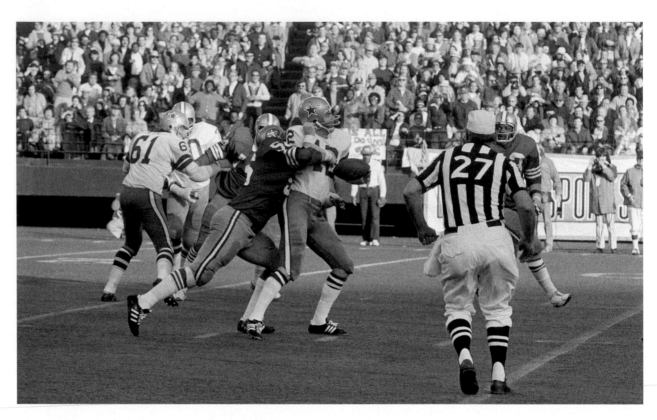

Cowboys quarter-back Roger Staubach (12) is nailed by Charlie Krueger and Dick Witcher of the 49ers. (AP Photo)

Playing behind Craig Morton most of the season after suffering a separated shoulder, Dallas quarterback Roger Staubach had to stand and watch as San Francisco built a 28–13 lead in the 1972 NFC divisional playoff game in the Bay Area. Staubach was healthy, and he had led the Cowboys to their first Super Bowl title the year before, but he was not yet established as a Hall of Fame quarterback or as "Captain Comeback." Had the score been 28–24 entering the fourth quarter, he probably would not have played in what turned out to be a pivotal moment in NFL history.

But Cowboys coach Tom Landry, more comfortable with Morton's classic drop-back style than with the athletic Staubach's willingness to improvise, did have a breaking point. It came late in the third quarter when Staubach trotted onto the field,

forever changing the legacy of Staubach, the Cowboys, and even the NFL.

"I felt I had to do something to change the mood of the game," Landry said. "We hadn't been doing much for three quarters, and Roger has a way of turning things around. He was pretty rusty when he started, but then he came around. He really came around."

Former 49ers wide receiver Gene Washington made it clear many years later that he wished his team had not pushed Landry into a corner. "It was our ball game until this guy named Roger Staubach comes into the game," he said. "If Craig Morton stays in the game, we win."

That wasn't so obvious in 1972. On this particular day in San Francisco, Staubach's impact was far from immediate. It was a 48-yard Calvin

Hill run—not any Staubach magic—that set up a Toni Fritsch 27-yard field goal, cutting the deficit to 28–16 early in the fourth quarter. Not much went right for the next 12 minutes, and only 1:53 remained when a short punt gave the Cowboys the ball at their 45, still down 12 points.

And then it happened. Staubach got hot and showed the world why he would later be recognized as one of the great clutch quarterbacks in NFL history. "I had nothing to lose," he said. "I was trying to make up for that whole season in that one game."

Knowing it was now or never, Staubach connected on three passes, then found Billy Parks on a 20-yard post pattern for a touchdown. It was 28–23, and the Cowboys suddenly had a glimmer of hope if they could somehow get the ball back. They did just that on the ensuing onside kick, artfully done by Fritsch, who would say in his Austrian accent, "The other teams, they don't know which way comes the ball." The ball squirted loose from Preston Riley, and Mel Renfro recovered, giving Dallas the ball at midfield with 1:03 left.

A lot of the fans had already left the stadium, thinking their 49ers were heading toward the NFC title game. Turns out, some of the San Francisco assistant coaches had the same belief. "The 49ers coaches had already left the press box because they thought the game was over," then–Cowboys running back Dan Reeves said years later.

Staubach scrambled for 21 yards to the 49ers' 29 as only "Roger the Dodger" could. Then he hit Parks down the sidelines for a first down at the 10. On the next play, Staubach saw a blitz coming, and he found Ron Sellers in the middle of the end zone for a 10-yard touchdown.

Just like that, the Cowboys had the lead, 30–28, with 52 seconds left—barely a minute after Stau-

bach launched a comeback that began with San Francisco 12 points up. A Charlie Waters interception of a desperate John Brodie pass secured the stunning triumph.

The Cowboys would lose the next week to the Redskins, but the comeback set in motion a decade of NFL history. Staubach would lead the Cowboys to three Super Bowls, Morton would be traded to Denver—where he would lose to Staubach in the 1977 Super Bowl—and by the late '70s Dallas would go on to be crowned "America's Team."

Dallas Cowboys mob Ron Sellers (in center with hand on head) after he catches the winning touchdown pass, thrown by Staubach during the last minute of play against the 49ers. The jubilant Cowboys are Cliff Harris (43), George Andrie (66, in back waving arm), Jethro Pugh (75), and Bob Hayes (22). At left is a very sad Jimmy Johnson of the 49ers. (Bettmann/Corbis)

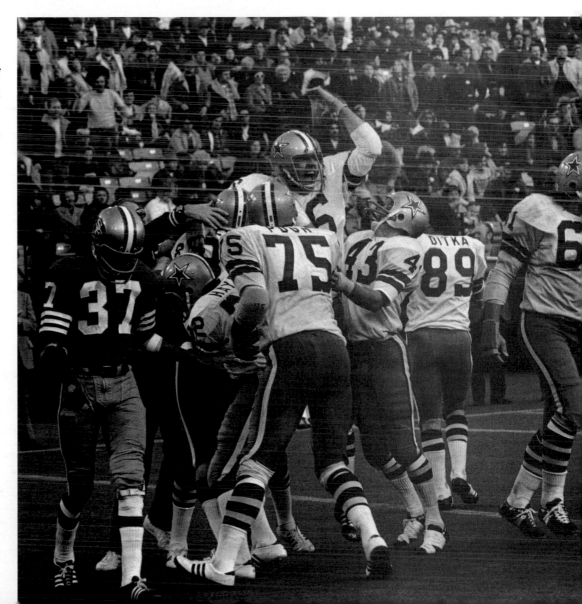

4 | SEPTEMBER 24, 1989
49ERS 38, EAGLES 28

Eagles running back Mark Higgs runs upfield against the 49ers. (AP Photo/ NFL Photos)

Joe Montana (16) drops back to pass. (AP Photo/Paul Spinelli)

It was Eagles coach Buddy Ryan, the defensive guru who refined the "Blitzkrieg 46" scheme that made life hell on quarterbacks in the '80s, against Joe Montana at the peak of his Hall of Fame powers.

Ray Didinger, a Pro Football Hall of Fame writer, was so impressed that he told NFL Films, "I saw Joe Montana play a ton of games, including all the way back to Notre Dame. I saw all his games in San Francisco, all the Super Bowls, everything. But I don't think I ever saw him play better than he did in the fourth quarter of that Eagles game."

Montana, by then established as one of the great clutch quarterbacks of all time, was sacked eight times by the Eagles, who featured the ferocious Reggie White at defensive end. He was also hit countless other times as he threw, but he still finished the game 25-34 for 428 yards and five touchdowns, four coming during a stunning display

of fourth-quarter perfection. Montana threw 12 passes in the final 15 minutes, completing 11 for 227 yards and 28 points against a mauling defense that knew he was going to throw and attacked him relentlessly.

In terms of superlatives, Montana did admit to one thing while recalling one of his 26 fourth-quarter comebacks in San Francisco. "That was the sorest I've ever been after a game," he said. "We got mauled, especially me. They had Reggie White and that big front four, and all I remember is getting my ass beat all day."

After the Eagles went ahead, 28–17, halfway through the fourth quarter, however, Montana turned the pain into gain for the defending Super Bowl champions. Overcoming sore ribs that were wrapped after he threw a 70-yard scoring pass to John Taylor early in the fourth quarter, "Joe Cool" completed scoring passes to fullback Tom Rathman (eight yards), wide receiver Brent Jones (24 yards), and Jerry Rice (33 yards). The final TD gave Rice (6-164, two TDs) and Taylor (6-136, one TD) a combined 12 receptions for 300 yards and three TDs.

"I was the secondary receiver on both my touchdowns," Rice said. "Joe Montana continues to amaze me."

The late-game onslaught stunned Ryan, who had said during the week that Montana couldn't hurt the Eagles if he was on his back. "Well, I guess they showed us why they are the world champions," he said. "Twenty-eight points ought to be enough to win in this league."

Not against Joe Montana on his best day. Put another way, 49ers cornerback Eric Wright joked, "I guess Joe is a pretty good passer, even on his butt, huh."

5 | OCTOBER 23, 2000
JETS 40, DOLPHINS 37

Jets quarterback Vinny Testaverde looks to pass during the second quarter against the Dolphins. (AP Photo/ John T. Greilick)

The Jets came into this Monday night showdown 5-1, but played more like a 1-5 team for three quarters. The Miami Dolphins were 5-1 as well, but they actually played like it. They intercepted three passes while running up a 30–7 lead against their division rival, prompting Jets announcer Howard David to proclaim, "And with a whole quarter to go, this game is over."

Fans from America's biggest city don't tolerate lousy performances, so they quickly made it clear that they agreed with David. They started leaving Giants Stadium en masse early in the fourth quarter. Then, incredibly, they started to come back—at least those who weren't already heading home on the Jersey Turnpike—and many of the stadium's empty seats were empty no more even as the clock ticked well past midnight.

What they returned to see was a finish so amazing that NFL fans would later select the wildly improbable battle the greatest game in *Monday Night Football* history when the series celebrated its 500th telecast on November 11, 2002.

"They booed us, they booed us, and then they booed us some more, and then they left," wide receiver Laveranues Coles said a decade later. "And then we started coming back, and then you start seeing people filter back into the stands, and I think with just half the stadium empty, that's probably about the loudest I ever heard it. I mean, it was very exciting. There was so much energy in the stadium for the guys."

The Jets' comeback became known as "the Monday Night Miracle"—or as some preferred, "the Miracle in the Meadowlands."

Vinny Testaverde threw for 235 yards and four TD passes in the fourth quarter alone. Three of those TD passes went to players (Coles, Jermaine Wiggins, Jumbo Elliott) who had never before scored an NFL touchdown. The 6'7", 315-pound Elliott scored the game-tying TD in the final 42 seconds on a tackle-eligible play, bobbling the ball twice before securing Testaverde's three-yard lob. And Coles sparked the comeback by somehow snatching the 30-yard scoring pass out of cornerback Sam Madison's hands in the end zone.

Then there was Arnold Schwarzenegger, making one of those *MNF* halftime appearances reserved for celebrities. He boldly predicted that "Wayne Chrebet is going to pull it off. I think as usual the Jets are going to come from behind,

you will see. I think the Dolphins have to be terminated." Chrebet scored on a 24-yard pass from Testaverde to make it 30–30.

A decade later, Testaverde told *New York Daily News* writer Rich Cimini, "I've heard about being in the zone. In those 15 minutes, I felt I was as close to being in the zone as I've ever come."

After Marcus Coleman's second interception in overtime (he fumbled away the first), John Hall christened the game an official sports miracle with a 40-yard field goal—putting the Jets alone in first place on Tuesday morning.

"People always tell me they were there or they stayed up to watch it," Testaverde said. "It brings back some great memories. I still get goose bumps thinking about it."

Some of the Dolphins had a physical reaction to the outcome. "For them to come back on us [after] we had the game on a lock . . . and Jumbo Elliott catching the ball, that just topped everything," linebacker Zach Thomas said, "and it made me sick."

Jets offensive lineman John "Jumbo" Elliot pulls in a touchdown pass with 42 seconds left in the fourth quarter against the Dolphins. (AP Photo/Bill Kostroun)

Dolphins kicker Olindo Mare (10) and teammate Jerry Wilson react after their 40–37 loss in overtime. (AP Photo/John T. Greilick)

6 | NOVEMBER 23, 2003
RAVENS 44, SEAHAWKS 41

Marcus Robinson (left) makes a nine-yard fourth-quarter touchdown reception in front of Seahawks cornerback Marcus Trufant. (AP Photo/Nick Wass)

Seahawks cornerback Marcus Trufant (23) keeps Ravens wide receiver Marcus Robinson from making the catch in the second quarter. (AP Photo/Nick Wass)

First, quarterback Anthony Wright, just 2-5 as a starter, delivered the greatest comeback in Baltimore history. Then his wife delivered a baby girl, the couple's second child. All in a historic day's work for Mr. Wright.

After throwing for 319 yards and a career-best four touchdowns (all to Marcus Robinson), and helping the Ravens score 10 points in the final 72 seconds of regulation to force overtime, it was no wonder Wright delivered an emotional "we didn't quit" speech in the postgame locker room and then burst into tears. It took coach Brian Billick, filmed by NFL cameras he had allowed in the locker room, to remind Wright that "that's all well and good, but you're having a baby in three hours."

You could forgive Seattle coach Mike Holmgren if he wasn't caught up in the heartwarming and downright thrilling story. "We let them back in the football game," he said. "It was just a bizarre, bizarre ending."

A lot about this game was bizarre. Start with the fact that Wright had been a third-string quarterback in the recent past and would be a starter in only one other season (2005) after 2003 came to an end. Didn't matter. On this day, it was as if Johnny Unitas had returned to Baltimore.

Then consider the Seahawks' loss despite a career-high five touchdowns from quarterback Matt Hasselbeck, who was 23-41 for 333 yards. "Just one more play," Hasselbeck said. "We needed one more play, and we couldn't make it."

Then there was the whirlwind 17-point comeback itself.

Trailing 38–21, Baltimore scored unexpectedly when Ed Reed blocked a punt and returned it 16 yards for a score. Then the Ravens methodically marched 71 yards against the Seahawks' prevent defense and scored on Wright's fourth TD pass to Robinson, making it 38–35 with 1:12 left. After an onside kick flopped, it should have been all over, but the Seahawks unwisely went for it on fourth-and-1 and failed.

With time running out, Wright heaved a deep pass, and the Ravens got the benefit of a questionable 40-yard pass interference penalty. That set up a Matt Stover 40-yard field goal, and the scoreboard read: 38–38, :00.

Minutes later, Stover's 42-yard field goal capped the unreal comeback in overtime.

"This is something that you dream of," Wright said. "This is something that you write in books. For us to come back and win this game was unimaginable." Days later, Wright smiled and said the unbelievable victory coming on the day his daughter was born was "great. It's definitely something I can tell her about when she's older."

7 | JANUARY 5, 2003
49ERS 39, GIANTS 38

The 49ers' Jeff Garcia reacts after he scores a fourth-quarter touchdown. (AP Photo/Ben Margot)

All modern-day 49ers quarterbacks must labor in the shadow of Joe Montana, and perhaps even Steve Young, but on this particular NFC wild-card day, Jeff Garcia shined in the spotlight as few ever have. Garcia threw like Montana (27-44, 331 yards, three TDs) and scrambled like Young (8-60, one TD) while leading the 49ers to victory in the second biggest comeback in NFL playoff history.

And he did most of his damage after he was booed off the field midway through the third quarter, with the Giants seemingly on their way to a wild-card rout on the road. The 49ers didn't really begin their incredible 25-point rally until they went to a two-minute offense late in the third quarter, and Garcia turned a sputtering offense into an unstoppable juggernaut.

"His mother was crying," Garcia's father, Bob, told the *New York Times.* "Our whole section was getting teary-eyed. I hope this makes people appreciate him more."

Garcia, who grew up an hour's drive south of San Francisco, knew full well the history he was following. "It's one of those things where you're in the park playing with your buddies," he said. "You try to emulate what the great ones do, what Joe Montana and Steve Young did. Now I'm that guy. Maybe some kid wants to be Jeff Garcia. That's an awesome feeling."

In the space of 17 minutes, the 49ers put together consecutive scoring drives of 70, 27, 72, and 68 yards for three touchdowns, two two-point conversions, and a short field goal. Garcia was brilliant, and so was Terrell Owens, who ended the day with nine catches for 177 yards and two TDs (76 and 26 yards). Garcia capped the relentless rally with a 13-yard TD pass to Tai Streets, putting the 49ers ahead by a point with just over a minute left.

The Giants wasted a great game by Kerry Collins (29-43, 342 yards, four TDs), but they gave the 49ers' fickle fans a scare in the final seconds.

They had a shot at a potential last-second winning field goal, but that ended on a bad snap by Trey Junkin—a 41-year-old veteran signed earlier in the week to replace injured snapper Dan O'Leary—and a controversial penalty the 49ers declined.

When it was over, Garcia had led the 49ers from a 24-point deficit, 38–14, to a 39–38 victory. "As long as you live, you might never see a game better than that," 49ers coach Steve Mariucci said. "It's kind of hard to remember everything right now, but I remember how it ended."

The 49ers' Ahmed Plummer reacts after the Giants miss their last-minute field goal. (AP Photo/Ben Margot)

The 49ers' Terrell Owens (81) runs for a 76-yard touchdown as the Giants' Omar Stoutmire gives chase. (AP Photo/ Marcio Jose Sanchez)

8 | OCTOBER 16, 2006
BEARS 24, CARDINALS 23

Bears defenders leap as the field goal attempt by Cardinals placekicker Neil Rackers goes wide with less than a minute left in the game. (AP Photo/ Paul Connors)

Bears running back Thomas Jones (20) leaps but cannot avoid the tackle by Cardinals cornerback Eric Green. (AP Photo/Paul Connors)

The Bears, then 5-0 and destined to reach the Super Bowl despite an inconsistent offense, trailed, 20–0, at the half. They rallied to win, 24–23, despite four interceptions by quarterback Rex Grossman, who also lost two fumbles, and an offense that failed to score even one TD.

The punchless comeback was built on the Bears' return of two fumbles for TDs. The first came when Mark Anderson blindsided rookie quarterback Matt Leinart and Mike Brown went three yards to make it 23–10. The second fumble, caused by Brian Urlacher and returned 40 yards by Charles Tillman, made it 23–17 with five minutes left. Then, after the Bears defense again came through, punt returner Devin Hester broke a couple of arm tackles and raced 83 yards for the go-ahead TD with 2:58 remaining.

Wired for sound by the NFL, Kurt Warner was heard telling Leinart, who was 24-42 for 232 yards in his second start, "It's unbelievable. I've never seen anything like this."

Warner hadn't seen everything, though. The Cardinals still had a chance to win, but Pro Bowl kicker Neil Rackers, after connecting from 41, 28, and 29 yards out, hit the ground first with his leg and flubbed a 41-yarder in the final minute.

"Sometimes, when you're a team of destiny, things like that happen," Chicago coach Lovie Smith said. Bears defensive end Alex Brown put it another way. "In the NFL, when you have six turnovers, you lose," he said. "If you're fortunate enough to win, somebody upstairs is looking out for you."

On this day, Da Bears clearly had Da One Big Fan on their side.

First, the Cardinals blew a 20–0 halftime lead. Then coach Dennis Green blew his stack. And to make matters worse for then-lowly Arizona, one of the NFL's strangest comebacks occurred on *Monday Night Football* in the franchise's brandnew Cardinals Stadium.

"The Bears are who we thought they were," Green said, visibly enraged at the postgame press conference. "That's why we took the damn field. If you want to crown them, then crown their ass. But they are who we thought they were. And we let 'em off the hook."

Green then hit the podium with his left hand and walked out, an act of frustration that made for great sound bites in the ensuing days. After this crazy comeback, though, it was understandable.

9 | OCTOBER 3, 2003
COLTS 38, BUCCANEERS 35

Playing on their home field and leading by three touchdowns, 35–14, with less than five minutes left, the defending Super Bowl champion Buccaneers had to believe they had gotten the best of the Colts and quarterback Peyton Manning on *Monday Night Football*. Former Bucs coach Tony Dungy's homecoming wasn't going to be a joyous occasion—for him or his Colts.

"This is a no-brainer," said Bucs radio announcer Gene Deckerhoff. "We're going to win this football game."

Not so fast.

A 90-yard kick return by Brad Pyatt, an obscure 30-year-old rookie, got the sluggish Colts going. Then a recovered onside kick, Manning's magic, and a fortunate set of circumstances, including Mike Vanderjagt's 29-yard field goal in overtime, enabled the Colts to become the only team in NFL history to overcome a 21-point deficit in the final four minutes of regulation. And they did it, incredibly, against what was at that time the NFL's stingiest defense.

"I never lost confidence," insisted Manning, who then bowed to the truth. "But I'm not going to lie. It didn't look good." Even Manning admitted that "the old cliché [of playing for 60 minutes], sometimes it's hard to keep believing that."

After Pyatt's return, James Mungro scored on a one-yard plunge to make it 35–21 with 3:37 left. After the onside kick worked, Manning hit Marvin Harrison with a 28-yard TD pass, and it was 35–28 with 2:29 left. After the Colts defense held, Manning drove the Colts 85 yards in 65 seconds, and Ricky Williams plowed through from the 1 to tie it with 35 seconds left.

Harrison ended up with 11 catches for 176 yards and two TDs. Manning was 34-47 for 386 yards and two TDs. "A lot of those plays, I tip my hat to Manning," Bucs coach Jon Gruden said. "He made some miraculous throws, and they made some incredible catches."

But fate worked its will on the outcome as well.

Colts head coach Tony Dungy (left) shakes hands with Tampa Bay head coach Jon Gruden before the start of the game. (AP Photo/ Steve Nesius)

Colts kicker Mike Vanderjagt (13) kicks the game-winning field goal from the hold by Hunter Smith (17) in overtime. (AP Photo/Chris O'Meara)

The Colts' Ricky Williams (35) takes the handoff from quarterback Peyton Manning (18) to score against the Buccaneers' Derrick Brooks (55). (AP Photo/Chris O'Meara)

In overtime, Harrison's 52-yard catch set up a 34-yard field goal for Vanderjagt. He missed, but the Bucs were called for a controversial leaping penalty that the NFL later admitted wasn't appropriate. Then Vanderjagt's chip-shot 29-yard kick looked like it might go wide right, but it was redirected by a tip at the line of scrimmage, hit the right upright, and went through.

"We've got great chemistry," Dungy said, "and I just had the feeling the Lord was going to do something, and He certainly did."

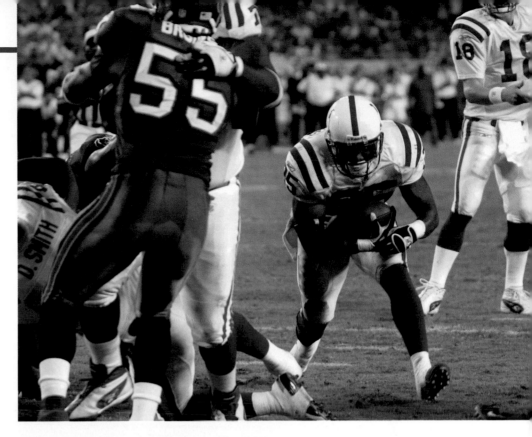

10 | SEPTEMBER 17, 2006
GIANTS 30, EAGLES 24

Giants quarterback Eli Manning (10) is sacked for a five-yard loss by Eagles tackle Darwin Walker (97) in the first quarter. (AP Photo/Rusty Kennedy)

Giants receiver Plaxico Burress (17) hauls in an Eli Manning touchdown pass to beat Eagles cornerback Sheldon Brown (24). (AP Photo/George Widman)

The New York Giants and their young quarterback, Eli Manning, were coming off a tough season-opening loss to his big brother Peyton's team, the Indianapolis Colts. Worse, they were down 17 points early in the fourth quarter at archrival Philadelphia, home to some of the NFL's nastiest fans.

Manning, who would complete 31 of 43 passes for a career-high 371 yards and three TDs despite being sacked eight times, lit a fire under the Giants and sparked the most dramatic comeback in franchise history. Jay Feely's 35-yard field goal, coming after a no-time-out, 63-yard drive in the final minute, tied the game with seven seconds left. Then Manning, going a perfect 8-8 for 83 yards after regulation, won it with 3:11 left in the overtime period when he saw a blitz coming and lobbed a 31-yard touchdown pass to a single-covered Plaxico Burress.

"It was a huge win," said Manning, who knew only too well this was because "it wasn't the prettiest win. It was downright ugly for a while."

Amani Toomer, who caught a career-high 12 passes for 137 yards and two TDs, talked about what the victory would mean to the Giants in the Manning era. "It's just a good feeling to be on a team where you know no matter what happens in the first three quarters, you're always going to have an opportunity in the fourth quarter to come back," he said.

A crazy play sparked the comeback. Manning hit Burress for a 23-yard gain to the Eagles' 16, where a fumble bounced forward and was almost recovered by both teams. The ball finally ended up in the end zone, where the Giants' Tim Carter fell on it to make it 24–14.

The Eagles didn't see one of the NFL's great

comebacks coming any more than anyone could have predicted Carter's TD. "After the first half, I never thought in a million years those guys would come back and beat us," Eagles linebacker Jeremiah Trotter said.

That just made it even sweeter for Giants defensive end Michael Strahan. "The fans are cursing at us, screaming at us, yelling obscenities at us, mooning us on the way into the locker," he said. "To win in this hostile territory and have it end on such a good play . . . [it's] priceless."

Priceless for him and New York's Eli Manning era.

Giants receiver Amani Toomer celebrates after catching a pass for a 22-yard touchdown against the Eagles late in the fourth quarter. (AP Photo/George Widman, File)

Giants coach Tom Coughlin celebrates stopping the Eagles on a fourth-and-1 running play in the fourth quarter. (AP Photo/Rusty Kennedy)

8 | FRANK REICH—"MR. COMEBACK"

Colts quarterback Peyton Manning (right) talks with Reich during a 2008 practice. (AP Photo/ Michael Conroy)

Soft-spoken or not, Frank Reich is a believer, a follower, and a leader all at the same time. And there's no reason to doubt his versatility or his sincerity. He's earned the street cred.

Reich is, above all else, a devout Christian who isn't shy about telling the world why he believes Jesus Christ is the source of his strength and happiness. But he is also a former quarterback whose belief in miraculous comebacks on the gridiron should never be doubted.

If anyone has earned the nickname Mr. Comeback, it is Reich, the man ESPN announcer Chris Berman once dubbed "Frank Lloyd Reich, Architect of Comebacks."

The soft-spoken, cool-as-a-cucumber Reich is best remembered as the backup quarterback who started for the injured Jim Kelly and led Buffalo to the biggest comeback in NFL history, a 41–38 triumph over Hous-

ton that overcame a 32-point deficit at the January 3, 1993, AFC wild-card game. Not quite as well known is the fact that Reich also starred in what was then the greatest comeback in college football history—coming off the bench at halftime and leading Maryland from a 31–0 deficit to a shocking 42–40 victory over Miami on November 10, 1984.

Asked about being known primarily for the two comebacks, Reich said, "Well, there's not a whole lot of other things. The truth of the matter was, I was a backup. What opportunities I had, I'm grateful for those."

Perhaps Reich's humble approach to football and life is what links both football miracles. There was no ego involved in either comeback, just the ability to be lost in the moment, take it one play at a time, and keep the faith that he could lead his team to victory.

Reflecting on Buffalo first and then on both comebacks, Reich said, "It was a great memory certainly, but not the individual accomplishment. What made it so great was that it was a team effort, and then being able to share that victory with our families and friends. . . .

"I was never the star and I wasn't looking to be. So it worked out pretty well."

Reich was the starter his senior year at Maryland, but a shoulder injury gave Stan Gelbaugh the opening he needed. He remained the starter from week 5 until the late-season Miami game, when a disastrous first half prompted coach Ralph Friedgen to put Reich in. By then, Reich had made peace with being a backup, so he took the field with nothing to prove. He completed 12 of 16 passes for 260 yards and three TDs, ran for another, and led the Terrapins to a 42–9 second half that secured a crazy win.

"It was through that injury that God rocked my world," Reich said, "and He really brought me to a place where I needed to fall on my knees before Him and confess that football was (incorrectly) first in my life."

Eight years later, that dramatic comeback would play a role in the Bills' comeback as well. Teammates came up to Reich during the game and said, "You did it in college, you can do it again today!" When he did just that, Reich knew who to thank. He opened the post-game press conference in rare fashion, reading the lyrics from "In Christ Alone" before taking questions.

Reich, who started just 15 regular-season games during a 14-year NFL career, has been a professional speaker for more than a decade. He returned to football in 2008 as the quarterbacks coach for the Indianapolis Colts, where he helps Peyton Manning continue to build his legacy.

"It's been a great journey," he said. "Having been at Maryland during some really good years and then moving on to the NFL, going to Buffalo, was just a dream come true. . . . And then I had an opportunity to get in here with a great organization. So, three pretty good stops."

Considering that Reich was out of football for many years, that's three pretty good comebacks too.

Bills quarterback Frank Reich cocks his arm to pass during Super Bowl XXVII. (AP Photo/ NFL Photos)

COACHING GREATS

A life of frustration is inevitable for any coach whose main enjoyment is winning.
—Chuck Noll, NFL coach

1 | VINCE LOMBARDI

When he said, "Winning isn't everything—it's the only thing," he was uttering the words that guided his mission in life.

In his book *Run to Daylight*, Lombardi described his drive to work in Green Bay: "There is a traffic light at the corner of Monroe and Mason and I stop behind a line of cars in the left lane. . . . Six days a week, this traffic light is the one thing that invades my consciousness as I drive to work, that constantly interrupts that single purpose of winning next Sunday's game."

"I don't think Vince was ever a child," said his wife Marie. "I think he was born conscientious."

Lombardi's sense of purpose was forged in his father's Brooklyn butcher shop, where the younger Lombardi hauled slabs of beef and cut up carcasses. He admired the work ethic of his father, Enrico Harry Lombardi, but lacked enthusiasm for that job.

The hard labor added bulk and muscle to Lombardi's frame, giving him the confidence to pursue his love of sports. Despite standing only 5'8", Lombardi, playing guard, became one of "the Seven Blocks of Granite," the nickname for Fordham University's offensive line.

While still a teenager, Lombardi also considered a spiritual life as a priest.

He was, wrote columnist Red Smith, "neither a saint nor a sadist, but a human being who could

Vince Lombardi was an undersized guard (5'8", 185 pounds) on the Fordham University Rams' famed "Seven Blocks of Granite" offensive line in the 1930s. (AP Photo/NFL Photos)

Lombardi is carried off the field after his team defeated the Raiders, 33–14, in Super Bowl II. Packers guard Jerry Kramer (64) is at right. (AP Photo)

Paul Hornung loved to test his boundaries, both on and off the field. Nobody seemed to faze the high-stepping, high-living Green Bay Packers running back.

Nobody, that is, except his coach. For Hornung, Vince Lombardi's boundaries were sacrosanct.

"If the coach wants everybody in the bus in five minutes," Hornung said, "I'll be in the bus. If he says everyone walks to practice, I walk. If he says everyone runs to practice, I run. If he says everyone swims the Fox River to practice, I swim the damned river."

All his players agreed it would be foolhardy to question Lombardi, the epitome of discipline, diligence, and determination.

sometimes seem to be one and sometimes the other. Vince Lombardi was a deeply moral man, pure of thought and speech and habit, who studied two years for the priesthood and was inwardly as violent as a crime of passion."

Wellington Mara, owner of the New York Giants, for whom Lombardi served as an assistant coach, said that he could have been either a pope or a president.

Instead, Lombardi opted for a whistle and a clipboard.

He became head coach of the Packers in 1959 and led them to three NFL championships in the seven years before the creation of the Super Bowl. The advent of that game offered Lombardi an even bigger stage, and he took advantage of it. Lombardi's Packers won Super Bowl I (35–10 over the Kansas City Chiefs in 1967) and II (33–14 over the Oakland Raiders in 1968).

He wasn't, of course, the first coach obsessed with winning, nor the last. But because Lombardi was in his prime at the birth of the Super Bowl, the man and the event are forever linked as twin standards of excellence. So it is only fitting that the ultimate football triumph, victory in the Super Bowl, is rewarded with the Vince Lombardi Trophy. And it is only natural that what has followed is his elevation to legendary status.

Anybody who ever played for Lombardi re-members him as a taskmaster always in search of perfection. His style was a result of his belief that success was more dependent on what his team would do than what the other team was planning.

Lombardi would not have been bothered with calling the opposing coach to check on his work habits.

Hall of Famer Forrest Gregg, a tough offen-sive tackle, wasn't so tough or confident when he arrived for his first training camp under Lom-bardi.

"I came . . . with my bags packed," Gregg said.

"Coach Lombardi made practice so difficult and so demanding," said Hall of Fame defensive end Willie Davis, "that the game itself was fun."

Gregg recalled that, when defeat came to Lombardi, as it inevitably does to all coaches, "he wasn't tough. He was ferocious."

The Green Bay power sweep is a perfect ex-ample of Lombardi's philosophy. It was a simple play — the running back, his blockers perfectly aligned in front of him, sweeping around the end. Lombardi believed that, if it was perfectly ex-ecuted, no defense could stop it.

"There can never be enough emphasis on repetition," Lombardi said. "I want my players to be able to run this sweep in their sleep. If we call the sweep 20 times, I'll expect it to work 20 times. Not 18, not 19."

Lombardi's supreme confidence in his system was never better illustrated than on the final play of the Ice Bowl, the game for which he is best remembered.

Played in Arctic-like conditions on New Year's Eve 1967 at Green Bay's Lambeau Field, the game was between the Packers and the Dallas Cowboys for the NFL championship. The temperature was 13 below zero, but with the windchill figured in it was 46 below.

The game came down to one play, 16 seconds remaining, Cowboys leading 17–14, Packers with the ball inside the Dallas 1-yard line. The clock was stopped, but Green Bay had no time-outs remaining.

Rather than trying for a game-tying field goal or even a pass play that could at least stop the clock if it was incomplete, Lombardi went for all or nothing with a run.

To Lombardi, it was not a gamble. In his mind, there was no way any defense on earth could stop one of his plays, if perfectly executed, from gaining a yard.

Sure enough, quarterback Bart Starr squeezed through the defensive line for the game-winning touchdown.

That gave the Packers a slot in the Super Bowl and Lombardi his place in the NFL's coaching pantheon. When Starr squeezed through the hole, he felt the chill of the snow in the end zone on his cheek and the thrill of victory in his frozen veins.

Final score: Green Bay 21, Dallas 17.

Lombardi coached the Packers in only one more game, Super Bowl II, then left the sideline to serve as general manager.

But a year later, offered the Washington Redskins' head coaching job, along with full control of the team and the chance to purchase a substantial share of stock in the franchise, Lombardi accepted.

He coached the Redskins for just one year before dying of colon cancer in 1970 at the age of 57.

When Lombardi lay dying in a hospital bed, Vince Promuto, a Redskin guard, told his coach, "I thank God that you came my way, even if it was for just a short year."

Lombardi finished with a 96-34-6 regular-season record and a 9-1 mark in the postseason.

He won't be forgotten. Every year the Super Bowl–winning coach raises the Lombardi Trophy in victory, reigniting the memory of the first coach to ever do so.

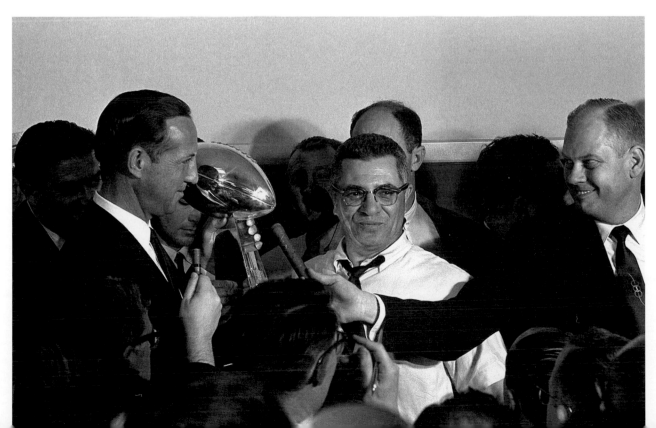

Football commissioner Pete Rozelle (left) presents the trophy to Lombardi after the Packers trounced the Kansas City Chiefs, 35–21, in the first Super Bowl game. (AP Photo)

2 | BILL WALSH

49ers quarterback Joe Montana and Bill Walsh smile for photographers during the closing moments of their playoff game against the Vikings on January 4, 1989. (AP Photo)

Walsh is hoisted on the shoulders of his team after defeating the Miami Dolphins, 38–16, in Super Bowl XIX. (AP Photo/File)

Of all the coaches in the Pro Football Hall of Fame, only one was known as "the Genius."

Bill Walsh was a winner, leading the San Francisco 49ers to victory in all three Super Bowls in which he coached.

Walsh was a superb judge of talent, drafting two all-time greats, Joe Montana (third round) and Jerry Rice (28th pick), after many others had passed on them. Montana has said of Walsh, "Outside of my dad, he was probably the most influential person in my life."

"He was always there for me," added Rice, "when I was dropping balls, doing everything, when the media were trying to crucify him, 'Why did you go draft this small college player out of Mississippi Valley State?' He hung in there with me."

Walsh was also a slick trader, getting Steve Young, for instance, in exchange for draft choices from the Tampa Bay Buccaneers.

Walsh was an effective teacher. The list of assistant coaches going on to success of their own after learning by his side includes Mike Holmgren, George Seifert, Sam Wyche, Ray Rhodes, and Dennis Green.

Walsh was an inspirational leader. After inheriting a 2-14 San Francisco club in 1979, he took it to a Super Bowl just three seasons later.

Many of his peers in the hallowed halls of Canton, Ohio, can boast of similar accomplishments. So what makes Walsh a genius?

It can be summed up in three words: West Coast Offense.

act across the bay where Al Davis was dedicated to the vaunted vertical game for his Oakland Raiders. Davis drafted strong-armed quarterbacks and fleet-footed receivers, and he employed a wide-open, stretch-the-defense passing attack. With sky-scraping throws, deep pass patterns, and frequent reliance on an all-or-nothing, bombs-away strategy, regardless of down or distance, the opposing end zone could be vulnerable on any play.

But risk didn't always result in reward. Costly interceptions and lost momentum were the downside of the vertical game.

Walsh favored a more controlled approach, meaning more receivers in shorter patterns with a lot of slants and curls. And of course, when a receiver like Rice got his hands on the ball, a trip to the end zone was always a possibility.

Such a finely tuned scheme would work only with a brilliant football mind running it. While good chess players may be six, seven, or more moves ahead of their opponents, Walsh was perhaps 15 plays ahead on the football field, his game plan scrupulously scripted before the opening kickoff.

When Walsh first employed the West Coast Offense at Stanford, it was known as the "dink and dunk."

With a name like that, it would have been difficult to convince his college players that they were working on the offense of the future.

Yet they were. The West Coast Offense has been copied over and over by Walsh's far-flung disciples and others, appearing on the gridirons of cities far from the West Coast.

"The essence of Bill Walsh was that he was an extraordinary teacher," NFL commissioner Roger Goodell said. "If you gave him a blackboard and a piece of chalk, he would become a whirlwind of wisdom." Walsh's influence far exceeded his own tenure in the NFL. He coached the 49ers for only a decade, leaving in 1988 after winning his third Super Bowl.

He was only 56, and later Walsh conceded that he might have stepped aside too soon.

That was evident in the ensuing seasons when

It was an idea formulated in Cincinnati, where Walsh was a Bengals assistant under Paul Brown, and instituted at Stanford when Walsh was head coach there.

Walsh didn't feel comfortable taking credit for the idea. As a matter of fact, he said, in all fairness, it should have been called "the Cincinnati Offense."

But it was at San Francisco that Walsh perfected the offense and thus launched an era.

"With his meticulously crafted organization and cerebral practice regimens, to his daring personnel decisions and his visionary offensive schemes, he created an enduring model," wrote Michael Silver of Walsh in a *Sports Illustrated* article. "Today, the West Coast Offense, with its reliance on short passes, precisely timed routes and intricately planned progressions, is the NFL's preeminent scheme. But in the early 1980s, it merely drove opposing coaches nuts."

Silver referred to Walsh as the "most influential football man of his era" and a "transcendent ringmaster."

On the surface, Walsh's offense seemed almost simplistic, a low-risk alternative to the high-wire

George Seifert, taking over the controls of Walsh's creation, coached San Francisco to two more Super Bowl victories.

To satisfy his urge to be back on the sidelines, Walsh returned to Stanford at age 60 and coached three additional seasons.

He died in 2007 of leukemia at the age of 75.

"He knew me well before I knew myself and knew what I could accomplish well before I knew that I could accomplish it," said Hall of Fame quarterback Steve Young. "That's a coach. That's the ultimate talent anyone could have. I said in my Hall of Fame speech that he was the most important person in football in the last 25 years, and I don't think there's any debate about that."

Steve Young speaks at a memorial service for Walsh on August 9, 2007. (AP Photo/David Gonzales, Pool)

3 | CHUCK NOLL

Who is the winningest coach in Super Bowl history?

Bill Walsh?

Vince Lombardi?

Bill Belichick?

Forget all the usual suspects. The biggest winner is Chuck Noll.

That elicits another question from all but the most die-hard Pittsburgh Steeler fans: Who?

Think of the Steelers of the '70s and names like Lynn Swann, "Mean Joe" Greene, Franco Harris, and Terry Bradshaw come easily to mind.

Yet Chuck Noll, the coach behind "the Steel Curtain," the man who stands alone atop the Super Bowl coaching class with four wins in as many tries, is largely a forgotten figure.

That's understandable considering Noll was a coach who much preferred holding the spotlight to standing in it. He wanted his players to get the attention.

Nevertheless, remembering his first meeting with Noll, Bradshaw recalled the coach's "tight lips" and "seething eyes."

Surely he must have had an ego.

"Ego is tough to satisfy," he said.

Despite his modesty, Noll deserves much of the credit for the powerhouse Steelers of the 1970s no matter how much he has tried to avoid it. Art Rooney Jr., whose family owns the Steelers, and whose father, Art Sr., hired Noll as coach, summed up Noll's importance to the franchise when he said, "Chuck Noll is the best thing to happen to the Rooneys since they got on the boat in Ireland."

This wasn't a coach who inherited a team of superstars and relaxed on the sidelines while they excelled on the field.

When Noll became Pittsburgh's coach in 1969, the Steelers had been dreadful throughout most of their history. They had never, in their 40 years of existence, won so much as a division title. Pittsburgh had had just four winning seasons in its previous 19 seasons and hadn't been over .500 in five years.

Noll wasn't intimidated. "I don't view football historically . . . the key to a winning season is focusing on one opponent at a time," he said. "Winning one week at a time. Never look back and never look ahead."

Noll knew better than to look back. Growing up in Cleveland, he worked in a meat market for 55 cents an hour in order to earn the $150 annual tuition fee required to attend Benedictine High School.

He wound up playing his college football at the University of Dayton after first attending Notre Dame. When Noll suffered an epileptic seizure prior

Pittsburgh Steelers head coach
Chuck Noll in 1974. (AP Photo)

Noll with John Stallworth (82)
and Lynn Swann (88) in 1978.
(AP Photo)

to his freshman year at Notre Dame, his coach, Frank Leahy, was hesitant about putting him on the field.

Pittsburgh fans were also hesitant about Noll at the beginning. In his first season, the Steelers were 1-13. And in his first three seasons, they failed to get to .500.

That was something Noll had never experienced in his seven seasons playing under coach Paul Brown as a guard/linebacker for the Cleveland Browns.

At the end of Noll's fourth year as Steelers coach, Pittsburgh was on the receiving end of one of the most unforgettable plays in NFL history, a sign that, perhaps at long last, the fortunes of the woebegone Steelers were turning around.

It came against the Oakland Raiders in Pittsburgh's first postseason game in a decade.

On a play disputed to this day, Franco Harris made what became known as "the Immaculate Reception" and raced into the end zone with the deciding points in a 13–7 Steelers victory.

Pittsburgh went on to lose to the Miami Dolphins in the AFC championship game that season, but Noll had gained something even more valuable for the long term. He had brought a winning attitude into a locker room where losing had long been a way of life.

Attitude, however, only goes so far without the talent to bolster it.

Noll and the Steelers bolstered their roster in 1974 with arguably the greatest draft in NFL history. Four of their first five picks—receivers Lynn Swann and John Stallworth, linebacker Jack Lambert, and center Mike Webster—wound up in the Hall of Fame.

At the end of that season, Noll cashed in on his investment as Pittsburgh beat the Minnesota Vikings in Super Bowl IX.

It was the beginning of an incredible run that produced four Super Bowl titles for Pittsburgh in six seasons.

Over that span, Noll did not win the Coach of the Year Award a single time.

"I think that was one of the worst disgraces by those who voted for the award throughout the '70s," Swann told the *Cleveland Plain Dealer*.

Noll never cashed in on his own name. It's not like he didn't have his chances. When he was approached about doing commercial endorsements, he'd always have the same response.

See if one of my assistants wants to do it.

Joe Gordon, a Steelers public relations director during the Noll era, told ESPN that he figured Noll probably turned down what would amount to a million dollars today in endorsement money.

"He's a very private person," Gordon said, "and his sole interest was coaching football. He wasn't interested in extraneous stuff. If Chuck had his way, after the game on Sundays he would've just taken a shower, packed his briefcase, and gone home without doing any interviews."

"I lived a block away from him, literally, for six years of my career," Steelers safety Mike Wagner told the *Plain Dealer*. "He didn't say, 'Hey, come on over anytime you have questions.' He kept his social life private and his interests to himself."

Don't think, however, that Noll didn't have a method of communicating with his players.

"If you were on the wrong end of a Chuck Noll glare," Pittsburgh offensive lineman Craig Wolfley said, "that was all the proper motivation you needed."

In all, Noll coached the Steelers for 23 seasons, finishing with a record of 193-148-1 in the regular season and 16-8 in the postseason.

Noll doesn't need to brag about his accomplishments. His record says it all for him.

Noll and Steelers quarterback Terry Bradshaw (12) watch the Dolphins offense on the field during the second quarter of a game in the Orange Bowl in Miami on September 10, 1981. (AP Photo/Kathy Willens)

A happy coach Noll leaves the field with Jim Allen (45) after defeating the Cowboys, 21–17, in Super Bowl X. (AP Photo/Phil Sandlin)

4 | DON SHULA

Don Shula played defensive back for the Baltimore Colts from 1953 to 1956. (AP Photo/NFL Photos)

Shula is carried on his team's shoulders after his 325th victory, at Philadelphia's Veterans Stadium on November 14, 1993. (AP Photo/Amy Sancetta, File)

He began as the boy wonder, one of the youngest head coaches in NFL history when he assumed command of the Baltimore Colts in 1963 at age 33.

Shula had first joined the team 10 years earlier as a defensive back, part of a 15-player trade with the Cleveland Browns.

His playing career had been over for six years, and he was the defensive coordinator of the Detroit Lions when the Colts came calling again. They needed a head coach.

"[Defensive lineman] Gino [Marchetti] was the one who got me the job," said Shula. "[Owner] Carroll Rosenbloom loved Gino. Carroll told him, 'I'm letting Weeb [Ewbank] go. Who should I hire?'

"'There's only one guy,' Gino said.

"'Who's that?'

"'Shula.'

"'You mean the guy who played defensive back for us?'

"Carroll called me up to say, 'You've been recommended.'"

Rosenbloom wasn't totally convinced.

"You're going to be the youngest coach in the National Football League. Do you think that you are ready for the job?" he asked Shula.

"Carroll," Shula replied, "the only way that you'll find out is if you hire me and give me the opportunity."

Shula later said, "He liked that answer. He gave me the job."

It wasn't as big a gamble as Rosenbloom thought. Back when Shula was still playing for the Colts, columnist John Steadman had written, "Shula was all but a defensive coach without portfolio."

Despite all the promise, Shula could have become a has-been before his 40th birthday, the glow of his early years prematurely dimmed by the league's greatest upset.

The 1968 Colts were 13-1 heading into Super Bowl III against the New York Jets, who played for the upstart American Football League, generally considered an inferior rival.

That's what the oddsmakers were figuring when they made Baltimore an 18-point favorite.

The stunning 16–7 victory by the Jets forever shattered the image of NFL superiority, and a merger soon followed between the two leagues.

The Colts still seemed haunted by that loss the following season. After losing only two games in two years, Baltimore stumbled to an 8-5-1 mark in 1969.

Would Shula be able to bring them back to the top? He didn't wait around to find out when Miami Dolphins owner Joe Robbie came knocking on his door.

After making overtures to Bear Bryant and Ara Parseghian as well, Robbie hired Shula, luring him away by offering him a 10 percent slice of the team's ownership. So rather than attempting to restore the Colts to greatness, Shula accepted an even bigger challenge, heading south to become the coach of

Shula strategizes with quarterback Dan Marino (13) and reserve quarterback Don Strock (10) during Super Bowl XIX against the San Francisco 49ers. (AP Photo)

a struggling young team devoid of the success and tradition of the Colts.

Said Shula, "Success is not forever, and failure isn't fatal."

Nevertheless, he was starting all over again. The Dolphins had been in existence for only four years. They had never had a winning record and were coming off a 3-10-1 season.

To think—Shula had believed he had troubles in Baltimore.

"We played our first preseason game at Pittsburgh and won the game, and they gave me the game ball—after working them the way I had," Shula said. "That told me I had a group that was willing to work and willing to do the things I thought necessary."

What looked like a time-consuming fixer-upper,

however, turned out to be, under Shula's guidance, a quick fix. And the onetime boy wonder turned out to be a coach for the ages.

In Shula's first season in Miami, the Dolphins were 10-4 and made the playoffs. In his second season, they were 10-3-1 and made it all the way to the Super Bowl, where they lost to the Dallas Cowboys.

Nevertheless, in just two years Shula had turned an expansion team into an NFL powerhouse. And he was just beginning.

"Styles changed over the years, situations changed, and players changed. That's the nature of the game," said coach Marty Schottenheimer. "What never changed was Don's ability to win, no matter what the circumstances might be."

The Dolphins' Super Bowl appearance was only the first of three straight trips to pro football's big-

gest show. Miami would win the next two, beating the Washington Redskins, 14–7, in Super Bowl VII and the Minnesota Vikings, 24–7, in Super Bowl VIII.

Shula also took Miami to Super Bowl XVII and XIX, but failed to win either. His six Super Bowl appearances, however, remain a coaching record.

"Anytime the league has had to have somebody step up and have a vision for the future, it has been Don," said coach Tom Landry.

Shula also set two other all-time records, one that may never be broken and one that can never be broken.

He surpassed the regular-season record for coaching victories, set by George Halas with 324 wins. Combining his years in Baltimore and Miami, Shula finished with a 328-156-6 record.

"He's like the Lou Gehrig of the NFL," coach Ted Marchibroda said. "But I don't think there will ever be a Cal Ripken to break Don's record."

In 1972, just his third year in Miami, Shula led the Dolphins to the NFL's only perfect season, Miami's victory over Washington in the Super Bowl giving the Dolphins a 17-0 mark.

"It's hard to compare this team with other great teams of the past, but this team has gone into an area that no other team has gone into before," Shula said. "In the past, there was always the feeling of not having achieved the ultimate. This is the ultimate."

Shula retired from the game after the 1995 season. At 65, he had been an NFL head coach for 33 years, the final 26 in Miami.

The kid coach had proved to be better than all his elders.

Baltimore Colts head coach Don Shula on the sidelines during Super Bowl III. (AP Photo/NFL Photos)

5 | BILL BELICHICK

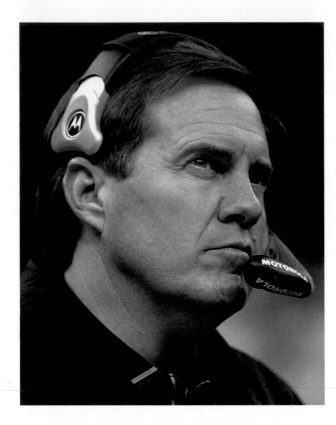

Bill Belichick watches the action from the sideline. (AP Photo/Robert E. Klein)

Belichick celebrates his team's victory, along with players David Givens (87) and Tedy Bruschi (54), after winning Super Bowl XXXVIII, 32–29, against the Carolina Panthers. (AP Photo/Eric Gay)

He's never going to win any awards for sartorial splendor.

He hasn't won over too many members of the media.

And he's had a difficult time winning the argument that his brilliant coaching record doesn't merit an asterisk after he was found guilty and punished by the NFL for illegally videotaping the defensive signals of opponents.

"What we have here is a football version of Watergate," wrote *Boston Globe* columnist Bob Ryan. "Bill Belichick is Richard Nixon. Brilliant. Tormented. Paranoid. Controlling. Highly suspicious of the media."

But none of that can keep Bill Belichick off the list of the top coaches in NFL history as long as he keeps winning in the area that counts most: the football field.

And win he does.

He won three Super Bowls with the New England Patriots and remains the only coach to achieve that accomplishment over a span of four seasons. He held up the Vince Lombardi Trophy in triumph after Super Bowls XXXVI, XXXVIII, and XXXIX.

He is the only coach to have a 16-0 regular-season record. That was in 2007 when Belichick's Patriots were denied a perfect season by the New York Giants, who upset them in the Super Bowl, 17–14.

Belichick has racked up all sorts of dazzling numbers in the win column. He won 112 games in the first decade of the 21st century, the most by any coach in any decade in league history. From 2003 to 2008, Belichick's Patriots had an 82-18 mark, the best record ever over a 100-game span.

Under Belichick, New England quarterback Tom Brady set the all-time single-season record with 50 touchdown passes.

On and on it goes, but tossing numbers in Belichick's direction is not the way to get his attention.

"Stats are for losers," he says. "The final score is for winners."

That attitude defines Belichick, who seems like he must be wearing invisible blinders, his unwavering focus on victory obscuring any and all possible distractions.

Perhaps that's why even on the sideline he always looks as if he's running a practice, having apparently given little thought to his outfit while dressing on game day.

Perhaps that's why he doesn't schmooze with the media, an activity that might rob him of some of the precious time he uses to make sure every X and O in his game plan is in place.

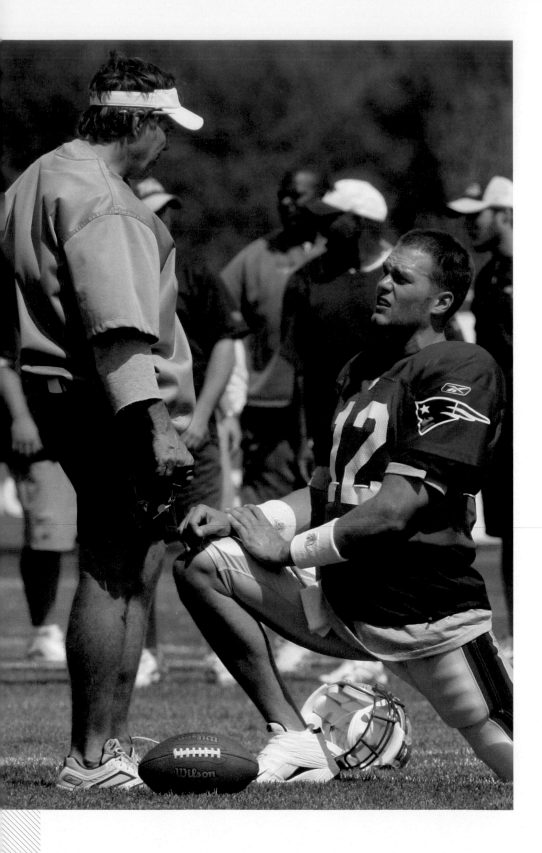

"I try to be detail-conscious so that the little things don't end up becoming big things you miss," Belichick said.

One thing Belichick certainly doesn't want to miss is the right player to pick when the Patriots' turn comes up in the draft. But for him, it's not necessarily the best player still available.

"It's not about collecting talent," Belichick said. "It's about building a team. Some players fit better into one system or style of play than they do in another."

Belichick is not big on adorning his locker room with inspirational slogans. But he does have one he treasures. These words of Chinese general Sun Tzu are as applicable today as they were when he said them in 540 BC — "Every battle is won before it is ever fought."

New Orleans Saints coach Sean Payton is so impressed with Belichick that Payton decided to impersonate him, down to the smallest details, in preparing his team to play New England.

"I made a careful note of how he scrunched up his face and how he tilted his head," Payton wrote of Belichick in his book *Home Team: Coaching the Saints and New Orleans Back to Life.* "I became Bill Belichick. The hair greased over to the side and darkened. The blue hoodie with the New England Patriots logo. The khakis and the tennis shoes.

"[I] listened [to Belichick's voice] three or four times until I had that flat, tightly wound, slightly psycho-sounding monotone exactly right."

Detroit Lions coach Jim Schwartz likens his

Belichick talks with quarterback Tom Brady during practice. (AP Photo/ Robert E. Klein) years as an assistant under Belichick to "getting a degree in football-ology."

Belichick got his own degree in the sport as a result of being around it all his life. His father, Steve, played fullback for the Lions and coached at the Naval Academy for 33 seasons.

The younger Belichick has been on an NFL sideline for 35 years as either a head or assistant coach. He was head coach of the Cleveland Browns for five years and has led the Patriots for the last 10.

There's no evidence that the years have mellowed him. Nor do all the triumphs seem to have satisfied him.

Blinders in place, he's still fiercely in search of his next win.

Belichick watches from the sideline during Super Bowl XXXVI. (AP Photo/ Amy Sancetta)

6 | TOM LANDRY

Dallas Cowboys coach Tom Landry in 1982. (AP Photo/Pete Leabo)

The silhouette alone gave him away.

With his lean figure, stylish suits, and trademark Stetson fedora firmly set on his head, Tom Landry was as distinct a figure as ever walked an NFL sideline.

A sharp contrast to today's era, when warm-up suits and running shoes are standard sideline attire for many coaches, Landry exuded class and decorum in his 29 years as head coach of the Dallas Cowboys.

Before Jimmy Johnson and Jerry Jones, Barry Switzer and Bill Parcells, Landry *was* the Cowboys, the only coach the team had in its first three decades of existence.

He took Dallas to five Super Bowls, won two of them, and made the Cowboys "America's Team."

It wasn't easy at first. Given an expansion team consisting largely of wannabes and never-weres, Landry didn't win a game his first season, going 0-11-1. He didn't have a winning season until his seventh year.

But he persevered, his stoic manner and tight-lipped nature serving him well as he built his team, position by position. Like any fine craftsman, Landry constructed a sturdy product geared to last through all the inevitable storms that buffet any team.

And last it did. Once Landry got on the winning side of the ledger, he stayed there for two decades with 20 consecutive winning seasons, including 19 playoff appearances and 13 division titles.

He finished with a regular-season record of 250-162-6, trailing only Don Shula and George Halas in the win column.

Despite all the triumphs, there were, of course, setbacks. Landry believed in an even keel, win or lose.

"Right after the game, say as little as possible," he would advise.

But when Landry did finally speak after a loss, it was with a view of the future rather than the past.

"Today," he would say, "you have 100 percent of your life left."

Landry attributed his self-discipline and sense of propriety to his deep faith. "Outside of football and my family," he once said, "I spend most of my time speaking to various organizations about the joy and fulfillment of having Christ in your heart." A signed portrait of Billy Graham, the evangelist, hung on his office wall.

Self-discipline was not always a Landry attribute.

"As a kid, I ran free," he said. "No supervision. That's how you learned. Of course, I was spanked like the devil when I did wrong. Things are changing these days, and so are football players. There's more freedom. But freedom must have boundaries. Man is not made strong enough not to have boundaries. Without boundaries, you have the breakdown of the individual and then of society, and then you have chaos. With boundaries, people are happy."

Landry had offensive stars like Roger Staubach and Tony Dorsett, but he was initially known as a defensive coach.

Every football fan is familiar with the 4-3 defense, a standard among NFL teams. Landry invented it when he was the defensive coordina-

Landry confers with quarterback Roger Staubach (12) toward the end of the 1972 NFC championship game. (AP Photo)

tor of the New York Giants. In Dallas, it evolved under Landry into the "Flex Defense," part of what became known as the "Doomsday Defense."

Landry wasn't one to gush about his players. The highest compliment he would bestow would be to say, "He's a pro."

Coming from Tom Landry, that was all the praise a player could ever want.

"I have strong emotional feelings," Landry insisted. "The reason I take on the appearance of being unemotional is I don't believe you can be emotional and concentrate the way you must to be effective. When I see a great play from the sidelines, I can't cheer it. I'm a couple of plays ahead, thinking."

"Tom is not the type you can be buddy-buddy with," said Dallas linebacker Lee Roy Jordan. "But no successful head coach can hang around and drink with his players and be their pal. That relationship is bound to spoil."

"I used to be able to tell when I made him mad messing around on the field or in meetings," said Cowboys receiver Pete Gent. "The muscles beneath his ears would pop out and his eyes would sort of glaze over."

Those muscles popped out more and more toward the end of Landry's career. He had losing records in his final three seasons with the Cowboys and was fired by Jones when he bought the team.

Landry died of leukemia in the year 2000 at the age of 75.

But his legacy endures.

"I think Tom will always make the Dallas Cowboys," Staubach said, "more than a football team."

Landry looks dejected as the clock ticks down in the NFC divisional playoff game with the Los Angeles Rams on January 4, 1986. (AP Photo/Lennox McLendon)

Giants defensive backfield coach Tom Landry, during a workout at
Yankee Stadium, with (left to right, kneeling) linebacker Harland Svare,
middle guard Sam Huff, and back Cliff Livingston, and (standing) backs
Carl Karilivacz, Jim Patton, and Emlen Tunnell, linebacker Bill Svoboda,
and back Lindon Crow. (AP Photo/John Lindsay)

7 | JOE GIBBS

Joe Gibbs yells to his players during a game against the Tampa Bay Buccaneers on September 12, 2004. (AP Photo/ Evan Vucci)

Washington Redskins head coach Joe Gibbs in 1983. (AP Photo)

levels before he got his first head coaching position, signed by the Redskins at age 40.

"You can find a lot of fine assistant coaches, but there are few assistants who can lead," said Washington general manager Bobby Beathard when he hired Gibbs. "Joe has an unusual talent to get along with players. . . . He really knows how to bring the best out of the guys he's worked with."

After beating the Miami Dolphins, 27–17, in Super Bowl XVII in 1983, the Redskins were back the next year, but lost to the L.A. Raiders, 38–9. Gibbs subsequently led Washington to a 42–10 win over the Denver Broncos in Super Bowl XXII in 1988 and a 37–24 triumph over the Buffalo Bills in Super Bowl XXVI in 1992.

A year later, however, mentally exhausted and desirous of spending more time with his family, Gibbs stepped down.

The fans weren't happy about his departure. Even the nation's number-one fan had an opinion.

"I think Joe Gibbs is a very great football coach and, in my lifetime, one of the best I ever saw," said President Bill Clinton, in office less than two months when Gibbs retired. "I'm kind of sad, because I just moved here, you know, and I was looking forward to going to the games, and I'm a big football fan, and I think he's a very gifted man. I wish him well."

"Sooner or later it gets to you," said coach Dick Vermeil of the pressures of the job. "I'd say no one would compare with Joe Gibbs in the 1980s except Bill Walsh. They were the [best] of the NFL."

Explaining his decision, Gibbs told the *Washington Post* about seeing his son Coy in college and realizing that "he wasn't my little boy any-

To the current generation, Joe Gibbs was a failed coach who struggled with the Washington Redskins, going 30-34 over a four-season span beginning in 2004.

He was also a recognizable figure on the NASCAR circuit as the owner of Joe Gibbs Racing.

But back before all that, in the first stage of his NFL coaching career, there was far more brilliance than struggle. In a 12-year run with the Redskins beginning in 1981, Gibbs took Washington to four Super Bowls and won three of them.

Gibbs played college football at San Diego State and stayed on as a graduate assistant. He was an assistant coach for 17 years at the college and pro

more, and I had missed too much of that."

Turning to auto racing was a logical step for Gibbs.

"I love cars, and I love working on cars," he said. "I plan to spend some time with each of the guys at the shop on the days I'm there. I'd like to change a tire, but I'm not sure if I'll ever get enough confidence."

As it turned out, though, Gibbs missed football more than he thought he would. Even though his racing teams were very successful and Coy and his brother, J.D., were part of his NASCAR operation, Gibbs decided, at age 63, to return to the Redskins' sideline for the 2004 season.

"The desire to coach has always been with me, even after being away from the game for 11 years," he said.

In 2008, Gibbs again retired, again because of family concerns. His three-year-old grandson, Taylor, was suffering from leukemia.

Gibbs said his first priority was to devote himself "to the most important thing I'm going to leave on this earth."

Taylor has since been declared free of the disease.

Despite the sub-.500 mark for his return engagement with the team, the Redskins were 154-94 (.621 winning percentage) during the regular season in Gibbs's 16 years at the helm and 17-7 (.708) in the postseason.

Neither his two retirements nor his long absence from the game can lessen the excellence of Gibbs's first tour of duty with Washington. In just a dozen years, he won only one Super Bowl less than Chuck Noll, the NFL's all-time leader.

8 | PAUL BROWN

Browns coach Paul Brown diagrams one of his pass plays on September 26, 1947. (AP Photo)

Cincinnati Bengals head coach Brown, operating a movie projector, in 1969. (AP Photo/Harvey Eugene Smith)

Paul Brown never won a Super Bowl. But it's fair to say that, without Paul Brown, there might not be a Super Bowl.

More than any other figure, it was Brown who built pro football into the national pastime by creating many of the elements of the game that are taken for granted today.

He was as much a teacher as a coach. Brown gave his players notebooks and taught them in a classroom setting. He used intelligence tests to ascertain a player's learning ability.

He was just as demanding of himself as he

was of his players. Brown compiled film clips of both opposing teams, to study their game plans, and his own players, to grade them, and he created a sophisticated scouting system to analyze college players.

None of this revolutionary approach to the game, making it as much an intellectual pursuit as a physical one, should come as a surprise. Education was a big part of Brown's life. He earned a bachelor's degree in education at Miami of Ohio and a master's in education at Ohio State.

"A sloppy notebook means a sloppy player," he

told his Browns. "Star or rookie, you will be gone."

Other pro football innovations begun by Brown included the housing of players in hotels the night before home games as well as before road games, sending in plays from the sidelines by alternating two guards, and attaching protective face masks to the players' helmets.

It was hard to argue with success, and Brown had been successful at every level he coached from high school to college to military-service teams.

After leading Ohio State in 1942 to its first national championship — the Buckeyes ranked number one after finishing 9-1 — Brown took over the Cleveland Browns in the new All-America Football Conference. Brown served the team not only as its head coach but also as president and general manager.

He couldn't have done more: winning the AAFC championship in all four years of the conference's existence, Cleveland lost a total of only four games in those four seasons.

After the Browns lost a game in 1949 following 29 straight victories, any player thinking his coach would salute the squad for going nearly two years without a defeat found that he was deluding himself.

"I'm telling you this, and it's cold turkey," said Brown to his squad. "If those of you who fell down on the job don't bounce back, I'll sell you."

In 1950 the Browns were accepted into the NFL and immediately proved they were good enough to play with the big boys of the established league. They won the conference championship in each of their first six seasons in the league and won the NFL title—the equivalent of a Super Bowl victory in those days—in three of those seasons, 1950, 1954, and 1955.

Combining his AAFC and NFL years, Brown had a streak of five straight league titles and 10 conference crowns in a row. Overall, including the postseason, Cleveland's record under Brown was 167-53-8.

After 17 years as the Browns coach, with only one losing season among them, Brown stepped down after the 1962 season at the age of 54.

But six years later he was back where he loved to be, on the sideline. Even though he had already been elected to the Pro Football Hall of Fame, Brown became head coach of an expansion team, the Cincinnati Bengals.

"It was terrible," he said of his time away from the game. "I had everything a man can want: leisure, enough money, a wonderful family. Yet with all that, I was eating my heart out. Football has been my life. I had a strong desire to become alive again."

The Bengals struggled at first, as every expansion team does, but in the latter half of this final phase of his illustrious career, Brown eventually returned to the win column. Cincinnati had a winning record in three of his last four seasons, including an 11-3 mark in 1975, his last season before retiring at 67 after 41 years of coaching.

Brown left an enduring legacy: pro football as we know it today.

Browns coach Brown (left, kneeling) poses with players (front, left to right) Dante Lavelli, Lin Houston, Frank Gatski, and George Young, and (left to right, standing) Marion Motley, Otto Graham, Mac Speedie, Lou Groza, and Bill Willis. (AP Photo/Julian Wilson)

Cincinnati Bengals head coach Brown talks to his players during a 27–21 victory over the Miami Dolphins on September 14, 1969. (AP Photo/NFL Photos)

Cleveland players cheer in their dressing room after their 56–10 victory over the Detroit Lions for the National Football League title on December 26, 1954. Coach Brown (wearing a hat) is in the center of the back row. (AP Photo)

9 | JOHN MADDEN

John Madden cheers on his team during their 21–17 Western Division championship win over Denver on December 16, 1973. (AP Photo)

Raiders head coach John Madden (left) and owner Al Davis talk with the media and display the Vince Lombardi Trophy after the Raiders' 32–14 victory over the Minnesota Vikings in Super Bowl XI. (AP Photo)

He won only one Super Bowl, had just a 9-7 postseason record, and was a head coach for only 10 years.

Yet the face and voice of John Madden are probably better known to this generation of football fans than those of Bill Walsh, Don Shula, and Chuck Noll. Vince Lombardi might just be a name on a trophy for some fans, but Madden is the name and the face fans saw for years every time they reached for a video game or flipped on a TV and watched a game or saw one of his many commercials.

Kids used to dream about playing in the NFL. That was reality for quarterback Michael Vick. But his dream was about virtual reality.

"This is a dream come true, for me to be on the cover of 'Madden NFL' and be part of the game," Vick told *The Sporting News*. "It's something you think about as a kid, but you don't think it will ever happen."

Many of those fans don't even know Madden paced a sideline back when his hair was darker and his waistline was slimmer.

Madden began in the trenches as a lineman at Cal Poly San Luis Obispo. He was good enough to be drafted by the Philadelphia Eagles, but unlucky enough to suffer a knee injury in his rookie season that ended his playing career.

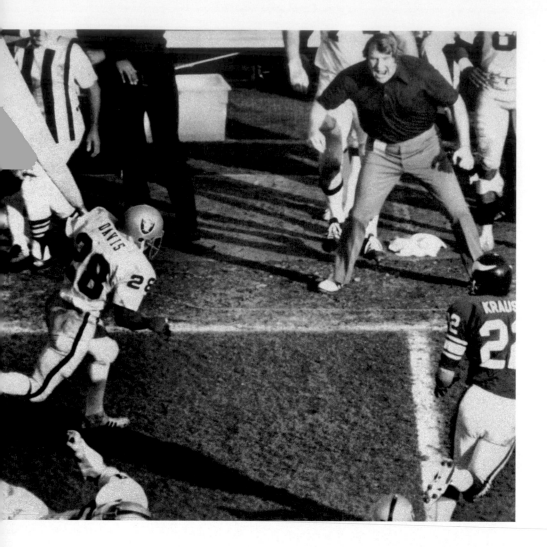

"[At first,] I didn't know how bad the injury was," Madden said. "I knew it was surgical. Then I got the cast, got an infection, and I was in the hospital for a long time. It didn't look very good. I knew I wasn't going to play that year."

Anxious to stay in the game after he realized he wasn't going to play again at all, Madden began coaching at Hancock Junior College in Santa Maria, California.

He eventually became a linebacker coach for the Oakland Raiders and was promoted to head coach at the age of 33.

"Al Davis has been the biggest influence in my professional football life," Madden said. "There weren't a lot of people that thought John Madden, the linebacker coach, was going to be the head coach of the Raiders. Al believed in me. . . . That was something very special. . . . He's just one of my best friends in life."

As a coach, Madden's rookie season went a lot better than it had as a player. The Raiders were 12-1-1 in their first season under Madden.

He never had a losing season, had a double-digit win total in six of his 10 seasons, made the playoffs in eight of those seasons, had 17 straight victories at one point, and won a Super Bowl at the age of 40, the Raiders beating the Minnesota Vikings, 32–14, in Super Bowl XI.

"The next week I was at a banquet," Madden said. "Roger Staubach was there. He came up and shook my hand and said, 'For the rest of your life, they can never again say you can't win the big one.

"'That's your *Yeah, but.* . . . Yeah, this team wins a lot of games, wins divisions, but it never won the Super Bowl. When you win the Super Bowl, that eliminates all your *Yeah, buts.*'"

Madden left the game after the 1978 season

Madden can't contain himself on the sideline as his star running back, Clarence Davis (28), races down the field in Super Bowl XI. Minnesota safety Paul Krause (22) is coming over to force Davis out. (AP Photo)

Madden interviews Steelers All-Pro defenseman "Mean Joe" Greene for a CBS television program about the Super Bowl. (AP Photo)

Fox broadcasters Pat Summerall (left) and Madden in the broadcast booth at the Louisiana Superdome before Super Bowl XXXVI in New Orleans. (AP Photo/Ric Feld, File)

and embarked on a broadcasting career that stretched over a 30-year period from CBS to Fox to ABC to NBC.

"People ask, 'Is broadcasting the same as coaching?' I say, 'Hell, no.' Coaching, you win and lose," Madden said. "Broadcasting, you don't win or lose. Coaching was a lot bigger than broadcasting."

To his broadcasting bosses, Madden was a winner.

"He was so consistently entertaining—that guy you really wanted to have on the couch with you, but larger than life," said Dick Ebersol, head of NBC Sports. "I think people stayed with a rout or a bad game that Madden might have to broadcast in the second half [more] than they ever would have stayed with anybody else."

His "Madden Football" video game hit the market 22 years ago and has become the top-selling sports video game of all time, with 85 million units sold worldwide, generating $3 billion in revenue.

"I started the video game," Madden said, "before there were video games. . . . We were going to make a computer game. Then, boom, lo and behold, here comes the hardware for video games, and we already have the software. There we go. To say when I started that I knew it was going to happen, I didn't know. But no one else knew. We stumbled upon it. We're still going. It just gets bigger and bigger."

People have always loved listening to Madden, even if they weren't always sure what he was saying. And that included his players.

Before games, his battle cry was, "Don't worry about the horse being blind. Just load the wagon."

What did that mean?

His players weren't sure, but it sure inspired the heck out of them.

10 | TONY DUNGY

Tony Dungy acknowledges fans at a Super Bowl rally at the RCA Dome in Indianapolis on February 5, 2007. (AP Photo/Tom Strickland)

Tony Dungy rode around Miami's Dolphin Stadium on the shoulders of his players following the Colts' 29–17 victory over the Chicago Bears in Super Bowl XLI.

To the celebrating fans surrounding him and a national television audience, it was a short, joyous trip. But to Dungy the 2007 triumph was also the culmination of a long and arduous journey that began before he was even born.

"It means probably more to him than it does to any of us," said Colts defensive end Dwight Freeney. "He has waited a long time."

So had many others.

Not only was Dungy's victory the crowning moment of a 27-year coaching career, including 11

as a head coach, but it was also the first time in 41 Super Bowls that an African American had been the winning coach.

The breaking of that color barrier had already been guaranteed before the opening kickoff. No African American head coach had even made it to football's ultimate game before that day, but two had qualified for Super Bowl XLI, with Lovie Smith on the opposing sideline as the Bears' coach.

When he accepted the Vince Lombardi Trophy after the game, Dungy, while praising his players, also took time to remember other African American coaches who had preceded him and upon whose shoulders he had stood in order to reach the historic moment.

"Great coaches that I know could have done this if they had been given the opportunity," Dungy said. "I feel good I was the first to do it and represent the guys who came before me. I dedicate the game to them. . . . There's a lot of African American men that can do the job."

Born to Wilbur and Cleomae Dungy, both educators, in Jackson, Michigan, Tony, one of four children, played football at the University of Minnesota and in the NFL with the Pittsburgh Steelers and San Francisco 49ers. He was an assistant coach for 16 seasons before landing his first head coaching job with the Tampa Bay Buccaneers. Dungy spent six seasons in Tampa Bay. Fired by the Buccaneers after the 2001 season, Dungy was hired a week later by the Colts.

The week before his Super Bowl appearance, Dungy called Pittsburgh owner Dan Rooney, whose Steelers had signed Dungy as a free agent out of college.

"Tony called to thank me," said Rooney. "That's

all he wanted to do. He said, 'You guys gave me a shot. I was a free agent, and you brought me in. You later brought me back as a coach, and I got to be a defensive coordinator.'"

Dungy says Pittsburgh coach Chuck Noll made a big impression on him.

"Chuck's philosophy," Dungy said, "was to convince every guy on the team that his role was important. If you came in as a free agent and were just a gunner on the punt team or the third safety, you were doing something the team needed to win. . . . It was his way of emphasizing that no one is irreplaceable."

Dungy coached the Colts for two more seasons after winning the Super Bowl, then retired and headed into broadcasting. In spite of his departure from the sideline, Peyton Manning said of his former coach, "Tony's going to consult me for the rest of his life."

At the end of Dungy's final season, Mike Tomlin, another African American, coached the Pittsburgh Steelers to victory in Super Bowl XLIII.

Dungy could retire in peace, knowing that others were following in his footsteps across a color barrier that never should have been erected in the first place.

Dungy is hoisted above the crowd after the Colts' victory in Super Bowl XLI. (AP Photo/ David J. Phillip)

Bears owner/ coach George Halas watches in disgust as a pass falls incomplete. (AP Photo/Ernest K. Bennett)

Jets coach Weeb Ewbank congratulates quarterback Joe Namath at the end of the Jets' upset of the Colts in Super Bowl III. (AP Photo)

From the first snap in the first NFL game to the last snap of the most recent Super Bowl, there have been great coaches poised on the sideline, inspiring their players and influencing the game.

Three more in particular, whose careers span the NFL's existence, deserve mention.

George Halas

In the beginning, there was George Halas. Beginning in 1920, he was player/coach of the Decatur Staleys, named for the A. E. Staley Food Starch Company of Decatur, Illinois, and he was involved in the formation of the American Professional Football Association, which became the National Football League.

In 1921 the Decatur Staleys became the Chicago Staleys in their second season. Halas purchased the club from the Staley company and changed the name to the Chicago Bears a year later.

Halas was their coach for 40 years, finishing with six NFL championships and 318 regular-season wins, the second-highest total in league history.

How did he last so long? Bears running back Gale Sayers found out when he played for Halas as a rookie. Halas was 69.

"I couldn't believe a man that age coaching football," Sayers said. "He shocked me and he motivated me. I admired him for his age. We had a lot of cold winters in Chicago, and he'd be the first one on the field and the last one off it. We had guys 21, 22 years old. They'd catch a cold and couldn't play. He was always there."

Weeb Ewbank

Weeb Ewbank was a key contributor in the middle years, winning the NFL's two most important games, games that led to pro football's rise to become the country's biggest sport.

Ewbank was head coach of the Baltimore Colts when they faced the New York Giants in the 1958 NFL championship game. The Colts won, 23–17, in the first sudden-death game ever played.

Pro football's popularity soared after what became known as "the Greatest Game Ever Played."

Eleven years later, Ewbank was on the other side, leading the New York Jets to a 16–7 victory over the 18-point-favorite Colts in Super Bowl III.

It was the first Super Bowl victory for the supposedly inferior American Football League, and the merger that ensured NFL dominance in the American sports market soon followed.

Sportswriters loved Ewbank for his colorful quotes in situations such as:

- Becoming head coach of the then-struggling New York Jets: "I kept telling people I'd seen sicker cows get well."
- Discussing a Joe Namath injury: "I wouldn't say that Joe has a sore arm per se, but his arm is kind of sore."
- Sending in the next move at a crucial moment in a Colts game: "Tell John [Unitas] to score a touchdown."

Ewbank may have generated his share of laughs, but when it came to the serious business of winning football games, nobody has ever won bigger ones than did Ewbank.

Sean Payton

Sean Payton led the New Orleans Saints to victory in 2010 in Super Bowl XLIV.

Nearly four and a half years after Hurricane Katrina cut a path of death and devastation through that city, Payton's team, in winning its first Super Bowl, gave the residents of New Orleans new hope that their city could have a promising and prosperous future.

There is no way to separate the man from the city. That is evident as Payton, in his book, describes the fans lining the streets of New Orleans for the Saints' victory parade after the Super Bowl triumph.

They were cheering for their team. They were cheering for their city. They were cheering for themselves. And we were cheering right back at them. These were the people we'd been playing for—people who'd lost so much and struggled so valiantly, literally crying tears of joy.

Halas, Ewbank, and Payton—three coaches who join so many others in leaving an indelible mark on the game they made their life's work.

Saints coach Sean Payton talks with his players before a game against Atlanta on December 13, 2009. (AP Photo/ John Bazemore)

ACKNOWLEDGMENTS

Like each of the memorable moments chronicled in this collection, it took a "team" to do this book and they all deserve my deepest gratitude.

Beginning with Bob Costas, the *gold standard* in broadcasting, for his friendship, his incomparable talent and encyclopedic knowledge of sports. Bob has been an invaluable ally through the years, along with his thoughtful and meticulous team of Pam Davis and Kay Reller, and his agent Sandy Montag at IMG.

Joe Montana, the greatest quarterback ever, and a true gentleman. I cannot imagine anyone more appropriate to provide the first words in this book.

Al Zuckerman, my agent at Writer's House, for his unwavering and enthusiastic support, creative and business insight, candor, and guidance; and his assistant Mickey Novak for keeping our communication flowing.

Craig Ellenport, Senior Editor of NFL.com and NFL Publishing, for giving this book the "green light," consulting on our story choices, and for unreservedly sharing his insights and knowledge about the history of the league.

Jim Castle for his friendship, expert creative eye, and "we'll get it done no matter what" attitude.

The visionaries at Houghton Mifflin Harcourt, beginning with publisher Bruce Nichols for believing in the book, my editor Susan Canavan whose talent and passion for developing great sports stories has made this book even richer. I also want to thank Ashley Gilliam, Laura Brady, Christina Mamangakis, and Hannah Harlow for deftly and affably managing the enormous workflow, and Melissa Lotfy and Clif Stoltze Design for the interior and jacket designs.

Mike Shayotovich at AP Images for working as hard as anyone to make sure we had access to the best NFL photography.

Aaron Cohen, Stuart Miller, Steve Springer, and Jim Thomas for their passion for sports, creativity and superior storytelling talents.

Linda Sponaugle and everyone at NFL Films for making sure we had the best game footage to bring these stories to life.

Max Segal and Suzy Brunink at HBO Archives for helping gather additional footage of the great NFL players and coaches of the past.

Bill Kurtis, acclaimed journalist and documentarian, for generously agreeing to lend his talent to my first book which started me on this amazing journey in publishing more than a decade ago.

Barry Freeman, Lark Baskerville, and John and Sharman Borncamp, my dear friends, for their truly invaluable support, love and encouragement.

Joe Deems, my attorney (more like *consigliere*), for his wise, unbridled and principled advice and his true friendship.

My Mom and Dad, Jim and Betty Garner, for their inspiration, unconditional love, and steadfast encouragement to always follow my dreams.

My two children, James (J.B.) and Jillian, I am proud to be their Dad and grateful for their love and unfaltering faith in their father.

And finally, Laura Swanson, for inspiring me every day with her infectious enthusiasm and optimism, sharp intuitive business sense, boundless friendship, and her amazing love.

INDEX

Page numbers in *italics* refer to photograph caption page